Julie Candler Hayes offers an ambitious reinterpretation of a crucial aspect of Enlightenment thought, the rationalizing and classifying impulse. Taking issue both with traditional liberal and contemporary critical accounts of the Enlightenment, she analyzes the writings of Denis Diderot, Emilie Du Châtelet, the Abbé de Condillac, Buffon, d'Alembert, and numerous others, to argue for a new understanding of "systematic reason" as complex, paradoxical, and ultimately liberating. Hayes examines the tensions between freedom and constraint, abstraction and materialism, linear and synoptic order, that pervade not only philosophic and scientific discourse, but also epistolary writing, fiction, and criticism. Drawing on the insights of a wide range of theorists from Adorno, Habermas, and Foucault to Deleuze and Derrida, she offers a dialogue between the eighteenth century and our own, an ongoing exploration of the question, "What is Enlightenment?"

Julie Candler Hayes is Associate Professor of French at the University of Richmond, Virginia. She is author of *Identity and Ideology: Diderot, Sade, and the Serious Genre* (1991) and of numerous articles on various aspects of eighteenth-century literature, philosophy, and culture.

CAMBRIDGE STUDIES IN FRENCH 60

READING THE FRENCH ENLIGHTENMENT

Recent titles in this series include

A complete list of books in the series is given at the end of the volume.

READING THE FRENCH ENLIGHTENMENT

System and Subversion

System and Subversion

JULIE CANDLER HAYES

CAMBRIDGE UNIVERSITY PRESS

CAMBRIDGE UNIVERSITY PRESS
Cambridge, New York, Melbourne, Madrid, Cape Town, Singapore, São Paulo

Cambridge University Press
The Edinburgh Building, Cambridge CB2 2RU, UK

Published in the United States of America by Cambridge University Press, New York

www.cambridge.org
Information on this title: www.cambridge.org/9780521651288

First published 1999
This digitally printed first paperback version 2006

A catalogue record for this publication is available from the British Library

ISBN-13 978-0-521-65128-8 hardback
ISBN-10 0-521-65128-X hardback

ISBN-13 978-0-521-03096-0 paperback
ISBN-10 0-521-03096-X paperback

Contents

Acknowledgments

A book is a network of relationships with the living and the dead, criss-crossed with conversations remembered and scenes of reading. My personal and intellectual debts are numerous. I am grateful to my colleagues and students at the University of Richmond for their encouraging comments, provocative questions and suggestions. Many an argument was tightened or rethought in response to a listener's question at a conference. The members of my family, especially my husband, Claude Bersano, and my sisters, Mary Leonard and Elizabeth Hayes, provided the emotional base without which this book certainly would never have been finished. I particularly want to thank those friends who read chapters and offered invaluable suggestions and comments at various stages along the way: Huguette Cohen, James Creech, Bernadette Fort, Madelyn Gutwirth, Jeff Loveland, Thomas Kavanagh, Downing Thomas, and Janie Vanpée. I am deeply grateful to Patrick Coleman, for many years of unfailing support, critical feedback, and epistolary conversation, and to Virginia Swain, who graciously (and heroically) volunteered to read and comment on the entire manuscript at a crucial stage. Thanks as well to the anonymous readers for Cambridge University Press for their insightful comments, and to Linda Bree for her editorial acumen and tact. The Faculty Research Committee at the University of Richmond supported this project with travel grants that enabled me to work at the Bibliothèque Nationale in 1989 and 1992, and with summer stipends in 1991 and 1995.

The book is dedicated to my son Daniel, who was kicking softly from within as I combed through the *fichier des anonymes* in the summer of 1989, and whose love and humor have sustained me ever since.

Author's note

Whenever possible, I have made use of the ongoing critical edition of Diderot's work edited by Herbert Dieckmann, Jacques Proust, Jean Varloot, *et al.* Full references appear in the bibliography; in the notes references to this edition are indicated by the abbreviation DPV. All translations are my own unless indicated otherwise.

Prologue – despotic Enlightenment

We are in the west of Ireland around the turn of the century. On his first day at school, a boy confronts a menacing schoolmaster.

After a while he directed a long yellow finger at me and said:
   – Phwat is your name?
   I did not understand what he said nor any other type of speech which is practised in foreign parts because I had only Gaelic as a mode of expression and as a protection against the difficulties of life . . . I heard a whisper at my back:
   – Your name he wants!
   My heart leaped with joy at this assistance and I was grateful to him who prompted me. I looked politely at the master and replied to him:
   – Bonaparte, son of Michelangelo, son of Peter, son of Owen, son of Thomas's Sarah, grand-daughter of John's Mary, grand-daughter of James, son of Dermot . . .

The recital is interrupted when the master sends his student reeling across the room with a violent blow to the head.

. . . before I became totally unconscious I heard him scream:
   – Yer nam, said he, is Jams O'Donnell!

The scene is repeated for each child in the school. As the narrator's mother later explains,

It was always said and written that every Gaelic youngster is hit on his first day of school because he doesn't understand English and the foreign form of his name and that no one has any respect for him because he's Gaelic to the marrow. There's no other business going on in school that day but punishment and revenge and the same fooling about *Jams O'Donnell*.[1]

The text is from chapter 3, "I go to School," of *An Béal Bocht*, by "Myles na Gopaleen," better known as "Flann O'Brien," the writer Brian O'Nolan. *The Poor Mouth* is a comic Bildungsroman, a pastiche of sentimental Gaelic revival texts, and an exercise in a kind of Irish magical realism.

In many respects, the schoolroom scene could be said to exemplify the worst features of what a number of twentieth-century thinkers see as coercive "enlightened" rationality: the school, ostensibly the haven of knowledge and progress, revealed as the brutal instrument of colonial aggression, where language and identity are destroyed. The passage also evokes the more general problematic, however, of Gilles Deleuze and Félix Guattari's "primal scene" of oedipalization, in which the analyst plays the role of the schoolmaster: "Dis que c'est Œdipe, sinon t'auras une gifle." ["Say that it's Œdipus or you'll get a slap in the face."][2] Theodor Adorno describes such imposition as 'identity logic,' making unlikes alike. The schoolmaster's brutality is as vivid as the specific correction he enforces is emblematic, when the alien, monolingual, morphologically minimal name interrupts and replaces the name-as-genealogical-performance, with its exotic allusions and unpredictable switches between patrilinear and matrilinear. In *The Poor Mouth*, however, names will ultimately not be conflated, nor language made one. The question of names and language extends beyond the scene depicted, to the situation of the novel itself, which is written in Gaelic and thus part of a linguistic revival that it parodies on the one hand and extends on the other, published after the author's death in the language of the colonizer; written by a man whose separate pseudonyms classify his production in Gaelic and English, and whose relation to his work (a history of lost, reconstructed, and transformed manuscripts) resembles one of his own works of comic modernism. Hovering between names, languages, and literary modes, O'Nolan and his work resist the reductionism inherent in "Jams O'Donnell."

The schoolmaster's blow resembles the essentializing work that has been done, by both critics and defenders of Enlightenment, through the assertion of a monological and unvarying form of rationality, the *esprit systématique*. History, language, and genealogy destabilize any such restrictive accounts.

Introduction – the critique of systematic reason

There have been many narratives of Enlightenment, ranging from euphoric accounts of intellectual courage and progress in the face of superstition and inequality, to dystopian unmaskings of reason's darker motives. In the second half of the twentieth century, from the early Frankfurt School to the work of Michel Foucault, and that of a number of feminist, Marxian and other historicist critics, the analysis of the covert strategies of domination inherent in our "enlightened" institutions cautions us against the liberal tradition's Age of Reason. A major focus for these critiques rests on the classical *episteme*'s drive toward classification and systematization as the discursive space for what Foucault called "disciplines" and "sciences of order." Although I am not taking issue per se with the work that has been done on the relationship between the purifying of classical reason and certain institutions, and strategies of domination, this intellectual current as a whole reminds me of another interpretative narrative.

The operative "story" is that of the *Anti-Œdipe*: desire is formless, partitionless, boundless, and "excessive" energy. It is the "unmasking" gesture of the analyst that actually imprints desire, defines its territory, grounds it in a master narrative. Now, according to Jean-François Lyotard (to take but one well-known example), Enlightenment is the source of many of our culture's coercive *grands récits*.[1] But I will argue here that "systematizing" is energy, unimpeded relationality, movement, emphasizing relations rather than entities, potential rather than fixity. The master narrative imposed on this activity, by Lyotard and others, has given it a name and a purpose. As mindful as one needs to be of disguised forms of domination and manipulation, there is also the danger of what Habermas calls "crystalline forms of arbitrary formations of discourse."[2] The bleak scenario is not the only one possible. Through an examination of the Enlightenment's own struggles with its

3

penchant for objectifying and systematizing – the celebrated *esprit systématique* – I read a subversive counter discourse, one which enfranchises energy and desire, and brings a salutary skepticism to our ability to know and control. It is this Enlightenment that, like Lyotard's postmodernism, "wages a war on totality."

This is a dialogue between the twentieth century and the eighteenth. Responses to the question, "What is Enlightenment?" have ranged from Kant's heroic *sapere aude* to Horkheimer and Adorno's grim assessment of the rise of instrumental reason. The question remains compelling, at least in part because, at the end of the twentieth century, we continue to seek understanding of many features of our own cultural landscape in those of the long eighteenth century. Whether one sees in the earlier period a model for creative artistic production and emancipatory social movements, or instead the mobilization of coercive, instrumentalizing rationality, interpretations become caught up in a commentary on the present. Furthermore, discussions of Enlightenment, or of "the" Enlightenment, tend to blur the distinction between a historically locatable phenomenon and a particular intellectual stance, however defined. As Foucault noted, this ambiguity already exists in Kant's 1784 essay, and it remains with us.[3] We need to be aware of these two aspects of the term, but the ambiguity has been in many respects a productive one and is not to be abolished out of hand. However much one may strive to understand the past "on its own terms," the ability for any terms to signify remains embedded within the context of inquiry; as the present interrogates the past, the past engages and solicits the present.

In his *Imagined Communities*, Benedict Anderson explores the contingencies, multiple itineraries, emotional investments, and complex webs of memory and forgetfulness that enter into the construction of the concept, "nation." Such formations "are to be distinguished, not by their falsity/genuineness, but by the style in which they are imagined."[4] The numerous accounts we give of Enlightenment similarly bespeak varied genealogies and historical vicissitudes. As Karlis Racevskis makes clear in *Postmodernism and the Search for Enlightenment*, the political stakes in the definition of "Enlightenment" have become quite high in the late twentieth-century United States.[5] Defining Enlightenment has become crucial to defining ourselves.

It is in part this sort of self-awareness, this concern with the ways in which the context and status of inquiry impinge on the object of inquiry, that constitute the appeal of (one version of) Enlightenment for certain contemporary writers. Foucault sees Enlightenment "not as faithfulness to doctrinal elements, but rather the permanent reactivation of an attitude" of "permanent critique" (42). More recently, Daniel Brewer (1993) claims in his book on Diderot that "[w]hat is contemporary about Enlightenment" is its critical theory, "self-reflexive, self-problematizing investigation into the real as it is produced in and by symbolic representation."[6] Thus, while my analysis in some respects offers still another "Answer to the question," it has become clear by now that there will never be a final answer, that the dialogue of the past and present is constantly reconfigured as it calls on us as readers to reread and reposition ourselves. It was Kant, of course, who referred to his century as "an age of criticism" [*Kritik*],[7] and so we like to think of our own.

What would it mean to carry out the critique of "systematic reason"? It is first of all to read the phrase as a double genitive: systematic reason is not only the object of critique, but is a powerful critical tool through its own discursive heterogeneity. The systematic spirit does not need to be seen in opposition to the various models that have been proposed to replace it. Just as Kant asserted that there were two sides to his First Critique, an inquiry both into the objects of understanding and into the "possibility and cognitive faculties" upon which pure reason rests (12), so too our critique operates both within and without the language of systematicity, both in the eighteenth century and in our own.

For the remainder of this introduction, I will turn to three texts that represent important ways in which Enlightenment has been imagined, both positively and negatively, in the eighteenth century and the twentieth: Horkheimer and Adorno's *Dialectic of Enlightenment*; Foucault's reading of Kant's "Answer to the Question: What is Enlightenment?"; a political fragment by Rousseau. Each points to areas of concern in the longer readings ahead. Horkheimer and Adorno consider Enlightenment's mythic dimension and provide a scheme that helps us understand the relations among a number of polarizing accounts of rationality. Foucault's desire both to counter and to retrieve Kant exemplifies conflicts we will observe later in many forms of "systematic" discourse. In particular, the tensions generated by an ideal of rational inquiry elaborated amidst a series of logical swerves and near-breakdowns in textual organization will reoccur in Buffon and d'Alembert. The Rousseau fragment allows us to historicize the issues at hand by showing how they were already being framed in the eighteenth century.

Let us turn first to what is still one of the richest and most compelling of the dark narratives of Enlightenment, Max Horkheimer and Theodor Adorno's 1944 work, *Dialectic of Enlightenment*. The central strategy of their account resembles what now would be viewed as a poststructuralist perspective.[8] Denying the constitutive opposition between "myth" and "enlightenment," they elaborate the ways in which "mythic" thought can be understood as explanatory, and "enlightened" thought seen as magical and fetishistic. As Adorno would later write in *Negative Dialectics*, "The antithesis of thought to whatever is heterogeneous to thought is reproduced in thought itself, as its immanent contradiction."[9] That is, systems are never truly stable, final, and closed, but instead both produce and contain their own immanent, material contradictions. The process takes this form in the *Dialectic*: Enlightenment seeks to extirpate myth, but is itself a product of myth and will return to myth, is entwined with myth. The dialectic supposes an important corollary: Enlightenment produces its opposite; "the fully enlightened earth radiates disaster triumphant."[10] The self-preservation of reason is self-alienation. We bring within ourselves a fatal estrangement of subject and object through the repression of the senses. Rationality, in this account, is discerning, systematizing, and hierarchizing; opposed to all that is undifferentiated and chaotic, it is dependent on separation, distanciation, and repression. "All objectification [also translated "reification"] is a forgetting," wrote Adorno (*Dialectic*, 230). Enlightenment collapses under the weight of its own blindness and exclusions.

To recapitulate the dialectic's stages:

Enlightenment arises in myth, but myth is already Enlightenment, already an explanatory device, "presentation, confirmation, explanation" (8). Although magic pursues its aims through a kind of participatory mimesis, rather than instrumentalizing distancing, the pursuance of intentions contains the germ of instrumental reason. This last insight distinguishes Horkheimer and Adorno's account from others whose opposition between the "participatory" and the instrumentalizing is similar in other respects, such as Foucault's discussion of the passage from a world of "signatures" to one of "representation" in *Les Mots et les choses* or the move from punishment exacted on the specific body of an individual like Damiens, to the carceral world created through the disciplinary practices of modern institutions in *Surveiller et punir*.[11] Horkheimer and Adorno offer an additional, more radical twist, in denying any clear break between "mythic" and "enlightened" thought: in their scenario, there is no lost golden age of "correspondence" or "participation," only a continuing dialectic of perspectives which are ineluctably bound up with one another.

For not only does myth produce Enlightenment, but Enlightenment also produces myth. Repeatability or predictability, the *sine qua non* of science, is "the principle of myth itself" (12). On another level, while liberating us from what Horkheimer and Adorno call "the old inequality – unmediated lordship and mastery," Enlightenment nonetheless perpetuates it through universal mediation, "the triumph of repressive equality" (13). Lastly, abstraction and the "universality of ideas" are described as "domination in the conceptual sphere" which develops alongside material domination. In the last stage, Enlightenment returns to mythology, as the "blank purity" of the administered, scientized world "assumes the numinous character which the ancient world attributed to demons" (28–9). No less than fate, abstraction nullifies the individual.

The discussion crystallizes in a reading of the Sirens episode in the *Odyssey*, touched on first in the general opening chapter on "The Concept of Enlightenment," and expanded in Adorno's excursus, "Odysseus or Myth and Enlightenment." In the first discussion of the episode, Odysseus's decision to stop the ears of his men and have himself bound to the mast in order to enjoy the Sirens' song represents self-preservation achieved through a denial of the senses, the estrangement of aesthetic enjoyment and the instauration of relations of control. Adorno extends this problem throughout the entire epic, where the Homeric narration is at pains to impose order on chaotic mythic material, just as Odysseus repeatedly must defend his integrity as a self against forces of undifferentiation and dissolution. Following Nietzsche, Adorno reads in this story the blueprint for western civilization's "introversion of sacrifice" (55). Through his cunning, Odysseus allows himself a restricted "mimetic participation" in otherness: he hears the Sirens' song, he sleeps with Circe, but only through self-impairment and the refusal to give himself. As will become clear in the readings ahead, I argue that the distinctions and sacrifices that Horkheimer and Adorno see as inherent to

Enlightenment are not ineluctable adjuncts of reason's unfolding. Rather, systematizing intelligence, passion, and the sensuous apprehension of the world remain productively entwined. And although like the Frankfurt School thinkers I too recognize the mutual implication of Enlightenment and purposive reason, I do not see any necessity in imposing narrative closure on that relationship, but instead regard each as a permanent possibility of the other.

Let us now glance at a few of the responses to the *Dialectic*. In what has been termed a "postmodern pastiche" of the *Dialectic*,[12] Peter Sloterdijk's *Critique of Cynical Reason* rereads the *Odyssey* and signals the culmination of the Cyclops episode as the supremely ironic moment when Odysseus's quest for self-preservation hinges on a loss of identity ("It was Nobody who blinded you!") – in Sloterdijk's word, "Being-as-Nobody."[13] As an alternative to the melancholy skepticism of the *Dialectic*, Sloterdijk proposes a "cynical consciousness" of disabused critique, which despite the supposedly "post-Enlightenment" stance is another formulation of Enlightenment as critical consciousness. Seyla Benhabib and Jürgen Habermas have criticized the *Dialectic* for its internal contradictions and historical locatedness; they propose instead models of "radical intersubjectivity" and "communicative rationality" in order to restore Enlightenment progressivism.[14]

Such models offer a great appeal. They propose to redeem the Enlightenment project and restore its emancipatory impetus by replacing its rationalizing, hierarchizing logic with logics of dialogue, positive change, and consensus.[15] Other schemas, sometimes coming from very different conceptual systems and employing very different vocabularies, have similarly decried the levelling, coercive effects of Baconian and Cartesian rationality, and suggested "a return to participating consciousness" (Berman, 1981), a reappropriation of "analog relationships" over and against digitized, quantified entities (Wilden, 1980).[16]

Despite the appeal of such approaches, it remains the case that they present Enlightenment systematicity on extremely narrow terms, and accept without question the bifurcation between a coercive classifying and systematizing rationality and a liberating model of responsiveness, inclusion, and dialogue. Thus Rorty speaks of retaining "Enlightenment liberalism while dropping Enlightenment rationalism" (*Contingency*, 57), as if such rationalism could only be understood in oppressive terms. It will be clear by now that I find this reading to be itself overly confining. Not that the modern consciousness, the "punctual self" in Charles Taylor's expression, has not suffered from internal and institutional discipline, thus confining itself to roles of either domination and oppression and impairing the possibility of action.[17] The demystification of these subtle forms of control is crucial in any number of contexts – social, institutional, epistemological. But it is also important to undo the monolithic and reductive understanding of classical rationality.

Foucault's late essay, "What is Enlightenment?" has been an important text for resituating the discussion. Although I will argue that the essay does not entirely escape its own dichotomizing logic, it offers with remarkable economy a reflection on both the contemporaneity and the paradoxical qualities of Enlightenment. While some have argued that the history of sexuality project that occupied Foucault's final years marked a radical departure from, if not a reversal of, his earlier work on "disciplinary" institutions such as the asylum, the hospital, and the prison, he himself maintained that both were similarly concerned with what he called "techniques of the self."[18] "What is Enlightenment?" should be seen in this context: not as a reversal of a previous position, but as an extension and refocussing of energy. The essay's tone, however, its "singularly affirmative understanding of modern philosophy," as Habermas put it,[19] the resonances between Foucault's project and Kant's, and Foucault's reappropriation of Enlightenment as the core of modernity, are striking. And yet the euphoria is hardly total, for the problems of freedom and systematizing control remain embedded throughout the text.

Foucault's essay presents a number of elements of significance for the present study. Foucault works through eighteenth- and nineteenth-century texts in order to establish the identity of "modernity" and "Enlightenment," and to assert that Enlightenment is both historically punctual and historically generalizable. Self-consciousness and self-elaboration take very different forms in Kant and Baudelaire, but are crucial links as well. Like a number of the works we will be looking at in the coming chapters, Foucault's text exemplifies the tension between the general scheme and the unruly particular. Just as Foucault is skeptical with regard to Kant's rational structures, so the various components of his essay tug at and resist the orderly formation he lays out. The tensions within that structure, however, do not undermine the argument so much as they exemplify it.

Foucault begins by offering a new version of the question proposed by the *Berlinische Monatschrift* and taken up by Kant in 1784. *Was ist Aufklärung?* becomes, "What is modern philosophy?" The essay circles back to this question and amplifies the original answer at several important junctures. We are first told that "modern philosophy is the philosophy that is attempting to answer the question raised so imprudently two centuries ago: *Was ist Aufklärung?*" (32). After a series of reflections on the Kant essay (and despite a disclaimer as to its constituting "an adequate description of Enlightenment"), Foucault examines at greater length the significance of Kant's engagement with his own present. The question posed in 1784, Foucault says, opened up a philosophical interrogation on the present that was distinct from earlier such historical inquiries in Plato, Augustine, or Vico: "It is in the reflection on 'today' as difference in history and as motive for a particular philosophical task that the novelty of this text appears to me to lie" (38). We have entered "the age of the critique."

The essay's second part proposes that we understand "modernity" (the term that has subsumed "enlightenment") less as a historical period than as an "attitude" or an "ethos," a term whose Greek context is explicitly underlined. In that context, "ethics" is intimately related to "character," and the individual in her or his material and social identity. This is the level of the "techniques of the self." In the discussion that follows, Foucault turns to Baudelaire's articulation of "modernity" as an awareness of temporal discontinuity that nonetheless involves an "ironic heroization of the present" and a complex, deliberate self-elaboration in *dandysme*. Like the section on Kant, this passage too is followed by a disclaimer ("I do not pretend to be summarizing in these few lines the complex historical event that was the Enlightenment . . . " 42), as if to remind us that what is being sought in Kant and Baudelaire is not control of a complete system, but fugitive, partial insights that echo one another. In a further parallel with the section on Kant, the discussion of Baudelaire leads Foucault to offer a further elaboration of his own project:

I have been seeking, on the one hand, to emphasize the extent to which a type of philosophical interrogation – one that simultaneously problematizes man's relation to the present, man's historical mode of being, and the constitution of the self as an autonomous subject – is rooted in the Enlightenment. On the other hand, I have been seeking to stress that the thread that may connect us with the Enlightenment is not faithfulness to doctrinal elements, but rather the permanent reactivation of an attitude – that is, of a philosophical ethos that could be described as a permanent critique of our historical being [*être*] ... (42)[20]

In these final pages, Foucault appears at his most Kantian, but also most deliberately distinguishes his unfolding project from Kant's by claiming that the "historical ontology of ourselves" is of necessity partial, experimental, and carried out within the limits of knowledge and in the absence of "grand systems and transcendental truths."[21] Whereas Kant, in Foucault's view, emphasizes "knowing what limits knowledge has to renounce transgressing," his own plan is "to transform the critique conducted in this form of necessary limitation into a practical critique that takes the form of a possible transgression" (45). In another passage, he speaks of his critical project as a "historico-practical test of the limits we may go beyond" (47). Both Kant and Baudelaire allow Foucault to emphasize intellectual distance and dislocation from the temporal as a crucial feature of modernity, whether through critique or irony. The Kant section allows him to render problematic the distinction between universals and particulars, whereas the Baudelaire section drives the point further through an emphasis on transgression, that is, the linking of categories hitherto thought to be distinct.

The notion of "transgression," key to much of Foucault's writing, has resonances elsewhere in this essay, in suggestions of "imprudence" and "audacity." When we are told that the original question, *Was ist Aufklärung?* was raised "so imprudently," this characterization anticipates the appearance of Kant's famous device, *Sapere aude*, a few paragraphs later. It has been pointed out that Foucault misquotes Kant and reverses the syntax, gallicizing it and privileging audacity over knowledge: "Aude sapere" (35).[22] "Imprudence," "audacity," and "transgression" have an echo in the discussion of Baudelairean modernity, which is described in terms of "a liberty that simultaneously respects [the] real and violates it" (41).

Some critics have argued that Foucault's essay fails in its emancipatory message because his genealogical critique undermines the possibility of human agency. "Who or what is left to transgress historical limits?" asks Richard Bernstein.[23] Bernstein's point has one kind of logical consistency. Kant, after all, takes as the starting point for the First Critique the problem of reason's self-overcoming, its propensity for generating problems it can neither answer nor

ignore. It does not, however, require an utter disruption of the
critical project to shift from dwelling on the need for a clear
definition of reason's limits, to emphasizing reason's paradoxes.
Foucault's account articulates another kind of consistency, a very real
feature of lived existence, of formal reason's relentless capacity both
to undermine itself and to argue for an ethical life. The constructedness of subjectivity and agency, their implication in the local
discursive terrain, do not render them any less powerfully experienced by individual men and women. In the world of "partial,
experimental" critique, there is no fall, no trap, no windowless
inescapable aporia: one simply proceeds as one has always proceeded. Similarly, the recognition of psychoanalysis that my desires
spring from innumerable labyrinthine origins, and pursue multiple
and often contradictory ends will never abolish the immediacy of:

I want you.

The form of argument that we find in Foucault, and the self-reflexive
critique that he found in Enlightenment, we will see in a variety of
contexts in the following chapters. Most notably perhaps in Diderot,
but in other writers as well, we encounter a fascination with
paradox, transgressively connected categories, teasing interrelations
among supposedly incommensurate objects.[24] Thus one radicalizes
the shift Kant envisaged in his well-known analogy with Copernicus,
who instead of studying how the stars revolved around the spectator,
"made the spectator revolve" (Second Preface, 22). Beyond such
family resemblances among these forms of critique, however, one
may read in Enlightenment texts such as those of Buffon, d'Alembert, Châtelet, Condillac, and others, answers to Norris's and
Bernstein's question, to see how indeed within the framework of an
ostensibly disciplinary discourse, *l'esprit systématique*, might arise
"active, self-shaping, volitional" subjectivities.

But while on the one hand Foucault's essay makes its strongest
case for experimental critique and "the undefined work of freedom"
(46), on the other hand it is caught amidst discursive regimes of
which it seems unaware. It has been argued, for example, that
despite Foucault's profound wariness of the political situation evoked
by Kant, he misses and even replicates Kant's repressive gender
dichotomies.[25] As Foucault says more than once in speaking of Kant,
despite its brevity and apparent simplicity, the essay is difficult and
on occasion ambiguous.[26] Neither Baudelaire nor Kant provides

Foucault with what might be called a basis for the social agenda he hints at in his final pages: Baudelaire envisages self-transformation only within the realm of art, and Kant's separation of public and private underpins what Foucault grimly refers to as a "contract with rational despotism" (37). But it is only in the case of Kant that Foucault refers to these tensions and shortcomings as "difficulties." During the discussion of Kant, some odd things happen to the rhetorical framework of Foucault's text. "What is Enlightenment?" offers the typographical peculiarity of being written in outline form: I. 1. 2. 3. a. b. c. etc. The discussion of Kant's essay falls in section I. 3, within which, however, the strict organizational structure begins to slip.

Foucault is suspicious of Kant; as I have noted, he refers several times to the text's "ambiguity" and misleading "appearances." He follows Kant carefully, enumerating his points ("three examples," "three critiques," "two conditions," etc.). Foucault's own points, however, are less clearly defined. He says he will "point out three or four features" of Kant's essay (34); three paragraphs later, however, the terminology shifts: "A third difficulty appears here ... " (35). The "third difficulty" is actually a series of difficulties with Kant's distinctions between public and private, immature and adult, etc., and it is only after complicated commentary that Foucault reaches his next point, "a fourth question that must be put to the text" (37). Whether "features," "difficulties," or "questions," Foucault's shifting points of contact with Kant's essay mark his ambivalence toward its proposals. For even if, as Foucault claims, Kant "shows how, at this very moment, each individual is responsible in a certain way for the overall [historical] process" (38), the relation between individuals and their context remains unclear, colored by the threat of despotism, however "rational."

While insisting on irregularities in Foucault's paragraph numbering may seem irrelevant or superficial, the fact remains that, as in his discussion of individual self-elaboration within larger historical structures, parts and wholes pull at one another in the innermost fabric of the essay. Thus, while the basic form appears to be I. 1. 2. 3. II. 1. 2. 3. 4., complex and uneven ramifications such as those in II. 3, and variant forms of textual hierarchization (bullets in Part I; A and B appearing in the second half of Part II) skew the regularity of the form.[27] The formal problems are particularly evident in the final pages. In the second part of II. 3, he claims that his project need not be carried out "in disorder and contingency," and that it has "its generality, its systematicity, its homogeneity, and its stakes" (47). The order is reversed in the development which follows, perhaps for increased rhetorical effect, but the relations among (a) stakes, (b) homogeneity, (c) systematicity, and (d) generality, are not congruent. We are told that (a) "leads to" (b), and that the "three broad areas" of (c) actually "stem from" (b). Furthermore, one of those areas or "axes" is ethics, which sounds suspiciously like the attitude or ethos that the entire section II. B purports to describe. Foucault speaks in these concluding paragraphs of "open series of questions," "indefinite number of inquiries," and "diverse inquiries," but the text is relentless in maintaining orderly categories, to the point of postulating three kinds of coherence in the final sentences. In this final paragraph Foucault takes leave of the term *Aufklärung* that he has used throughout the essay, and substitutes *les Lumières*, thus effecting a linguistic coherence kept ever so slightly at bay through use of the German word (*Dits et écrits* 4: 578).

It is an irony of Foucault's essay that it appears to lay forth its argument in clear, tangible outline form, yet the "argument" remains to a great degree implicit. Foucault proposes both critical-ironic distance and transgressive connections, both an overarching historical structure and a valorization of the momentary, the fragmentary, and the material; he places paradox at the heart of rationality. The project that Foucault sketches out, "in which the critique of what we are is at one and the same time the historical analysis of the limits that are imposed on us and an experiment with the possibility of going beyond them" (50) – this is a project that speaks urgently to me of the need for rereadings and reevaluations of Enlightenment texts. As in Foucault's own writing we will find there paradoxes and tensions among variant forms of order, or in relations between parts and wholes, attempts at categorization, and experiments in "going beyond."

The readings that follow will explore that complexity in a number of contexts: philosophy, science, fiction. Although the point of departure for the analysis is the twentieth century's struggle with the question, "What is Enlightenment?" I restrict my "answers" to texts from the French eighteenth century. I concur with Foucault on the need for historically specific, focussed tasks in carrying out the "historical–critical project." Twentieth-century critique has all too often moved to reject the past, or to see it from one perspective only

– a perspective that, however salutary it may be strategically, is nonetheless limiting, as we have seen. Part of my activity thus involves re-marking, seeing what was already there, but not necessarily relevant to earlier interpretations of the texts. "Limiting" the corpus of texts to be studied can thus paradoxically open up the range of possibilities of interpretation.

Let us consider one of the best-known of the pessimistic voices that answered the question, "What is Enlightenment?" from within eighteenth-century France: Jean-Jacques Rousseau. While it is beyond the scope of this discussion to consider the question fully in terms of the *Discours* or *Contrat social*, a number of relevant issues can be addressed by looking at a short piece related to both, the series of fragments from *Ecrits sur l'abbé de Saint-Pierre* called "L'Etat de guerre,"[28] which picks up arguments from the Second Discourse and foreshadows moments in the *Contrat social* and *Emile*, written a few years later. Frequently cited for its violent dismissals of Thomas Hobbes's notion of the "warre of every man against every man," the text also bespeaks unacknowledged affiliations between Rousseau and Hobbes, and between questions of order and passion, method and desire.

Hobbes appears on the one hand as "our sophist," author of a "horrible system," and on the other as "one of the greatest geniuses who ever lived." The attack on Hobbes is bound up in an attack on "systematic" philosophy,[29] which is perpetually associated with alienating abstraction, *abymes et mistères* (612). As he argued in the Second Discourse, Rousseau claims that Hobbes's natural "state of war" is only an importation into nature of the ills and tensions of society; the social structures that for Hobbes are intended to restrain natural aggressivity are instead the causes of violence and suffering. In a powerful passage, Rousseau contrasts the self-contained, placid formulations of "books" with the horrors of lived existence. After having read a fine theoretical account of justice and civil law and having "blessed the wisdom of public institutions," he goes outside and looks around:

... je vois des peuples infortunés gemissans sous un joug de fer, le genre humain ecrasé par une poignée d'oppresseurs, une foule affamée, accablée de peine et de faim, dont le riche boit en paix le sang et les larmes, et partout le fort armé contre le foible du redoutable pouvoir des loix. (609)

[I see unfortunate peoples groaning under an iron yoke, the human race crushed by a handful of oppressors, a starving mob, broken by pain and hunger, their blood and tears drunk by the rich, and everywhere the strong armed against the weak with the fearful power of the laws.]

The worst of it, Rousseau continues, is that "all this takes place peacefully and without resistance; with the tranquility of Ulysses' companions trapped in the Cyclops' cave, waiting to be devoured" (609). The passage derives much of its force from the trajectory of the speaker from the "classroom" to the outside and eventually to the horrors of war; from the quiet ironies of the opening phrases to a final ringing denunciation: "Barbarian philosopher! Come read us your book on the battlefield!" The dramatic effect is heightened all the more by contrast with the paragraph immediately preceding, which makes the point several times that, the state being an abstract entity, *un être moral*, one could theoretically "kill" it "without taking anyone's life" (608). Rousseau contrasts bloodless abstraction and hideous violence, intellectualizing apologetics and clearsighted denunciation.

Like many twentieth-century writers, then, Rousseau counters soulless systematic philosophy with vital historical reality, amoral speculation with moral passion. Robert Derathé has argued that the denunciation of Hobbes in "L'Etat de guerre" stemmed from a superficial knowledge of his work; that later, as Rousseau came to know Hobbes's work directly, he was more and more influenced by it.[30] Indeed, in "L'Etat de guerre," he appears to be working with a simplified Hobbes reduced to the notion of the war of each against all; much of the counter-argument hangs on establishing a distinction between the natural and the social, in order that the latter's depredations upon the former be cast into relief.

But does the distinction work? If we look a moment at Hobbes, for example, we see that in Parts I and II of the *Leviathan*, he confronts us with the unfolding political and psychological consequences of a universe of matter in motion; his geometrically ordered argument takes us through a chain constructing appetite and aversion, their ramified passions, speech, and thought, as voluntary motion. The "continuall progresse of the desire, from one object to another" is the mainstay of human happiness; and the "generall inclination of all mankind, a perpetuall and restlesse desire of Power after power, that ceaseth onely in Death."[31] As one commentator observes, the centrality of motion in Hobbes's world brings an end to the finite teleological systems of the Scholastics, opening up an infinite inertial universe.[32] Rousseau argued that Hobbes read features of social life into the state of nature, but his own account of the material world offers mechanisms similar to Hobbes's. As in the Second Discourse, the fragment on the state of war argues that the natural state of humanity is one of "rest," *repos*, but that the social body behaves according to physical laws of action and reaction, fueled by inequality, *inégalité*, understood in the full range of its meanings physical, moral, and social. The larger the social body, the less dramatic the contrasts of *inégalité*, the more inertia, or "frottement" would be noticeable in the machine.[33] The workings of the "law of conservation" blur the distinction between the natural and the social, as does the logic by which states are considered to be in a "state of nature" with regard to one another. It is the social that is accumulative and appetitive in Rousseau: "the more one obtains, the more one desires" (612).

It is hard to see how, for Rousseau, the operations of this universe of matter and motion could inflect the social sphere alone; indeed, in a series of concessions, he allows that violence arises in the state of nature, where people do sometimes kill one another "with either open force or stealth" (602).[34] Pain and violence in the state of nature can scarcely be articulated any more than "relational" concepts of vice and virtue; humans live without a sense of time or death, and only minimal notions of pain and pleasure (*Inégalité*, 3: 143–4). It is the development of language that gradually draws humankind from this atomistic perceptual mode; indeed, as Paul de Man has pointed out, the move to relationality and generality that defines "the political destiny of man" is already inscribed within the natural state itself.[35] Like the Hobbesian state of nature, life is disorderly, if not brutish, and short: "everything is in a continual flux" (602) between individuals whose "years are numbered" (604). What ultimately enables Rousseau to claim that no "warre" exists in the natural state is a rigorous redefinition of terms. For him, war "requires permanent relations" (602) and is, ultimately, a form of contract (615) – and hence ineradicably social. But this is hardly the war of each against all described by Hobbes.

Rousseau's attack on "systematic" philosophy is also suspect. Not only *Le Contrat social* (generally thought of as the most rigorously "systematic" of his political writings), but also "L'Etat de guerre," despite its fragmentary state, and *De l'inégalité* might be seen as having their own ties to systematic philosophy, particularly as *système* is associated with the geometrical demonstration and *méthode*. In the fragment, for example, Rousseau promises an examination based on basic "principles" that must compel belief (610, 612, etc.). But there is no great distance from the formal geometric exposition of axioms and proofs, to the fiction of the state of nature in *De l'inégalité*, a bare outline or set of *principes* from which social and political programs may be derived. The argument from such principles, however, cannot contain its own passion; the vivid denunciation of the "theater of murders" is staged as a departure from conventional philosophy, when Rousseau closes his books and walks outside.

Like Leibniz, whose thought owed much to him, Hobbes plays an odd background role in the period of this study; we can see in this brief look at Rousseau the extent to which Hobbes is simultaneously an adversary and a source. Rousseau's attempt to get around Hobbes replicates the object of his attack, and by so doing signals the degree to which systematic reason is inseparable from energy and desire, which constantly push and change the logical distinctions of the system even as they feed it.

In debates over the meaning and legacy of Enlightenment, neither the objects of admiration nor those under attack are quite what they appear to be at first glance. Foucault is right in warning of the futility of being "for" or "against" Enlightenment. Enlightenment is continuously articulated through the readings, interpretations, and interactions that are a constant feature of social practice. In looking at Horkheimer and Adorno, Foucault, and Rousseau, I have endeavored to show what is at stake in the interpretive choices from which we construct our Enlightenment and our modernity. These discussions also show the kind of textual work that provides the methodology of this analysis. Through close reading and a theoretical dialogue, I have tried to establish a "correspondence," in both senses of the term, between the eighteenth century and our own, a relation of both congruences and dialogical differences, in which Enlightenment is identifiable and recognizable, but also dynamic and open to change.

In the chapters to come, we shall see similar issues of order and logic, passion and containment, arising in a number of texts. We begin with an account of the semantic trajectories of the word *système* from the late Renaissance to the Revolution, the better to tune our hearing to the multiple contexts, associations, and language games in which the word is implicated. It is rather like learning a foreign language. Bilinguality is the condition under which we live when, as inhabitants of one century, we seek to understand the discourse and cultural conventions of another. We do not seek to "become" the historical other – a futile enterprise – but we can take advantage of our in-between status. Bilinguals, and translators, have access to insights that remain unavailable from a single, "monolingual" point of view (as Diderot observed in the *Lettre sur les aveugles*). Far from documenting the consolidation of a unified "classifying conscious-ness," this history underscores the ambivalence and multidirection-ality of systematizing discourse.

I take a similar approach in the second chapter on epistolary writing, moving away from intellectual history to examine a social, material correlate to the philosophical debate in the practice of letter-writing. Here, too, we find the period's preoccupation with rationality and order (in the horizon of expectations generated by genre, context, and the logic of response), the tendency in that order towards containment and coercion (in prescriptive how-to texts, and in subtler forms of politeness and expectation), and the ways in which epistolary networks, with their passions, projections, and permutations, function as the constant counterpart of the alternative discourse of systems explored in the previous chapter. The remaining chapters turn to the individual writers Du Châtelet, Condillac, and Diderot, to examine the different ways in which the discourse of systematic rationality could provide, not simply an "oppositional" critique of rationality, but rather an exploration of the role within reason of its ostensible others, passion and contingency. Diderot's writing, which includes fiction and aesthetics as well as philosophy and science, underscores the productive depth and range of this reevaluation of systematic reason.

In the conclusion, I take a new look at a favored metaphor for many of the writers of this study, the labyrinth. Although some, like d'Alembert, tend to see in the labyrinth the nightmare reversal of the system and an abyss of confusion, there are alternative views in Du Châtelet, and especially Diderot. It is the labyrinthine view of systematicity that constitutes the heterological tradition that I read in their works, and that enables us to see in the complexities and shadows of systematic reason, new possibilities and occasions for inclusiveness and progressive change. These readings constitute interventions in an ongoing dialogue between present and past; part of this version of the dialogue will involve not only the interaction of eighteenth- and twentieth-century interpretative frameworks, but also the occasional juxtaposition of various modern imaginative works – by O'Nolan, Barthelme, Cortázar, and others – with the eighteenth-century texts that are the focus of the study. The choices are eclectic, not systematic; meant more to suggest the lingering presence of certain problems and issues within the literary imagination, than to exhaust the comparison. As d'Alembert, Buffon, Condillac, Du Châtelet, and Diderot all discovered, the most rigorous analytic or systematic discourse produces and is produced by unpredictable areas of turbulence, analogical kinships, and vectors of desire. Thus this study will allow itself other avenues of exploration than the classically configured relation of "theory" and "text." The Enlightenment discourse of systems, so often taken as emblematic of reason's totalizing side, has within it as well "an entire discreet, thriving, flourishing world ... a secret garden"[36] where other perceptions, connections, and potentials are to be found.

Let us begin by reconsidering the *Odyssey*. Both Rousseau's insistence on the unresisting "tranquillity" of Odysseus's companions, and Horkheimer and Adorno's concentration on the hero's ruthlessness give a one-sided view. Despite the siren-like seduction of such readings and their usefulness in various contexts of philosophy and cultural analysis, it is nonetheless the case that this Odysseus whose single-minded quest has been read as the preservation of identity through purposive reason, and therefore taken as emblematic of the rationalizing process, was a very different sort of figure for the Greeks, who saw in him the thorough embodiment of *mêtis* or cunning intelligence. As Marcel Détienne and Jean-Pierre Vernant observe, *mêtis* is not part of the lexicon with which the Greeks describe their approach to logic, rationality, and knowledge; yet it permeates the world of "situations which are transient, shifting, disconcerting and ambiguous, situations which do not lend themselves to precise measurement."[37] *Mêtis* has little to do with *logos*. Rather than inaugurating a tradition of alienated punctual identity, Odysseus also belongs within a counter current that emphasizes cunning over truth and tactics over strategy.

The practice of systematicity outlined here can also be said in some respects to lie outside traditional accounts of Enlightenment thought and to provide a subversive counter-discourse to it. From another angle, however, the two are not so easily distinguished, and resist classifications such as "dominant" and "resistant."[38] The *philosophes* are both oppositional and permeated by the institutions and practices of the Old Regime; their program is emancipatory – and contains the potential for setting off a repressive dialectic. To reread the systematic discourse of the Enlightenment, to understand the potential subversiveness in its complexity and instability, is to see that systematizing and classifying reason could become hegemonic and coercive only to the extent to which significant strains within it are forgotten and repressed. It is important, therefore, to reread, reclaim, and rearticulate this logic which is both contestatory and productive.

CHAPTER I

"Système" – origins and itineraries

Système comes from a Latin word whose Greek roots mean "to stand
with" and which refers to a constituted group or organization. A
technical term in music theory, and later in astronomy and philosophy, its first recorded use in French is in Pontus de Tyard's 1555
Solitaire second ou discours sur la musique. The subject is of considerable
philosophic import. The proximity of music theory and philosophy
for the ancient world and Middle Ages is echoed in Tyard, who finds
in music "the image of all the Encyclopedia."[1] Looking back to this
text, one must be struck by the fortuitous resonance of music, the
original context of "system," and the evocation of the circle of
knowledge or encyclopedia in which the figurative derivations of
"system" would play so great a role. Tyard specifically calls attention
to the word *système* and indicates that it is a technical term that he
does not expect his interlocutor to know. The definition comes a few
pages later in the course of the discussion of *diasteme* ("a distance of
two or more intervals"): "among reputable Authors the word
System means several things, always however signifying a group or
assembly, and signifying among Musicians an assembly of voices
containing both intervals and Diastems" (90). The novelty of the
word is underscored when, after pages of highly technical discussion
of music theory, the Solitaire again feels called upon to define this
term in particular: "System is the name for any group or assembly of
intervals and sounds that produce a harmonious consonance ...
Nevertheless its true and most complete definition is a harmony
composed of at least two consonances or chords" (155). Even at this
early juncture, *système* is apparently thought of as containing a
certain margin for greater and lesser degrees of order and internal
organization. Much of the history of the term will take place in its
variance between the simple aggregate and complex symmetry.[2]

The work generally credited with bringing *système* into ordinary

French, however, is Marin Cureau de la Chambre's *Le Système de l'ame* of 1664,[3] a treatise presenting itself as defiantly scholastic in a Cartesian age ("I have never strayed from the principles received in the School [*des Principes receus dans l'Escole*]," [11]). The author spends a substantial part of his preface in justifying his use of the word *système*, "as extraordinary as it may seem in this context" (9). He sets up an elaborate analogy with astronomers who construct "the System of the World," or "order and disposition of the bodies which compose the world," observing that they do not take into account the "nature of those bodies," but simply their "situation, figure, size, and movements" (7). Cureau explains that he is similarly interested in the *situation, figure, grandeur,* and *mouvemens* of the soul, whose faculties are disposed as are the planets: "For the Understanding and the Will can be considered as the Planets and wandering or vagabond Stars; the Faculties attached to their organs are the fixed Stars; and each has its influence that it spreads throughout the body" (9).

In discussing the rather late appearance of "system" as a metaphor for mental or philosophical schemes, Walter J. Ong notes its relatively late application in cosmography, despite the antiquity of the term. The concept of the astronomical "system" is concomitant with the acceptance of the purely geometrical Copernican universe "in which no direction was more favored than any other,"[4] unlike older Aristotelian or Ptolemaic cosmologies, which favored an up-and-down orientation and whose conceptual "wholeness" was so absolute that the notion of divisible, analyzable parts was inconceivable. Cureau's use of the term to evoke a cosmos containing fixed and wandering stars that extend their "influence" afar suggests a curious survival – doubtless an effect of the author's allegiance to *l'Escole* – even as the modern visualist understanding has reoriented the scheme. His universe is clearly the modern one, composite and analyzable. In particular, its availability to abstraction, through the separation of "Situation, Figure, Grandeur, Mouvemens" from "le fond de sa Nature," places us well within the Cartesian era, whatever the professed beliefs of the author might be. Even so, the Thomistic distinction between natural and divine truths takes on the color of Weberian disenchantment, and Cureau strays into the proximity of philosophical skepticism in spite of *l'Escole.*

... dans l'incertitude où l'on sera toujours des veritables Principes de la

Nature, il estoit de tous les Systemes de la Philosophie, comme de ceux des
Astronomes, qui sont touts bons pourveu qu'ils rendent raison de tous les
Phaenomenes, & qu'ils ne choquent point la Religion ni l'Experience. Car
ce sont là les deux grans Luminaires qui nous doivent éclairer en cette vie;
l'un pour le jour des veritez eternelles, et l'autre pour la nuit & l'obscurité
de la Nature. ([12])

[… given the uncertainty that we will always have concerning the true
Principles of Nature, it was the case with all Philosophical Systems as with
those of the Astronomers, that they are all good provided that they explain
Phenomena, and that they contradict neither Religion nor Experience. For
those are the two great Luminaries that must shed light on our path; one
for the daylight of eternal truths, and the other for the night and obscurity
of Nature.]

The *vérité* whose discursive rehearsal would weaken it thus falls out of
language; Cureau is left with an abstract "order and situation"
bereft of value or substance and a series of indifferently useful
"systems" that will not yield any final answers.

In his 1675 *Remarques nouvelles sur la langue françoise*, Dominique
Bouhours credits Cureau with bringing *système* out of astronomy into
ordinary language.[5] Bouhours seems to distinguish two or perhaps
three levels of usage for *système*: a technical term in mathematics and
philosophy (evoking in passing its connection with the Copernican
universe), and a figurative expression with both accepted and non-
standard uses. If "Aristotle's system" and "a system of tragedy" [*le
systeme d'Aristote, un systeme de tragédie*"] are tolerated by people who
are sensitive to language [*des gens habiles en notre Langue*], while "the
system of the Court, the system of German affairs" [*le systeme de la
Cour, le systeme des affaires en Allemagne*] is not, it would appear to be a
question of the quasi-philosophical context of the former remaining
more easily permeable by the term's associations; something that the
context of the "world," conceived of as the Court or Germany,
resists.

A similar hesitation regarding the appropriate use of *système* can be
seen in turn of the century dictionaries. Incorporating the examples
from Bouhours in its definition of *système*, Richelet's 1680 dictionary
gives literal (astronomical) and figurative meanings (as "state or
constitution"), noting that the latter are not yet established. The
Academy dictionary of 1694 recognizes only the philosophical use of
système as a "supposition of one or more principles from which one
derives consequences and on which one establishes an opinion, a

doctrine, a dogma, etc." Although the definition emphasizes *système*'s philosophical use, the examples ("the system of Ptolemy, the system of Copernicus; he has founded a new system") show an interesting conflation of philosophy and astronomy. *Système* has become entirely abstract, referring not to the physical disposition of the universe envisioned by Ptolemy or Copernicus, but rather to their concept of it, their premisses and arguments. For Richelet, "C'est la figure du monde," the "figure of the world," a phrase which takes on its own metaphoric vibration: *système* is not only the world's "(con)figuration" but also a figurative world, an abstraction, a sign. Furetière's 1720 dictionary turns out to take the most conservative approach of the three, noting only that *système* comes from the Greek term for "composition" and has narrow technical uses in astronomy, medicine, and music.

Nevertheless, in the late seventeenth and early eighteenth centuries, the figurative uses of *système* had proliferated. Littré gives a phrase from Bossuet concerning the "nouveau dogme, ou, comme on parle à présent, du nouveau système de Luther" ["the new dogma, or, as they say these days, Luther's new system"]. As his aside indicates, Bossuet is clearly making a concession to popular jargon; that he would use the word at all, however, shows that it is not entirely beyond the pale. His reference to the "système de Luther" further indicates a certain trend – still present today – to associate "system" with a set of beliefs that one does not hold oneself, even that one finds inimical. The connotation is not absolute; the index to the 1720 edition of Bayle's dictionary gives instances of use that all appear to be in the neutral sense of any philosophical set of beliefs or theories ("le système des atômes," "le système des causes occasionnelles," etc.).

Nevertheless, the negative implications became attached to the term, which tends to crop up in theological tracts from the first half of the eighteenth century. A 1733 pamphlet, *Le Sisteme des anciens et des modernes*, apparently seeking to attract readers' attention through the use of trendy vocabulary,[6] uses the term rather loosely ("l'ancien Système de l'éternité de l'Enfer" ["the former system of the eternity of Hell"], 14). In an anonymous tract from 1735, *Le Système du melange dans l'oeuvre des convulsions*, the negative connotations of *système* are clearly in evidence, as is the ease with which the term permits a slide to the visual metaphor of a linked chain leading "au fanatisme & à la corruption des moeurs" ["fanaticism and moral corruption"].[7]

The *philosophes* often used *système* negatively to characterize scholastic thought and other objects of their enlightened disdain. In such an instance, a satirical poem of Voltaire's, God convokes various theologians and philosophers, and requests that they answer a simple question: "Dites-moi qui je suis? & comment je suis fait?" ["Tell me who I am, and how I am made?"]. Following a parody of Thomistic doctrine, the narrator summarizes,

> Chacun fit son sistême & leurs doctes leçons
> Semblaient partir tout droit des petites maisons.[8]

[Each explained his system, and their learned lessons seemed to come straight out of the madhouse.]

If the word *système* evoked a certain hostile alienness or unreality in the first part of the eighteenth century, it may be in part through association with the disastrous financial schemes of the Regency and the monetary *système* of John Law. Harshly alluded to in *Les Lettres persanes*, reflected in the normative and economic confusion of *Manon Lescaut*, the disruption spread by the *système* shook social and political institutions and fed into a general sense of ontological unease.[9]

A less threatening "neutral" philosophical sense of *système* occurs in a 1704 *Système du coeur* by grammarian-philosopher Etienne-Simon de Gamaches.[10] The title of the work is interesting in that it juxtaposes two terms that would increasingly be seen as incompatible as the century went on. Already in his dedicatory epistle to Fontenelle, Gamaches is attempting to bridge a perceived gulf between the scientific and the "human." Noting Fontenelle's importance in both the Academy of Sciences and the Académie Française, the author claims that "vous n'estes pas moins recherché pour le solide que pour le délicat," ["no less sought out for the solid as for the delicate"] ([III]). Like Cureau, he deftly shears theological questions from his field of study, averring that they "should not be mixed in with other sorts of questions, especially simple conjectures" ([XXV]). The purpose of the treatise, ostensibly understanding, is also regulation: "Wise conduct depends on the science of the heart [*la science du coeur*]" ([XIX]). Like Descartes, who in *Les Passions de l'âme* sought to give a dissection and anatomy of the emotions with a view toward "strengthening" the soul and hence avoiding the vagaries and dubious availability to the outside that constitutes "passion,"[11] Gamaches posits a Baconian equation of understanding and mastery, in which science, aligned with *système*, contrives to save and direct the heart. The conjunction of *système* and *coeur* thus takes on a more instrumentalizing sheen than originally suggested by the dedication's praise of Fontenelle's stylistic joining of the *solide* and *délicat*.

At the same time, the treatise manifests a certain tension between the controlling orderliness of the *système* and a disorderly world. The book has its origins, we are told, in the latter: "these were mere reflections randomly jotted down on paper, but ... they naturally found their places in my System" ([xvi]). The non-systematic, ostensibly banished as each idea found its "place," continues nonetheless to haunt the unnumbered pages of the "Avertissement." At one point, for example, Gamaches describes the types of people for whom he is *not* writing, all of whom rely on some fixed set of authorities or doctrines, or who substitute "un certain jargon qui roule sur des sentiments confus" ["jargon based on confused senti-ments"] for clear ideas ([vii–viii]). The ideal readers are those who are "free from prejudice" and "always ready to think" [*en état de penser*] ([xvi]). The irony is that the first types are all people who adhere to a predetermined plan of action or strategy for dealing with the world, in other words, a system. As for the last group, "toujours en état de penser" suggests an ongoing potential for change, difference, and a total indifference to "system," at least as far as "system" is conventionally understood.

The treatise's form also shows a problematic approach to orderli-ness. Far from the "systematic" exposition the Avertissement leads one to expect, the text comprises three rather loosely defined *discours*: "De l'amour en général," "De l'amour & de l'Amitié", "De l'Amour propre." Most surprising, however, is the table of contents appearing at the end of the volume. Instead of the distilled rendering of the *Système du coeur*'s internal organization, the "table" is a collection of reflexions and maxims, accompanied by page references to the body of the text, but following no discernible thematic, formal, or even alphabetic order: "How friendship some-times profits from losses in love"; "How a satisfying friendship is more secure than too happy a love"; "Idea of love in general," etc. In perusing these final pages of the *Système du coeur*, one has the impression that the "réflexions jettées au hazard sur du papier" from which the work supposedly originated, have again succeeded in freeing themselves from the author's system, although, given his practice, such a system seems to have been little more than wishful nostalgia for clarity, distinctness, and utterly unanswerable arguments.

The incipient paradox in Gamaches's Avertissement between unreflective, but "systematic," readers, and intelligent, but unpredictable, readers, is one that other writers will attempt to explicate and resolve. A famous example would be d'Alembert's distinction between a (desirable) *esprit systématique* and an (undesirable) *esprit de système* in his Preliminary Discourse to the *Encyclopédie*. Half a century earlier, however, Fontenelle, writing in the vulgarizing vein so admired by the author of the *Système du coeur*, had also come across two ways of looking at systematizing.

Fontenelle's basic aims in his essay, "Sur l'utilité des Mathématiques et de la Physique," are to establish the universality of *l'esprit géométrique* and to survey the present state of the sciences.[12] He is confident in the utility and aesthetic superiority of the systematic or "geometrical" approach.

L'ordre, la netteté, la précision, l'exactitude qui regnent dans les bons Livres depuis un certain temps, pourraient bien avoir leur premiere source dans cet Esprit Geometrique, qui se répand plus que jamais, & qui en quelque sorte se communique de proche en proche à ceux même qui ne connoissent pas la Geometrie. (14–15)

[The order, clarity, precision, and exactitude that have reigned in good Books in recent times might well have their source in the Geometric Spirit that is more widespread than ever, and that in some way communicates itself by proximity even to those who do not know Geometry.]

Fontenelle's *esprit géométrique* presents a certain self-consciousness of the classical *episteme*: temporally situated ("depuis un certain temps"), constituted in a discourse that does not require conscious knowledge of an object, but whose presuppositions subtend all utterances. The discussion of the state of the sciences seems to confirm this optimistic evaluation of systematic thought. In speaking of the "youthfulness" of physics, Fontenelle remarks that "systematic physics" must wait for "experimental physics" to "furnish its materials" (24). The distinction between *physique expérimentale* and *physique systématique* here clearly serves to privilege the latter as the other's goal or the *édifice* it seeks to construct. Fontenelle returns to his sequential model (first facts, then system) a few pages later, but another element enters the scene.

Jusqu'à présent l'Académie des Sciences ne prend la Nature que par petites parcelles. Nul Système général, de peur de tomber dans l'inconvénient des

Systêmes précipitez dont l'impatience de l'esprit humain ne s'accommode que trop bien, & qui étant une fois établis, s'opposent aux veritez qui surviennent. (25)

[Up until now the Academy of Sciences has only taken Nature by small pieces. No general System, for fear of falling into the disadvantage of those precipitous Systems that human impatience adopts all too easily, and that, once established, oppose the truths that come along later.]

A perversion of "systematic physics," the "precipitous systems" not only subvert the sequence of progress towards truth, but also derail Fontenelle's syntax. The architectural metaphor, with its implications of rational, orderly, and material progress, disappears, leaving us caught between two non-rational, emotional, forces: on the one hand, fear of the "precipitous systems," which prevent us from constructing the sought-after *Système général*, and on the other, the seductive appeal of those same precipitous systems to "human impatience."

In Fontenelle, we see an ambivalence regarding systematicity that will continue to be felt in other writers throughout the century. Although it is difficult to generalize – in the texts studied here the philosophical stakes and understanding of terms vary, despite a common vocabulary – one often finds pairs of terms, alternative aspects of systematizing, one valorized and pursued, one denigrated. Such polarization, however, only tends to maintain ambivalence, and there where it is the most energetically pursued, as we shall see in d'Alembert's *Discours préliminaire* to the *Encyclopédie*, it is often all the more impossible to maintain.

Before looking at d'Alembert, however, there is another crucial context for *système* that deserves our attention. By mid-century, the word *système* had acquired new polemical weight in the scientific community in the continuing debates over taxonomy and natural history, as it could automatically call to mind the work of Carl Linnaeus. With the publication of the *Systema naturae* in 1735, Linnaeus's classificatory system and binomial nomenclature spread rapidly throughout Europe.[13] Buffon's attack on Linnaeus in the "Premier discours" or introduction to the first volume of the monumental *Histoire naturelle*, was published in 1749. Although not without his partisans, Buffon's views were controversial even in France, and his arguments were long regarded as manifesting a misunderstanding of Linnaeus's project. More recently, Buffon's views have been re-evaluated as a significant critique, not only of

Linnaeus, but also of the entire taxonomic project.[14] Their contro-versy touches on numerous issues that continue to arise in the contemporary understanding of Enlightenment.

Much has been written over the past twenty years on the intensity of taxonomic enterprises in seventeenth- and eighteenth-century Europe; interest in the topic gained impetus in the 1970s from Foucault's account of the development of "sciences of order" in *Les Mots et les choses*. For Foucault, the withdrawal of language from "resemblance" or participation in the world is succeeded by lan-guage which "represents" and is conceived of in relation to the world. It is a short transition from Foucault's exploration of the manifold activities of the classical *episteme* – representation, classifica-tion, exchange – to his studies of "disciplinary" institutions and practices. Even given the criticism that Foucault's scheme renders overly uniform the set of practices subsumed under his concept of power,[15] philosophers, intellectual historians, and historians of science have found his a useful model for investigating the means by which science and epistemology configured themselves in the modern period. The desire to classify and set forth a rational world order reaches back as far as Aristotle; groupings of plants and animals based on external resemblances are an integral part of many early compendia of natural objects.[16] In the seventeenth and eighteenth centuries, however, the epistemological ramifications of such projects began to spread further afield. System-building was not simply a technique to facilitate the manipulation of the huge amount of new information concerning new species, but part of the cultural impulse toward rationalization and mathematicization.[17]

In the *Premier discours* to the *Histoire naturelle*, Buffon encounters many of the same ambiguities that have been attendant on the term *système* since it entered the language, and he amplifies the scope of the discussion. Buffon only explicitly states his views on Linnaeus's system twice in the course of the *Premier Discours*, and elsewhere does not mention him by name. The restricted use of Linnaeus's name, particularly in the discussion of plant taxonomy, points towards the wider horizons of Buffon's criticisms. Having noted certain practical uses of "systems" – in simplifying the naturalist's task, aiding memory, and offering "a sequence [*une suite*] of ideas" whose relatedness, however factitious, creates a livelier impression in the mind than could "detached objects [*des objets détachez*] without any relation"[18] – he proceeds to enumerate systems' disadvantages:

… de vouloir trop allonger ou trop resserrer la chaîne, de vouloir soûmettre à des loix arbitraires les loix de la Nature, de vouloir la diviser dans des points où elle est indivisible, & de vouloir mesurer ses forces par notre foible imagination. Un autre inconvenient qui n'est pas moins grand, & qui est le contraire du premier, c'est de s'assujettir à des méthodes trop particulières, de vouloir juger du tout par une seule partie, de réduire la Nature à des petits systèmes qui lui sont étrangers, & de ses ouvrages immenses en former arbitrairement autant d'assemblages détachez: enfin de rendre, en multipliant les noms & les representations, la langue de la science plus difficile que la Science elle-même. (9a)

[… wanting either to lengthen or to shorten the chain too much, wanting to submit the laws of Nature to arbitrary laws, wanting to divide Nature where it is indivisible, and wanting to use our puny imagination to measure its forces. Another disadvantage that is no less great, and which is the opposite of the first, is subjecting oneself to overly particular methods, wanting to judge the whole by its parts, to reduce Nature to little systems that are foreign to it, and arbitrarily to create detached assemblages from its immense works: finally, through the multiplication of names and representations, to render the language of Science more difficult than Science itself.]

It is not entirely clear how one should read this indictment. Certainly the split between "nature" and "system" that has been in some sense developing throughout the history of the word *système* is in evidence here, but other issues arise as well. It is interesting that, a few lines earlier, Buffon recognized systems' heuristic value in creating *rapports*, however illusory, among objects, but here he condemns them for truly creating *objets détachez*. A striking feature of this seeming series of criticisms is that it is supposedly reducible to two "disadvantages," one of which is furthermore said to be the contrary of the other. Neither the reduction nor the opposition is quite obvious on a first reading. One source of contrast can be found in the verbs *soûmettre* and *s'assujetir*, enjoining the naturalist neither to dominate nature nor to be dominated by rules. The terms are not symmetrical, but they suggest the need for some sort of "working relationship" between naturalists and the world and between naturalists and their technique.

The second group of disadvantages shows some degree of cohesion in the choice of terms: *particulières*, *partie*, *petits systèmes*, *assemblages détachez*. All indicate some form of "partiality" or limited vision. The first group, on the other hand, speaks to a misapprehension of the whole. And despite the dualistic arrangement implied by "a disadvantage/ another disadvantage," there seems to be a third term that cannot be subsumed or recuperated by the two others ("finally . . . making the language of Science more difficult than Science itself"). Concern for the language of science remains one of the principal leitmotivs of the *Discours*, as does Buffon's penchant for setting forth his views in slightly heterogeneous pairs, as we shall see.

To continue with Buffon's stated objections to the systematists: the passage we have just seen leads him to a reflection that serves as the basis for a series of progressively more radical versions of the same criticism. Claiming that systematizing activity is spurred by an innate human "penchant" to organize, group, and seek analogies among objects, however erroneous they may be ("faux rapports," 9a), Buffon holds up Linnaeus's system for ridicule for having "confused" such utterly different objects as "elms and carrots, roses and strawberries" (12a–b). Buffon makes the point even more vehemently in discussing Linnaeus's classifications of animals, speaking of his "classifying mania" [*manie de faire des classes*] and his "assemblages" as both gratuitous and bizarre (19a–b). Such systems are impossible, according to Buffon, first because nature, envisioned in terms of the Great Chain of Being, proceeds by "unknown gradations" that do not lend themselves to divisions (10b). Buffon returns to the idea of the incommensurability of plants, animals, and a "system" in the most radical formulation of his view: "il n'existe réellement dans la Nature que des individus, & . . . les genres, les ordres & les classes n'existent que dans notre imagination" ["in Nature exist only individuals . . . genera, order, and class exist only in our imagination"] (19a). Buffon's universe follows the law of Leibniz's principle of the identity of indiscernibles: all natural entities being, in fact, "discernible" from one another, their universal difference ineluctably condemns any grouping as an *assemblage bizarre*.

Buffon reproaches Linnaeus and other systematists for their failure, or refusal, to *see*. Whereas his own language is heavy in visualist metaphors – his preferred term for an idea is *vûe*, for cognition, *voir* – he accuses his opponents of neglecting sight through an over-emphasis on characteristics visible only through a microscope (12b). Buffon's scarcely veiled indignation at the thought that his own natural (in)sight might not suffice, that some artificial device might be needed to correct the evidence of the senses, reinforces the association of "system" with that which is alien, estranged from us as from nature. Buffon's preferred term for his own work is "method," although the distinction between "system" and "method" had not yet acquired the stability it would have in Lamarck's day.[19] Although Buffon occasionally uses the term "method" to refer to the work of his opponents (or "méthodiste," 12a), he consistently uses it in reference to his own enterprise, whereas he never applies the word "system" to his own work.

"Seeing" is at the heart of the venture, both in a conceptual and a literal sense: "On doit donc commencer par voir beaucoup & revoir souvent"["One should begin by viewing a great deal and by re-viewing often"] (8a). Given Buffon's emphasis on natural (in)sight and "lumière," his frustration with Linnaeus's abandonment of it is hardly surprising. Just as sight takes in whole objects in their context, while microscopes focus on specifically selected minutiae, Buffon insists repeatedly on the necessity for broad views, multiple aspects, and contexts. Rather than choosing one system or method to the exclusion of all others, one must "borrow insights from all sides" (8b), whereas one of the chief faults of the systematists is "wanting to judge the whole by a single part" (9a). Such was, indeed, one of the principal areas of contention between the theoreticians of a natural method such as Buffon or Adanson, and the proponents of artificial systems such as Linnaeus or (despite Buffon's defense of him) Tournefort.[20] At the heart of Buffon's method is the reminder that comparisons must be made "not of one part, but of the whole [*du tout ensemble*]" (13b) and that, given not only the infinity of differences in a universe composed of individuals, but also the limits of our own perceptions, all groupings are contingent and relative to the observer (10a). Thus, a few pages later, Buffon recommends grouping the animals according to their overall resemblance and their degree of familiarity to us (17). Such a grouping is no less arbitrary than artificial systems based on a single characteristic, but it has the advantage, in Buffon's view, of foregrounding the relationship between the naturalist and the observed world, rather than attempt-ing to suppress that relationship through an artificial exclusivity that makes no reference to the context of observations.

Those observations will take the (again, dual) form of a *description* and *histoire* of the object studied. The central section of the *Premier discours* takes up each of these aspects of the writing of natural history, past and present, emphasizing in particular the degree to which linguistic expression is an integral dimension of the enterprise. Observation is inclusive, synoptic, but communication is discursive, linear. Buffon, whose elegance of style has been much appreciated from his day to ours, returns on several occasions to the questions of writing and the relationship of language to the production and conduct of natural history. As we have seen, one of his complaints against the systematists is their misuse of language. His own proposed nomenclature will situate each object in its own specificity and in relation to others (13b). It is far from clear that such a nomenclature would simplify the language of science at all; certainly in comparison with Linnaeus's binomial system, Buffon's proposal – especially given his views on the universal difference of individuals – appears to generate an unending chain of names and qualifiers. If on practical terms this approach seems unwieldy, it is at least consistent with Buffon's desire to see a scientific language based on physical observation ("at a glance"), a relationship with the observer (on whom the criterion for "singularity" depends), and the specificity of the object in relation to other objects. Knowledge and its linguistic expression are closely related for Buffon, who discusses the need for a "complete," expressive language and a disciplined form of writing, both exemplified by the Greeks. The classical comparison reinforces Buffon's critique of Linnaean nomenclature. Knowledge is naming; naming is knowledge. Linnaeus's names, however, bring no knowledge and only increase difficulty. The Greeks knew the thing-in-the-world; Linnaeus can tell us only of the thing-in-the-system.

Buffon's attentiveness to language leads him to a style that counters the taxonomists as much as his manifest arguments. Buffon does not simply argue against "systematicity"; he practices a supple "linearity" that further serves to undo the system. His linearity takes many forms. We have seen that his natural history is couched in terms of a chain (18a), in which questions of order, placing items "before or after" one another, constantly reoccur. A most visible form of linearity is Buffon's insistence on the "discursivity" of the *Discours*. Not only does the text evoke public oral presentation through a studied use of *je* and *vous*, as well as emphasizing the verb *dire* ("Me seroit-il permis de dire," "ils ont dit," "je dis donc," etc.), but it also calls attention to the linear quality of discursive logic by repeatedly noting the order of ideas and events. Buffon's exposition relies heavily on terms of order (*d'abord, ensuite, passons au second ordre* ...) and transitions that emphasize the sequence of ideas ("Il résulte de ce que nous venons d'exposer," "comme nous l'avons dit," etc.).

The importance of sequence for Buffon can also be seen in his interest in epistemology, specifically in the order in which ideas are formed. Two passages in particular exemplify the trait. Buffon's introduction discusses the steps by which one begins the study of natural history, and features a "pedagogical" excursus distinguishing the stages of adult learning from that of children (8). Later, in a passage reminiscent of Condillac's famous statue in the *Traité des sensations*, Buffon asks the reader to imagine "a man who has forgotten everything" and proceeds to relate how that man perceives and begins to classify natural objects (16–17). Even in less elaborately developed passages, the tendency toward a narrative approach is strong. The text's tendency to narrative recalls Buffon's overall concern, setting him apart from his contemporaries, with chronology and history – less apparent here than in later parts of the *Histoire naturelle* or in such works as the *Époques de la nature*, but certainly present in the opposition of the titles *Histoire naturelle/Systema naturae*. Linearity infuses many of the metaphors Buffon uses to characterize his argument: *frayer des routes, chemin, chaîne*. Crucial in this regard is the term "method" itself, etymologically linked to the same series. (The *Encyclopédie* gives "par la voie" as the definition in the article "Méthode.") "Method" as path, is thus diametrically opposed to the "system" as aggregate or *assemblages détachez* Buffon warns about at the beginning of the *Discours*.

Even as it accents the linear, the text complicates the scheme by also manifesting an equally strong penchant for bifurcation and pairing. These too take numerous forms. On occasion the pair represents two equally undesirable extremes, as when Buffon speaks of the "two traps" [*écueils*] that the naturalist must avoid. Elsewhere pairs appear as positive and negative aspects of an object: "scrupulous attention," for example, can either be a help or a hindrance depending on one's state of knowledge (8a). Very rarely, Buffon resolves the duo into a third term, as when "description" and "history" are subsumed under the ultimate goal of explanation (22b). More often, however, he simply notes two aspects of an object or concept, and neither privileges one nor opposes them. He frequently "counts" his pairs himself, as when he refers to the "two qualities of mind" needed for the study of nature (7a) or organizes the obstacles to the study of nature under the terms "the first one" and "another" (7b). Elsewhere, he proposes two classes of science (15b), two possible objections to his method (17b), and two expository styles for writers (26b). Other pairs include the Lockean model of sensation and reflection (7b), two categories of observations of the world (17), and two kinds of truth (Buffon notes a third, moral truth, but does not discuss it here, 23–4).[21] As we have seen, this predilection for pairs can disguise a real plurality, as when Buffon presents "one disadvantage" and "another disadvantage" of artificial systems.

The text's relentless binarism continues, however, in Buffon's preferred stylistic devices. The epigraph from Pliny sets the tone:

Res ardua vetustis novitatem dare, novis auctoritatem, obsoletis nitorem, obscuris lucem, fastidiis gratiam, dubiis fidem, omnibus verô naturam, & naturae suae omnia.

[It is a difficult thing to give novelty to the old, authority to the new, brilliance to the worn, light to the obscure, grace to the unpleasant, faith to the dubious, to all things (their) true nature, and to Nature itself all things.]

His favorite tactic for criticizing Linnaeus consists of spinning series of absurd pairs of mis-matched objects (12a–b, 19b) and in general his prose tends towards the elegant equilibrium of pairs and the dramatic tension of antitheses. To give one example among many:

Les plus grands Philosophes ont senti la nécessité de cette méthode, & même ils ont voulu nous en donner des principes et des essais; mais les uns ne nous ont laissé que l'histoire de leurs pensées, & les autres la fable de leur imagination ... la méthode de bien conduire son esprit dans les Sciences est encore à trouver: au défaut des préceptes on a substitué des exemples, au lieu de principes on a employé des définitions, au lieu de faits averez, des suppositions hasardées. (23a)

[The greatest Philosophers have sensed the need for this method, and they have even given us principles and preliminaries; but some have left us only the account of their own thoughts, and others the product of their imagination ... The method for correctly directing one's mind in the Sciences is yet to be found: in the absence of precepts we have substituted examples, instead of principles we have used definitions, instead of solid facts, speculative suppositions.]

In spite of the preponderance of twos, however, Buffon's universe remains complex, rather than neatly dualistic. His primary challenge to classificatory systems, after all, rests in the principle that something invariably escapes classification, falls between the categories, in the domain of "imperceptible nuances", "middling species" [*espèces moyennes*], and "hybrid objects" [*objets mi-partis*], all of which "necessarily disturb the project of a general system" (10b). Buffon's linearity is a refusal of the *système*, but it does not constitute a refusal of complexity. The line is infinitely divisible; as in one of Zeno's paradoxes, it does not seem possible to get from point A to point B without becoming lost in the abyss of *objets mi-partis*. Furthermore, the line is rarely simple or single. Instead Buffon constantly proposes pairs, options, other aspects, binaries that rarely work into oppositions, but instead present a variety of relationships, resulting in the opening up of a kind of depth or space for dialogue.[22]

While Buffon is largely successful in setting forth his complex form of linearity as an alternative to taxonomic systematicity as a model for order, there remain several ambiguous areas, qualities which he condemns in the systematists, for example, but which are common to his model as well. One such quality is arbitrariness. Buffon makes an interesting distinction between arbitrariness and artificiality: Linnaeus's system is condemned not simply because it is arbitrary, but because it is artificial, equally estranged from nature and humanity. Buffon's groupings and orderings are admittedly no less artificial, but can be considered "natural" in his view, insofar as they are based on humans' relationships with the natural world. As we shall see, the issue of arbitrariness is an important one for d'Alembert and Diderot; Buffon's acceptance of arbitrariness in passages such as the one just referred to places him closer to Diderot's eventual approach, but this acceptance does not prevent him from condemning Linnaean taxonomy as "not merely arbitrary, but very badly thought out" (19a). Similarly, mathematical truths are "arbitrary and relative," whereas physical truths are "not at all arbitrary" (24a). An analogous tension exists between Buffon's empiricist skepticism and his essentialist hope for a method "that supports the very order of nature" (23a).

Another quality common to method and system is their relationship with "taste" [*goût*] or *penchant*. Early on, as we have seen, Buffon ascribes the use of systems to "man's penchant for finding resemblances among the most varied objects" (9b), and his most energetic attack on Linnaeus is liberally sprinkled with similar insinuations, speaking of his "classifying mania" and his "gratuitous assemblage" (19). "Penchant" or unreasoning desire is shown in numerous instances to run counter to the interests of good science, as we saw earlier in the case of Fontenelle. Were Buffon to remain with such examples, he could be seen as deconstructing the systematists' project by showing it to be founded upon that which it ostensibly excludes. But the scenario is complicated by Buffon's observation that *goût* or desire is the necessary starting point for all scientific curiosity (7a, 8b). The principal criticism, that scientific objectivity and abstraction are driven by desire and *manie*, is an important one, but in his haste to condemn *penchant* in others, Buffon remains open to the charge that he holds an idea of scientific rationality that is open to the same critique.

As much might be said of Buffon's negative assessment of the geometric method's techniques of abstraction or *dépouillement*, which leads to "suppositions contrary to Nature" and "an abstract being that no longer resembles the real being" (26a). The critique of abstraction in the *Dialectic of Enlightenment* makes much the same point, adding that the stripping away of qualities is the prime condition for negating the object and instigating systems of repression. The opposite move, to reinstate the object in its own context and its own materiality, also seems to find an echo in Buffon's demand that objects be studied and grouped with regard to the totality of their characteristics, without artificial exclusions. But Buffon also sees areas where exclusionary tactics are acceptable, even necessary. His long discussion on the writing of natural history includes numerous warnings and counter examples against "excess" [*fatras d'écritures*] and "irrelevance." Such judgements must, by his own reasoning, be as arbitrary and ideologically or willfully motivated as any he condemns. Furthermore, Buffon is perfectly willing to admit abstraction and *dépouillement* in his epistemological program (in the passages on the imaginary amnesiac or the student of natural history in the opening pages). Here, as in his drive against excess in writing, Buffon's method pursues the same path as that which he criticizes: arriving at truth through abstraction and exclusion.

Buffon's inclusionary logic also reaches its limits on one of the basic issues in his refusal of "systems." Although on the one hand he feels that there is no clean way of classifying reality, there remains at least one dividing line of absolute categories: "distinguish what is real ... from what we put into it" (26a), subject and object, us and it. Perception may be unreliable, arbitrary, and contingent, the effect of unknown causes, but the disjunction between the center of consciousness and the world is sharp and unambiguous. Thus

Buffon's method, while presenting a formidable critique of and alternative to the totalizing effects of abstract taxonomy, maintains a certain complicity with its potential for creating patterns of estrangement and domination.

D'ALEMBERT – ESPRIT SYSTÉMATIQUE VS. ESPRIT DE SYSTÈME

D'Alembert's *Discours préliminaire* to the *Encyclopédie* is the text which most fully articulates the tensions we have seen emerging through the first half of the eighteenth century. The *Discours* is a problematic text. It makes claims about itself, its purpose, and its expository order that it does not carry out. The *Discours* aims at setting forth and justifying the encyclopedic Tree or *Système figuré des connaissances*, but the path it takes to arrive at the Tree is circuitous indeed. In a pair of articles, Walter Moser has studied the attention given to self-reference in the *Discours préliminaire*, its proliferation of "orders" (variously qualified as *philosophique, métaphysique, historique, genéalogique, ordre de l'invention* ...) and the text's inability to integrate the discursive and the synoptic.[23] I am interested in many of the same phenomena, particularly the proliferation of orders, but with a different motivation. The fissure between discursive succession and figural simultaneity is part of a larger problem. Both these incommensurable elements participate in the text's guiding model, *l'esprit systématique* (*esprit*: discursive reason; *système*: figural complexity), as well as in its nemesis, *l'esprit de système*. Exemplifying the one, criticizing the other, are crucial to d'Alembert's enterprise. Unfortunately, what becomes increasingly clear in the *Discours préliminaire* is that the two are inextricably entwined. I want to examine the predicament and to see what alternatives there might be to this problematic account of rationality.

The *Discours* is in two main sections, each said to deal with a different aspect of the work in question: as Encyclopedia and as Dictionary. Each of these main sections falls into two sub-sections, the first of which is said to be of help [*un secours*] for generating the second in both cases. Throughout, d'Alembert uses a variety of terms to describe the exposition of his argument: genealogy, philosophy, history, metaphysics, encyclopedia, and dictionary. But the lexical distinctions are not in themselves enough to preserve clarity. The *Encyclopédie* is said to have two objects: as Encyclopedia it must present "the order and linking of human knowledge" [*l'ordre &*

l'enchaînement des connoissances humaines]; as Dictionary, it should contain both the "general principles" and the "essential details" of the arts and sciences.[24] These two "points of view" are to give "le plan & la division" of the *Discours préliminaire*, where they will be considered – as d'Alembert invariably points out – one after another. Knowledge's two aspects – "order and links" on the one hand, "general principles" on the other – liken it to language, with its syntagmatic and paradigmatic axes. The *Discours préliminaire* makes the paradigmatic its stated goal, through its privileging of *connaissance* over *système*, and its stated belief in the unified truth [*unique vérité*] of the universe, but the emphasis throughout remains order and *enchaînement*. This is not to deny that the dissemination of real positive knowledge is part of the encyclopedic project; but such knowledge cannot properly make it into the metadiscourse that is the *Discours préliminaire*: it must be enacted, performed. Comment *on* it invariably turns into a question of order, relation, succession, and transmission.

It is at the point of forming the Tree that the *Discours* nearly breaks down. "L'ordre philosophique de ce discours" is beset by the need to backtrack, restate, rename, and reconsider. It is hardly surprising that the image of the labyrinth reoccurs here. In a famous series of metaphors, d'Alembert claims that the encyclopedic order saves us from the constraints of successivity by placing the Philosopher:

au-dessus de ce vaste labyrinthe dans un point de vûe fort élevé d'où il puisse apperçevoir à la fois les Sciences & les Arts principaux ... C'est une espèce de Mappemonde qui doit montrer les principaux pays, leur position & leur dépendance mutuelle ... (xv)

[... in a high place above this vast labyrinth, from which he can see both the Sciences and principal Arts ... It is a sort of World Map that shows the principal countries, their position and interdependency...]

Yet no sooner has the enabling image of the *Mappemonde* appeared, than d'Alembert realizes how contingent such maps are, and that there are "as many different systems of knowledge as there are cartographic projections" each with its own advantage (xv). Nature, he tells us, is composed entirely of particulars without order, or whose order will always be hidden from us; any order imposed by us remains "arbitrary" (xv).

L'Univers n'est qu'un vaste Océan, sur la surface duquel nous appercevons quelques îles plus ou moins grandes, dont la liaison avec le continent nous est cachée. (xv)

[The Universe is but a vast Ocean, on the surface of which we perceive islands of varying size whose relation to the continent is hidden from us.]

Logically, this realization should signal the dissolution of his project, but d'Alembert begins again: "One might form the tree thus ..." He proposes a new series of divisions of knowledge based on epistemology. This approach eventually permits him to ground the Tree in the three faculties of Memory, Reason, and Imagination. The main branches of the Tree are described, its differences from Bacon's Tree duly noted and explained, the happy correspondence between the three faculties and the three divisions of the literary world ("Erudits, Philosophes, & Beaux-Esprits," xviii) discussed. Part i ends with a somewhat forced reconciliation of encyclopedic and alphabetic order and d'Alembert's assertion that classificatory systems (described as "frivolous enumeration") and even the Tree are less important than real existing particulars; and that the *ordre encyclopédique* of the *Système figuré* is "very different from the genealogical order of the operations of the mind."

D'Alembert's second part, which was supposed to consider the work at hand as *Dictionnaire raisonné*, consciously sets up a parallel with Part i: as the "metaphysical exposition" aided in the derivation of the Tree, so here a "historical exposition" will help show how to "transmit" the knowledge that the public desires (xix). D'Alembert is forced almost immediately to observe that actual history since the Renaissance does not correspond either to his early genealogical or epistemological orders, or to the encyclopedic order; he nonetheless qualifies it as having developed "naturally." Following his Great Man – actually, Great Philosopher – version of modern history with praise for his own philosophic century, d'Alembert proceeds to insert Diderot's Prospectus. The text is no longer the exposition of "general principles" that we were earlier led to expect, but instead a discussion of how knowledge is transmitted. Revised from the published 1750 version, the Prospectus contains new material concerning the use of alphabetical order and it lacks a passage that Diderot will later recuperate for use in his article "Encyclopédie."

La nature ne nous offre que des choses particulières, infinies en nombre & sans aucune division fixe & déterminée. Tous s'y succède par des nuances insensibles. Et sur cette mer d'objets qui nous environne, s'il en paraît quelques-uns, comme des pointes des rochers, qui semblent percer la surface & dominer les autres, ils ne doivent cet avantage qu'à certains événements étrangers à l'arrangement physique des êtres, & aux vraies institutions de la philosophie.[25]

[Nature offers us only particulars, infinite in number and lacking any fixed and determinate division. Everything proceeds by imperceptible nuances. And on this immense sea of objects that surrounds us, even if a few occasionally appear that, like the peaks of boulders that pierce through and dominate the surface, they owe their advantage to external events only, and not to the physical arrangement of entities or to the true institutions of philosophy.]

One reason for cutting the passage is that it has already appeared, as it was clearly the inspiration for d'Alembert's moment of "oceanic" doubt just before the construction of his Tree.[26] Repetitiveness aside, the passage is missing because the *Discours préliminaire* has by now surmounted those doubts, constructed a Tree, decided its history. The remainder of the text is concerned with *work*: assigning and researching the articles, publishing the volumes. The *Discours* ends with the list of contributors to the project. The text has thus moved from "a few philosophical reflections" to the division of labor and production of *l'Ouvrage*, the accomplishment of its task has not been without cost, and the encyclopedic order has only been achieved amidst some logical confusion.

As I have suggested, I think that d'Alembert's confusion is related to the account of rationality that he gives and ostensibly enacts in the *Discours*; let us examine his discussion of *l'esprit systématique* in detail. The subject appears twice, in the first section of each main part of the *Discours*. In the discussion of experimental reason that ends the sequence on the genealogy of the sciences, we are told that Nature will never be known by "vague and arbitrary hypotheses," but rather "by the art of reducing to the greatest extent possible a large number of phenomena to a single one which may be seen as a principle"; it is this reduction which "constitutes the veritable systematic spirit [*esprit systématique*], not to be confused with the spirit of systems [*esprit de système*]" (vi). The second occurrence comes near the end of the historical exposition of Part ii, as d'Alembert evokes his "philosophical century."

... le goût des systèmes, plus propre à flatter l'imagination qu'à éclairer la raison, est aujourd'hui presqu'absolument banni des bons Ouvrages. L'esprit d'hypothèse & de conjecture pouvoit être autrefois fort utile, &

avoit même été nécessaire pour la renaissance de la Philosophie; parce
qu'alors il s'agissoit encore moins de bien penser, que d'apprendre à penser
par soi-même ... (XXXI)

[... the taste for systems, more apt to flatter the imagination than to
enlighten reason, is nowadays almost entirely banished from serious Works.
The spirit of hypothesis and conjecture could at one time be extremely
useful, and was even necessary for the rebirth of Philosophy, because in
those days it was less a matter of thinking clearly, than of learning to think
for oneself ...]

In the first passage, d'Alembert has defined *esprit systématique* as the
"reduction" of multiple phenomena to their fundamental "principles," a process he opposes to "vague and arbitrary hypotheses."
The second passage, mainly concerned with criticizing the *esprit de
système*, informs us about the *esprit systématique* only indirectly, if we
may assume that it is what the other is not. Thus, as he goes on to
tell us, the one "flatters the imagination," while the other "en-
lightens reason"; the one can sometimes "put us on the path to
truth," but only the other can "lead us there"; the one occasionally
"glimpses the causes of things," but the other can "assure us of the
causes' existence." *Esprit de système* is again aligned with hypothesis
and conjecture, and, importantly, it is relegated to the past. D'Alembert underscores the past usefulness of the *esprit de système* for
"learning to think," but it is now only a hindrance: "times have
changed, and a Writer who would defend Systems today would be
too late."

The *esprit de système* is part of the current *esprit systématique*'s past.
Part of the "renaissance de la Philosophie," it is how we learned to
think. D'Alembert condemns it primarily as no longer useful: "The
advantages ... are too few to outweigh the disadvantages."
"Denuded" of direct contact with experience, it is no more than
"frivolous conjecture." Systematic philosophy, earlier described as
"abstractions and abuse of signs" (XXVII), takes on its most sinister
aspect when a heroic Descartes defies Scholasticism: "He can be
seen as the leader of a conspiracy who first had the courage to rise
up against a despotic and arbitrary power" (XXVI). It will be noted
that *arbitraire* is a term that tends to appear in discussions of *esprit de
système*. As the passage portraying Descartes as a freedom-fighter
suggests, the word has a heavy political connotation. *Arbitraire* is
defined in the *Encyclopédie* as "that which has neither law nor
constitution; which is left up to the judgement of individuals

[*particuliers*]." The etymology is given as the Latin for "will," and all save one of the cross-references are political: *cause, pouvoir arbitraire, despotisme, monarchie.* It is the tyranny of particulars, the oppression by the unexpected.

These resonances seem to have been present to Ernst Cassirer when he gave the distinction between *esprit systématique* and *esprit de système* a privileged role in defining what he called the "universal process of philosophizing" in the eighteenth century.

Instead of confining philosophy within the limits of a systematic doctrinal structure, instead of tying it to definite immutable axioms and deductions from them, the Enlightenment wants philosophy to move freely and in this immanent activity to discover the fundamental form of reality: the form of all natural and spiritual being.[27]

Cassirer's "universal process" and "fundamental form" are certainly in keeping with d'Alembert's view that the universe could – potentially – be seen as "a single fact and an overarching truth" (ix), with which they have much in common. In this account, a unified (and personified) Enlightenment eschews "limits" and "doctrine" and seeks to "move freely" and "discover."

As we have seen, d'Alembert's repeated efforts to draw genealogical, encyclopedic, or historical order from the anarchy of phenomena is constantly threatened by the persistence of the arbitrary, indifferent to whatever "laws" or "constitutions" may be proposed by the geometer. The project of forming the encyclopedic Tree is threatened by total annihilation. He imagines his philosopher confronting "the general system of the sciences and the arts" as "a sort of labyrinth," to which he applies himself in a series of complicated moves, "une suite d'opérations dont la génération même de ses idées rend la discontinuité nécessaire. Mais ce désordre, tout philosophique qu'il est de la part de l'âme, défigureroit, ou plutôt anéantiroit entièrement un Arbre encyclopédique dans lequel on voudroit le représenter" ["a series of operations rendered discontinuous by the very generation of his ideas. But this disorder, as philosophical as it is for the mind, would disfigure, or even completely annihilate an encyclopedic Tree in which one attempted to represent it."] (xiv). A "disfigured" *Système figuré* is nothing at all; and in the passage which follows, as we have seen, the partial solution of "Mappemonde" cannot dispel the labyrinth, which in turn degenerates into ocean. To form the Tree, it is necessary to begin a new paragraph and pay no heed to any of the preceding discussion: "nous sommes trop convaincus de l'arbitraire qui régnera toûjours dans une pareille division, pour croire que notre système soit l'unique ou le meilleur" ["we are too convinced of the arbitrariness that will always reign in such a division to believe that our system is either the only or the best one possible"] (xv–xvi). Indeed, despite the text's efforts to separate them, *arbre, arbitraire,* and *labyrinthe* have more in common than a certain phonemic harmony. Order is not to be derived from the manifold, but imposed by a select few, "les bons esprits" (xvi). D'Alembert downplays the importance of this move by denigrating taxonomists in general, but the fact remains that the entire *Discours* is geared towards demonstrating the contrary: obsessed with "encyclopedic" *ordre de l'enchaînement*, never quite arriving at the Dictionary's *principes généraux*; assigning the former to the *gens éclairés*, the latter to the *multitude* (xix).

If not entirely fictive, then, the *esprit systématique* is at least highly unstable. We are told that it arises from within the *esprit de système*, as the example of Descartes shows, but that it fails to prevent the tyranny of the arbitrary and that it must produce its opposite, as d'Alembert's practice reveals. The entwinement of *esprit de système* and *esprit systématique* thus parallels the "dialectic of Enlightenment" described by Horkheimer and Adorno, a model which also allows us to see d'Alembert's *Discours* in terms of its own *histoire*, the struggle to produce a master metaphor, the Tree. The main battle in the struggle: keeping *l'arbitraire* at bay. Numerous commentators have related the rise of mathematicization and probabilistic thinking in the seventeenth and eighteenth centuries to the repression of absolute, unknowable chance, and an affirmation of mastery.[28] True to this picture, the *Encyclopédie* defines chance, *le hasard*, as "that of which we are ignorant of the cause," thus reducing unfathomable randomness to a simple question of yet-to-be-completed knowledge. I would argue, however, that something of that primordial undifferentiated confusion is contained precisely in the *arbitraire* that dogs the *Arbre*. D'Alembert seeks to generate a natural, non-arbitrary Tree; failing that, he appropriates arbitrariness and proceeds apace. In order to develop, knowledge suppresses consciousness of its own facticity, but at a price. The Tree – the *esprit systématique* – is rooted both in the urge to liberation and progress, as well as in its totalizing power of the *esprit de système*.

For Deleuze and Guattari, trees, roots, and "arborescent structures" are key among the many figures of domination that they
examine: centered systems, territorialization, fixed attributes, hierar-
chies, unified "molar" systems. To the systematizing, subordinating
Tree they oppose the rhizome of connection and heterogeneity:

In contrast to centered (even polycentric) systems with hierarchical modes
of communication and pre-established paths, the rhizome is an acentered,
nonhierarchical, nonsignifying system without a General and without an
organizing memory or central automaton, defined solely by a circulation of
states.[29]

In view of their remarks on rhizomatic connectivity or the "logic
of AND," it is interesting to notice how, in the course of d'Alembert's
Discours, conjunction becomes less and less important, although he
seems willing early on to consider the multiple aspects of an object
(as when he asks whether logic is "an art or a science" (xii)). To be
sure, this rejection of a limiting choice is immediately undercut by a
wish for clear limits and "clear and precise" definitions. The actual
derivation of the Tree is performed with a razor-sharp series of
either/or propositions: "Our mind attends to objects that are either
spiritual or material, and it attends to them either by direct ideas or
reflective ideas ... Reason is of two sorts ...; either based on direct
ideas, or in imitation of them" (xvi).

Despite the importance given it in the *Discours*, the Tree is not the
most notable organizational figure for anyone looking at the actual
Encyclopédie. While endeavoring to preserve the complete circle of
knowledge (Diderot's and d'Alembert's etymology for "encyclopedia") the editors must render it usable and accessible by means of
alphabetical order. "Usefulness" is not, of course, what is fundamentally at stake. The systematizing Tree remains *hors texte*. Despite the
reminiscences of the *système figuré* in the rubrics of individual articles,
alphabetical order announces the heterogeneity and arbitrariness of
the world intelligible through language.[30] The "ridiculous disorder
of an alphabetic nomenclature" denounced by the anti-philosophe
Charles Palissot[31] is further balanced by the system of *renvois* which
for d'Alembert indicates real connections, *la liaison des matieres* (xviii).

D'Alembert's hesitancy here is cast into relief when we contrast
his approach with that of Diderot in his article "Encyclopédie."
Although I will reserve a fuller discussion of this important text until
later, it is worth noting here that, following a discussion that

characterizes language as the source of meaning to individuals rather than the reflection of transcendent truth, Diderot attacks the question of organization in very much the same terms as d'Alembert, but from the perspective of what Georges Benrekassa calls "a salutary practice of *disorientation*."[32] Diderot's elaboration of the use of *renvois* has come in particular to be regarded not so much as the imposed predetermined set of *liaisons* suggested in the *Discours préliminaire*, but instead as the site of discursive liberation and "philosophical contraband."[33] Thus the *renvois* will, in Diderot's oft-cited phrase, "changer la façon commune de penser" ["change the usual way of thinking"] (DPV 7:222).

Wilda Anderson, in a recent study of Diderot, offers a reading in which these two texts appear in almost total opposition, and I agree with her on many points.[34] It seems difficult to imagine a gap wider than that between d'Alembert's notion of an encyclopedia, "une belle machine de savoir ordonné," fixed in its "crystalline" – Anderson's happy expression – grandeur, and Diderot's complex and changing *machine infinie*. Diderot also embraces the very image that d'Alembert feels obliged to suppress, in his evocation of the *Encyclopédie* as a network of labyrinthine connections from which "it is impossible to banish arbitrariness" (DPV 7: 210–11).

Still, I think it would be a mistake to see too monological a discourse in the *Discours*, too dramatic a dichotomy between d'Alembert and Diderot. As Deleuze and Guattari observe, "There are knots of arborescence in rhizomes, and rhizomatic offshoots in roots" (*A Thousand Plateaus*, 20). The point is not to set up a dualism doomed to deconstruction, but to appreciate the diversity and fluidity of the "systematic" models, which like Diderot's participatory *modèle idéal* are perpetually evolving.

So let us look again at the *Discours préliminaire*. What can it offer us as alternative to its failed project of erecting an all-encompassing *esprit systématique*?

Certainly there are possibilities in that which the *Discours* attempts to exclude. The oceanic labyrinth of particulars that gives such vertiginous force to Diderot's article is present in the *Discours*, where it is neither recuperated nor combatted, but simply ignored. The systematizing activity itself generates a productive consideration of connections, of AND rather than OR. Still, the overall tendency continues to be, as Deleuze and Guattari would say, to subordinate the line to the point.[35] As we have seen, d'Alembert is ambivalent

about the status of the very *enchaînement* that he is discussing. If on the
one hand he sometimes emphasizes connectivity, by suggesting that
the best encyclopedic tree is the one with the greatest number of
connections (xv), he reimposes limits on the other: "Encyclopedic
order does not assume that all the Sciences are directly related to
one another" (xv). A similar ambivalence can be seen on the
question of whether or not the entire systematizing project is as
important as the determination with which d'Alembert pursues it
would suggest, or is merely "frivolous enumeration" (xix). The
relative importance of distinction and connection is utterly undecid-
able when d'Alembert considers the universe at its most rhizomatic
(just before calling it an "ocean"): "les objets se succèderoient par
des nuances insensibles qui servent à la fois à les séparer & à les
unir" (xv) ["objects would follow one another by impalpable
nuances that both separate and unite them."] In this passage, it is
clear that the links being proposed are not at all those of the
totalizing "identity logic," or desire to make unlikes alike, criticized
by Adorno, but instead bespeak the preservation of heterogeneity.

The text's ambivalence can further be seen in its alternation
between the linguistic poles of metonymy and metaphor. The
original disposition proposed by d'Alembert would seem to give
equal weight to each: discussion in Part I of syntagmatic "order and
links"; in Part II, of paradigmatic "general principles." As we have
seen, the *principes* are constantly deferred. The text resists closure,
proliferates structures, chains, sequences, genealogies. It also
abounds in figures and metaphors, however, and it is one of these,
the Tree, which becomes the master metaphor that imposes closure
on the *Discours*. D'Alembert's text imposes its own limits on just how
much alternative discourse it can be seen as generating. The
discussion of eloquence or genius is a site for such tension. Whereas
the systematizing impulse does not know what to do with that which
seemingly has no rules, no *principes*, eloquence "imposes silence on
reason itself" (x). Rhetoric, the attempt to formulate rules of
eloquence, is denigrated as "pedantic puerility" that d'Alembert
would like to see "banished" from *la connoissance humaine* (x). Later, in
discussing the arts of imitation, d'Alembert notes the flaws in all
philosophizing on the fine arts, since such analysis "can only be the
work of genius, and genius prefers to create than to analyze" (xvi).
One could perhaps argue that d'Alembert's banishment of rhetoric
and totalization of *génie* constitute another means of rendering

absolute the speaking subject by removing him from the categories of analysis that he projects on the world. At the same time, it is no less true that the dismissal of rhetoric marks a recognition of the limits of analysis. D'Alembert further complicates the issue by following the comments on genius with a passage he refers to as a "digression," in which he observes that the creative imagination is no less important to geometers than to poets. Analysis is the geometer's principal activity, but it does not alone permit creativity. D'Alembert's apology, "I hope that the reader will pardon a Geometer who loves his art" (xvi), calls attention to this perceived imperfection in his methodical discourse – an imperfection that approaches him to that master of digression, Diderot – and brings me to the last important element of non-discursivity.

"Un Géomètre qui aime son art . . . " Not just love, but the body's feelings in general are among the sub-currents in the *Discours*.

De tous les objets qui nous affectent par leur présence, notre propre corps est celui dont l'existence nous frappe le plus, parce qu'elle nous appartient plus intimement. (ii)

[Of all the objects which affect us by their presence, our own body is the one whose existence strikes us the most, because it belongs to us more intimately.]

In d'Alembert's genealogy of thought, awareness of the body and awareness of the world are simultaneous, and the motivating force impelling us to understand them is pain, "the liveliest sentiment within us" (iii). The "sovereign good" is reduced to "freedom from pain." If the necessity and the avoidance of pain are at the origin of the study of nature, however, pleasure and superfluity also have roles.

En effet, si un grand nombre de connoissances agréables suffisoit pour consoler de la privation d'une vérité utile, on pourroit dire que l'étude de la Nature, quand elle nous refuse le nécessaire, fournit du moins avec profusion à nos plaisirs: c'est une espèce de superflu qui supplée, quoique très-imparfaitement, à ce qui nous manque. (iv)

[If it were the case that a great deal of agreeable knowledge sufficed to make up for the lack of one useful truth, one could claim that the study of Nature, even when it refuses us the necessary, still provides for our pleasure with profusion: a sort of superfluity that supplies, however imperfectly, what we lack.]

This is an interesting, even revisionary, notion of "fact," permeated as it is by a discourse (*utile/agréable*) generally reserved for aesthetic contexts. Furthermore, the logic of supplementarity – the "supplement" seen simultaneously as superfluous and as completing a lack – alerts us to other moments when the mention of pleasure interrupts the text and shifts its coherence. The constitution of knowledge, genetically linked to both pain and pleasure, is later referred to as "a painful, and yet so necessary and even so agreeable a search" (VII). The terms are not in contradiction, but the "however" acknowledges their contrariness. The adjectives indicate that the mental activity of collecting and arranging facts is not neutral, abstract, or indifferent, but instead produced from and productive of feeling. Elsewhere, as wandering as we have seen d'Alembert's expository style to be, in the only passage he owns to be "digressive," he links the slip to love of his craft. Thus, while the text does for the most part strive to present human history as the disembodied *progrès de l'esprit*, it nevertheless remains implicated in the non-discursive realm of genius and persuasion, passions and bodies, pain and pleasure, attraction and avoidance.

In this reading of the *Discours préliminaire*, I have had two main objects: to examine the implications of d'Alembert's difficulties in elaborating a "systematic" discourse, and to ask what sort of a counter-discourse might lie beyond the impasse of the *esprit systématique* and *esprit de système*. It is to that impasse, of course, that I have attributed d'Alembert's dilemma: his efforts to produce an account of human knowledge that is both natural and rational fails, or rather becomes engulfed in the very things he criticizes in the *esprit de système*, preconceptions and arbitrary limits. Nevertheless, d'Alembert's text too can be seen as generative of other options, through the place it allows forms of non-discursive reason and even through the operation of its very systematizing energy, through its exploration of connectivity, its recognition of heterogeneity, and its resistance to closure.

AFTER THE *ENCYCLOPÉDIE*

Given the amplitude of d'Alembert's use of *système* in the *Discours préliminaire*, it is interesting to discover him returning to more conventional usage in a text written a few years later, his 1754 *Recherches sur differens points importans du système du monde*. The phrase *système du monde* returns us, of course, to the field of astronomy, but a passage in the opening *discours* is worth lingering over for its presentation of the extended meaning of the term. Characterizing the work of ancient astronomers as "vague" and "mal prouvé," d'Alembert observes that:

On n'y trouve point ces détails précis, exacts & profonds qui sont la pierre de touche de la vérité d'un système, & que quelques Auteurs affectent d'en appeler l'appareil, mais qu'on en doit regarder comme le corps & la substance . . . [36]

[One will not find those precise, exact, and profound details that are the touchstone of a system's truth and that some Authors affect to call its apparatus, but that one should regard as its body and substance . . .]

D'Alembert's denigration of the term *appareil* as "affected" and his concomitant valorization of "body and substance" place us on familiar territory, opposing form to content and privileging the latter. The image of the touchstone similarly underscores the notion of interiority and structural integrity. Curiously, however, the same "details" which form the "substance" are also said to "contain" the system's proofs – an image more evocative of *appareil* than *substance*. The underlying equation, truth = proof, repeats the uneasy juxtaposition, attempting to conflate a unified, autonomous *vérité* with a series of systematically related propositions. D'Alembert prefers the foundational *substance*; he describes nonetheless a relational *appareil*.

The negative connotations of *système* are all the more interesting, given the term's connection with culturally approved forms of philosophy and science.[37] Such was the negative drift in which *système* was caught that d'Alembert in the *Discours préliminaire* substitutes "Théorie du monde" for Newton's *systema mundi*, "because I do not wish to say his 'system'" in his praise of Newton. He further underscores his lexical hierarchy when, speaking of the partial astronomical understanding of the ancients, he claims that "what for them was only a conjectural and imaginative system, became a demonstration in Newton's hands" (*Discours*, XXVI–XXVII). "System" thus points to that which is not demonstrable, but instead dogmatic and fantastic.

The lure and fundamental untrustworthiness of the philosophical system is evident in texts from the second half of the century by Bailly, d'Holbach, and Senebier. In his *Eloge de Leibnitz*, Jean-Sylvain Bailly clearly distinguishes between "our century" and Leibniz's "century of systems."[38] Here *système* functions as the dividing line:

not my kind of philosophy. On the other hand, Bailly takes precisely the opposite tack in his *Histoire de l'astronomie moderne*,[39] where he argues that "systems" as imaginary conjectures are actually essential to the conduct of science. His most elaborate metaphor is a familiar one: "Imagine two or three avenues that lead away from a common point ..." The avenues quickly ramify into "a labyrinth" with "infinite exits." Some people study the labyrinth from one end, some from the other.

Des hommes plus courageux, instruits de l'art de la divination & des conjectures (ce sont les auteurs des systèmes), se proposent de leur servir de guides. Nous avons remarqué, disent-ils, que l'enchaînement de ces rameaux suit une certaine loi ... Les plans se succèdent, les systèmes se perfectionnent, & l'on arrive au dernier plan, qui est celui du labyrinthe, ou au dernier système, qui est le véritable ordre de la nature. (1: 334–5)

[Courageous men, instructed in the art of intuition and conjecture (these are the authors of systems), propose to help them. We have noticed, they say, that the branches are related according to a certain law ... The plans succeed one another, the systems are perfected, and we come to the final plan or map, which is of the labyrinth itself, the final system, the veritable order of nature.]

Bailly contains the labyrinth motif more neatly than d'Alembert was able to. The rapid proliferation of an "infinity" of communicating paths does not create the textual breakdown we observed in the *Discours préliminaire*. Potential tension is first eased by the prospect of entering the labyrinth at the end where all paths meet; even when the paths are experienced in their complexity, superior minds determine that they manifest an orderly pattern, *une certaine loi*, rendering them predictable. In spite of the visualist orientation of this passage, Bailly maintains an approach more closely aligned with the linearity of Buffon than with d'Alembert's attempted synoptic systematicity. There is no high place from which one may comprehend the labyrinth. Complexity is understood only by means of the linear thread of Ariadne and the sequentially-produced plans. Bailly seems equally poised between a foundational calm faith in the essential order of things and a more feckless Diderotian appreciation of "divination et conjectures." Bailly, unlike Diderot, believes in a real unitary truth in nature, but he has a sanguine appreciation for "necessary error" and even an intimation that "systems" undo the distinction between real and imaginary: "Without systems we would never attain any general truth" (1: 335). It is a short step from this intuition to claiming *vérité* to be a creation of the imagination, a bridge between the factual and the factitious.

D'Holbach's *Système de la nature* vividly dramatizes the different uses to which *système* could be put. In his introductory chapter "De la nature," d'Holbach begins his materialist manifesto by decrying the errors and illusions committed by the unempirical study of the world: "all their systems, conjectures, reasonings, from which experience is banished, were but a long tissue of errors and absurdities."[40] Here and elsewhere, *système* refers to a (usually wrong) set of beliefs, a usage for which, as we have seen, Enlightenment writing offers ample precedent. But the *système* of d'Holbach's title is, of course, a different matter altogether and the very antithesis of the "absurdities" he condemns. The material universe is referred to as an "assemblage" composed strictly of matter and movement; *système* appears as a classificatory term as d'Holbach posits the rational order of the universal "organization": "Les différens systêmes des êtres, ou, si l'on veut, leurs *natures particulières*, dépendent du systême général du grand tout" ["The different systems of entities, or if you prefer, their particular natures, depend on the general system of the whole"] (1: 11). There is nothing particularly novel in either d'Holbach's understanding of *système* as a set of beliefs (complete with the traditionally negative association) or his collapsing the idea of natural order into a dead metaphor for the solar system. The latter lends his title and subsequent usage a certain force by subtly underlining the materiality of the nature in question. The semantic value of *système* remains unstable, even in a work in which it is clearly a key term of explosive polemical potential. Thus, even as it plays an important part in the eighteenth-century vocabulary, consciously chosen for analysis, attack, and defense, or simply as a linguistic marker indicating the level of theoretical sophistication in a text, it also perpetuates a kind of excess baggage, confusing issues when it is meant as a hallmark of clarity and distinctness, betraying the extent to which it is available to varying agendas.

One could not, in fact, find two agendas more opposed than those of the atheist d'Holbach and the Calvinist naturalist Jean Senebier.[41] It is a paradox, given Senebier's formal opposition to the atheistic orientation of French materialism, that *système* again becomes in his text a far more flexible and open-ended concept than in d'Holbach's or Bailly's. In his *Essai sur l'art d'observer,* originally published in 1775 and revised and augmented in 1802,

Senebier notes – like Diderot, Bailly, and others – that the physical universe is too large and too diverse for any one being other than God to be able to seize "the whole of the general system" [*l'ensemble du système général*].[42] Classificatory schemes such as Linnaeus's are thus good, practical tools as we attempt to study the multiplicity of natural objects. Senebier will have none of Buffon's doubts concerning either the feasibility or desirability of such projects. The study of nature becomes a more complicated affair in the chapter "Des systèmes." Senebier begins with a cogent résumé of *système*'s twin connotations, physical ("the disposition of one or several parts of nature") and abstract ("that happy combination of ideas based on facts and deduced from one another, that explain phenomena," 2:305). Primary is the notion that linkage – what Senebier calls *enchaînement* – confers and even constitutes meaning, a rationalistic view consistent with his idea that we cannot directly comprehend the totality of the universe, and instead must define what *rapports* we may. It is not a notion leading directly to an account of empirical discovery.

True, systems are fraught with danger, and "seduce by brilliant appearances" (2:312). On the other hand, they have produced undeniable results: "les systèmes ont fait entreprendre une foule de recherches pour les établir ou les détruire; ils ont encouragé mille efforts qu'on n'aurait pas fait sans eux" ["systems have spurred a great deal of research in order to prove or disprove them; they have encouraged many efforts that would not have been made otherwise"] (2:312). Unlike Bailly's nuanced approval of a system as a "necessary error" on the path to truth, Senebier accentuates the desirability of the activity of "searching" in itself. Ultimately, "L'esprit systématique est bien plus dangereux que les systèmes" ["the systematic spirit is more dangerous than systems"]. "Systems allow for critical comparisons, but a "systematic mind" is inflexible. Senebier does not actually want to place undetermined activity as the sole end of science; as limited as he feels perception to be, he has faith in an ultimate goal, a unique truth. At the same time, there are "many routes that lead there" (3:245), as he claims in his volume on the "general qualities of observation." Still, the emphasis on truth's singularity, despite a plurality of routes, is different in spirit from the reiterated call to "rechercher" in the chapter on systems. As we have seen in d'Alembert, a certain systematizing energy leads the text on a different course than one might expect from the more foundational values it elsewhere espouses. Symptomatic too of this discursive tendency to swerve off course is Senebier's use of the expression *esprit systématique* to mean exactly the opposite of what d'Alembert had in mind in using the phrase. Even as a consensus of vocabulary is missing among theoreticians of systems, so too there is more heterogeneity than accord in their discussion. After examining such texts, one can no longer return to Cassirer's serene account of the *esprit systématique* and the *esprit de système* –

The whole theory of knowledge of the eighteenth century strives to confirm this distinction. (8)

The problem lies deeper than occasional reversals of the terms. Rather "the whole theory of knowledge" is subverted by the fault lines and shifting sands of all the instances of the discourse of systems, where no clear distinctions remain for long. As much may be said of Foucault's claim that *mathesis, taxonomia,* and *genèse* constitute "a solid grid of kinships that defines the general configuration of knowledge in the Classical age" (*Order of Things,* 74). The master narratives need to open a space for movement, inconsistency, and heterogeneity.

I will cite as postscripts two texts that occur as *système* encounters the fate of many conceptually-laden terms that have entered into wide usage: reification and recuperation. *Le Système des colonies,* an anonymous pamphlet written in response to debates in the National Assembly in December, 1789, is "systematic" only insofar as its numbered paragraphs present a fairly simplistic account of the relations linking colonies to metropole, including a defense of the slave trade, as, one supposes, a chief component in that *système de rapports.*[43] A comedy first performed in the same month, *Lucie, ou le système d'amour,*[44] casts the term in high relief, an emphasis made all the more clear by *système*'s frequent appearance at the end of the lines of verse. Lucie's "system," or personal code of conduct, is to refuse to reveal her tender feelings for Delval. Confronted by her father Delmont, she resists:

DELMONT. Quelques mots échappés, une indiscrète enfin
    Ont trahi ton secret; ainsi sans être fin,
    Je puis, ma chère enfant, connoître ton système.
LUCIE. Un système! qui? moi!
DELMONT. Je suis certain, toi-même. (scene 5)

[D: A few careless words and an indiscreet friend have betrayed your secret; without being too clever, my dear child, I have discovered your system. L: A system! who? me! D: You yourself, I am sure of it.]

– but her eventual capitulation provides her father with the opportunity to spell out the moral.

LUCIE. Je cède, j'ai promis,
    Et je sens qu'il est doux d'avouer que l'on aime.
DELMONT. Plus d'erreurs. Plus de ruses. Abjure un faux système;
    Un songe de l'esprit vaut-il l'instinct du coeur?
    Prends de guides plus sûrs, la nature & l'honneur. (scene 20)

[L: I concede as I have promised, and I realize that it is sweet to confess that one loves. D: No more errors. No more ruses. Abjure a false system; is the mind's fantasy equal to the heart's instinct? Take surer guides, nature and honor.]

Lucie accedes to lucidity in allowing herself to be guided, not by another pair of abstractions, but by the two men, Delmont and Delval, who like their names both repeat and complement one another in masculine solidarity. Her "system," qualified as false, equated with *esprit*, and opposed to *coeur*, was in effect her independence. The text presents an ironic contrast to the political pamphlet, where "system" is cast in a positive light, but is a euphemism for slavery.

Nous dirions le bonheur, abstraction faite du sentiment de l'esclavage, dont les Nègres en général [ne] sont guères susceptibles, puisqu'ils sont nés dans cet état, en sorte qu'on peut dire que leur liberté leur seroit à charge, & qu'ils sont incapables de la recevoir & d'en jouir. (*Le Systême des colonies*, § XVII)

[Leaving aside their awareness of slavery, we would say that Negroes in general are scarcely susceptible of happiness, since they are born into that state, so that one could say that their freedom would weigh upon them and they would be incapable of receiving it and enjoying it.]

There is no place here for affectivity within the "system," whether we understand it as a psychological or a commercial configuration. It is precisely this capacity to *faire abstraction* of that which is most intimately human, stripping away meaning, that gave *système* the sinister resonance that confounded Lucie ("Qui! moi?"). Both the refusal here of the slaves' potential for *jouissance* and Lucie's discovery of emotional *douceur* participate in the suppression and over-writing of the subjects.

Système is an active player in many language games. If it participates in a discourse of control, it also shares in a discourse of conjecture and undecidability. Often equated with the non-natural, fictive, and arbitrary, it can nevertheless be either denounced as alien (Bailly on Leibniz) or approved as helpful in making sense of confusion (Bailly on astronomy) and in helping to uncover nature's fundamental order (Senebier). Nature can be seen as inherently systematic, but still opposed to the philosophical system as something irremediably estranged from it (d'Holbach). A related opposition is that of *système* and *coeur*; in *Lucie*, the heart triumphs, but the opposite occurs in Gamaches's *Système du coeur* – although not without ambiguity. Senebier warns of an *attachement opiniâtre* for systems, Fontenelle is concerned with *systêmes précipitez* and Buffon with both *goût* and *manie*. Despite the philosophical prestige of detachment, there is no clean break between the abstract and the emotional or irrational, as we have seen in d'Alembert. Throughout these texts, structures bend and allegiances waver. Traditional accounts in intellectual history have taken the systematic model as a unified cultural phenomenon, which has been interpreted as scientifically progressive or demonized as ideologically menacing, depending on the frameworks invoked. The "systematic model" is a much more mobile network, or constellation, of agreement, disagreement, change, inconsistency, and uncertainty. There is no one discourse of systems, no one vocal line, but instead polyphony.

CHAPTER 2

The epistolary machine

If the women and men of the Enlightenment felt an affinity for the *esprit systématique*, a sense of the importance of complex networks of mutually defining, yet mobile, relationships, this affinity was reflected in and reinforced or perhaps even prompted by their participation in the widespread and engrossing practice of letter writing, beyond any encounters with trees of knowledge or Linnaean classificatory schemes. For us to understand the power of systematic reason and its critique, it is important to look beyond the disciplinary boundaries of philosophy and science. Sorting, naming, and classifying are not the exclusive province of the taxonomists. As I hope to show in this and subsequent chapters, the gulf between the love letters of Julie de Lespinasse and the abbé de Condillac's *Traité de systèmes* is not as wide as one might think.

Both social history and literary criticism have had a great deal to say in recent years about correspondence, real or fictional, as one of the eighteenth century's primary expressive forms. Like the salon conversation with which it was closely allied, letter writing was both a personal and a public performance, a means of affirming the importance of social relations, and a vehicle for furthering the exchange of ideas, the imparting of information, and the construction of a self, beyond the contacts immediately available to one.[1] This is ground on which over-sharp distinctions of "public" and "private" founder. The most private, inward-looking letter is, as Terry Eagleton has remarked, "ineradicably social."[2] Letters are circulated on a wide variety of levels, in many forms, and within a complex web of relations and projects, from the overtly public open letter to the recopied, circulated, and perhaps published "personal" letter; from the staged exchange (as when Diderot and Falconnet correspond over the artist's relation to posterity) to the surreptitious *billet* slipped into a pocket, hastily read, and burned. The vogue of published correspondences creates a new possibility in the horizon of expectations of any letter writer, and the proliferation of letter manuals suggests the degree to which the form could be a significant device for self-representation and regulation.[3]

As the author of a mid-century self-help book, the *Manuel de l'homme du monde*, put it:

Le talent de bien écrire une lettre n'est pas commun, & cependant on a souvent lieu d'en faire usage: c'est en quelque sorte une autre façon de vivre avec les personnes qu'on aime, ou à qui on doit des égards. La plupart des Jeunes gens qui entrent dans le monde, & ceux même qui parlent bien, sont si peu formés à ce style qu'ils écrivent à peine raisonnablement: c'est une façon de décrier soi-même son esprit, qui lui fait toujours perdre de l'opinion favorable qu'on avoit conçue de lui dans la conversation ... Or le moyen unique de posséder parfaitement ces bienséances, ne peut s'acquérir que par la connoissance des usages du monde & dans tous les témoignages de devoirs ou d'égards qui forment le commerce de la Société.[4]

[True talent for letter-writing is uncommon, and yet one must often attempt it: it is a way of living with other people of whom one is fond, or to whom one owes respect. Most young people coming into the world, even those who speak well, have so little notion of this style that they can scarcely write reasonably; they discredit their own wit, and lose the favorable impression created by their conversation ... The acquisition of these rules of correctness can only be achieved by a knowledge of the world's customs and in the performance of the duties and obligations that form the commerce of Society.]

At first glance, the emphasis on conversation and *usage* appears to exercise the regulatory function of Vaugelas's *Remarques sur la langue françoise*, where linguistic purity derives from face-to-face association with "l'élite des voix."[5] Vaugelas's linguistics abet the cultural politics of the absolute monarchy, by making physical presence at court indispensable. The *Manuel*'s own preface, however, undercuts such a reading. It addresses itself to the young man who upon making his first entrance into society, "a Foreign Country whose language he hardly understands" (XIII), has not the time (or inclination) to read the "various Books" necessary to educate himself, nor the years of experience needed to acquire any kind of worldly polish. Fortunately, there is the *Manuel*:

La plûpart de ces connoissances, il est vrai, sont dispersées de côté & d'autre dans quantité de Livres; mais ne pourroit-on pas les rapprocher

dans un Ouvrage portatif, & procurer par cette collection un grand
avantage aux jeunes gens? (x–xi)

[It is true that most of this knowledge is dispersed here and there in large
numbers of Books; but could it not all be brought together in a portable
volume, thereby procuring a great benefit to young people?]

The act of reading can thus substitute for conversation and experience acquired over time. This knowledge, properly ingested, governs
both speech and writing: "To have a sense of [*sentir*] who one is, and
to whom one speaks, is the first requirement for good speaking, and
consequently for good writing. This sentiment should regulate what
one says and the manner of saying it" (317). "Knowing oneself and
others" is the ultimate goal of the *Manuel*, which construes such
insight as knowing one's place in the large order of social and
political things that it sets before the reader's eyes. This is a highly
specific, overtly ideological form of self-knowledge, yet even the
Manuel participates in the utopian vision of a contemporary educa-
tional project, the *Encyclopédie*, in shaping selves and changing "la
façon commune de penser."

The letter, whether as text disseminated throughout the world at
large or as missive from me to you, thus articulates the general
cultural impetus that invests textual transmission with the power and
authority formerly reserved for "l'élite des voix," and the intense,
punctually located energies (social, sexual, aesthetic, political) involved in constructing oneself in relation to others, others in relation
to oneself.

Dena Goodman offers this euphoric vision of the epistolary
machine:

the Parisian salons, the Republic of Letters based in them, and the
epistolary networks that ran through them, served as an implicit mode ...
to transform society ... neither hierarchical in its internal operations nor
closed or self-perpetuating as an elite. Rather [the Republic of Letters] was
egalitarian in form and democratic in inspiration.[6]

Why might this be? one still asks. Since letters do not, as such,
always represent or enact the democratic spirit, "openness" or
gender equality. The widely held belief that women were somehow
especially gifted for epistolary writing is accompanied, in the letter
novels that constitute some of the age's most acute critical reflection
on the dynamics of epistolary form, by a distinct preference for
letters/plots of the so-called "Portuguese type": the passionate cry of

the woman seduced and abandoned, a crucial figure in the period's construction of female sexuality. Power relations, manipulation, and duplicity are the prime movers of epistolary novels, and throughout the "public" realm of letters as well.[7]

In attempting to resolve this contradiction, I shall consider the dynamics of correspondence in more general terms, and propose some models under which both the euphoric and disabused accounts of epistolary discourse might function, as well as showing how this practice might offer a widely diffused alternative understanding of systematicity. My interest here is less in the qualities of the individual letter, its literariness or the authorial self-consciousness of the writer,[8] than in the ways in which letters relate to one another as elements within a dynamic system, criss-crossing Europe and venturing beyond, relating public and private, passion and convention. To participate in the system is to avail oneself of its creative, productive capacities, to become part of the epistolary "desiring machine."[9]

Parts indicate wholes in a correspondence; individual letters are implicated in a series, or at least in a presumed circuit of sender → receiver;[10] and correspondences, however banal or dramatic, are implicated in larger sets of social/discursive practices. We may read an isolated letter, or one side of a correspondence, yet these parts are implicated in wholes, they produce "wholes" if only as ideal entities. Writers produce readers, who in turn become writers themselves, exchanging roles. The choice of interlocutors from a spectrum of intellectual, familial, social, sexual, and commercial partners bespeaks both the world in which the correspondence takes place, and the writing subject who constructs and is constructed by these choices and connections. Having marked an interlocutor (producing "Dear X," but not "Dear Y or Z" for the first time) inaugurates an open-ended set of possibilities for variable affective, intellectual, or strategic investment in a given dialogue. Correspondence is the productive, dialogic genre *par excellence*, in which time, chance, and what Christie V. McDonald calls "the rusing strategies of the writing subject" either suggest or elicit new subjective configurations, further discursive energies.[11]

It is probably a mistake to over-emphasize "absence" as a feature of epistolarity. Certainly physical and temporal distance are thematized in the letter, where if they do not exist, they must be invented, as in the opening section of Rousseau's *Julie*, where the correspondents live under the same roof. In the same novel, however, "real" time and space are transfigured and overcome by the letter. "I received your letter with the same rapture that your presence would have caused, and at the height of my joy, a mere piece of paper took your place" (*Julie, ou La Nouvelle Héloïse*, part 2, letter 16). Saint-Preux is not a madman, nor even an *extravagant*. As Hume defines belief ("a lively idea related to or joined with a present impression," *Treatise*, Book I, part 2, § 7), so Saint-Preux should be justified in "believing" that he sees and touches Julie: the impression of the letter is associated with the liveliest of ideas. Janet Altman remarks that "Epistolary language, which is the language of absence, makes present only by make-believe,"[12] but there is no "only" here. Even a less radical empiricism than Hume's opens the door to an awareness of the constructedness of the perceptual world and a skeptical assessment of what it means to be "really" anywhere. What does it mean to "know" Julie, to be in physical contact with her, if her face and body seem as much a representation as the words on the page? The letter's productive absence produces presence.[13]

The first quality of the correspondence is its productive relation between parts and wholes. The second general rule concerns the significance of the correspondence as an act, or set of acts, of reading. Historical correspondences and letter novels provide numerous instances which foreground the process by which recipients of letters assimilate those texts into their own and display a variety of strategies for reading, interpreting, and responding. Their approaches range from the manic – as when the marquis de Sade, writing from prison, decides that his wife's letters are in a code whose key she "refuses" to reveal – to the more conventionally conversational, as when Diderot responds conscientiously to questions and comments from Sophie Volland.[14] We should, perhaps, speak of one act, "reading/writing," with regard to letters: one writes to be read and reads to find the writer, yet despite this near-fusion (which of course varies in intensity in the different modes of correspondence) slippage inevitably occurs.[15] The sender cannot ultimately control the use that will be made of the text: once out of my hands, it can be cited, explicated, and reread in unforeseen ways, as the marquise de Sade discovers to her chagrin when her husband finds puns and word-counts to be more significant than her stated intended meaning. Even the master epistolary strategists of *Les Liaisons dangereuses*, so adept in fitting message to receiver and predicting the response, see the game slip away from them as disorderly affective ripples send their plans off course.[16] The reader's attention is not under the writer's control, and unexpected sectors of the text are emphasized or ignored as they encounter the networks of associations and investments that constitute their recipient. Furthermore, subtle relations exist among differing circuits. Voltaire writes a dozen letters in one day, all covering the same "material" but adapting attitudes and speech to each correspondent. To consider the letters simultaneously creates a certain amount of interference among the circuits, not "noise" as the communications theorists have traditionally described it, since that involves a decrease in information, but a surplus of information neither wholly compatible nor wholly incompatible with itself. The polyvocity of the correspondence stems from both the sender and the receiver, as bits of information glide, become reinvested with meaning, detached for special scrutiny, and reattached in other associational contexts.[17]

The desire to interpret *correctly*, to pull forth an interlocutor from the words on the page and to know the truth, is not the exclusive property of epistolary writing/reading (as we shall see in Condillac). It is however a matter of particularly poignant intensity in correspondence, especially personal correspondence.

Je ne sais par quel affreux plaisir vous trouvez à porter le trouble dans mon âme: jamais vous ne cherchez à me rassurer, et même en me disant vrai, vous y mettez l'accent de quelqu'un qui trompe.[18]

[I know not what hideous pleasure incites you to trouble my soul; you never seek to reassure me, and even when you tell the truth, you sound as though you are lying.]

The seventeenth-century scholar Camillo Baldi's treatise on "how to know the nature and qualities of letter writers" offers to fulfill the hope of every letter reader.[19] Certainly it is an unusual text: any number of manuals and anthologies instruct one on how to *write* a proper letter, but a manual for interpreting makes other kinds of suppositions about the nature of the epistolary relation. As Janet Altman notes, the letter anthologies of the French seventeenth century "stake out a space for the letter which is essentially uniform, public, and limited to persons of a particular social status," in contrast to an earlier Erasmian concept of the letter as exemplifying the singularity of the individual.[20] Baldi comes somewhere between these notions: he discounts certain formulaic utterances and standar-

dized epistolary situations ("Tout type d'écrit ne permet pas de
déceler les moeurs de celui qui écrit," 85), but quickly elaborates a
system of epistolary semiosis that dispenses, for the most part, with
the manifest content of the text. Handwriting, word choice, sentence
length, punctuation, tropes, and style figure as prominently as what
a letter writer affects to "say." The results of the analysis are rarely
surprising: uneven, indolent, sinuous writing denotes a writer who is
"dominated by his inclinations" (108); passionate lovers tend to
overuse antitheses and repetitions (143), etc. Even as he suggests that
hidden meanings are reassuringly analogous to surface effects,
Baldi's project reveals a nervous desire to know more than the text
claims to be telling; an assumption that the writer will not or cannot
provide the knowledge that the reader seeks; and an appreciation for
the complex patterns and interconnections among social, tropological, and graphological signifying chains. The impossibility of the
knowledge sought spurs and energizes the exegetical project.

There are dangers, errors, in reading, especially for the "unintended reader" of a published correspondence. One danger, as we
have seen, is to assume too absolute a role for "absence." Another is
to underestimate the polyvocity of reading/writing, and to promul-
gate a law by which the letter must be apprehended. The most
egregious instance, of course, is the tendency to regard letters as
simple documents. The debates over whether Madame de Sévigné
was an *auteur épistolaire* or a more spontaneous *épistolière* have raised
critics' consciousness over the past twenty years regarding the
interpenetration of "real life" and *écriture* in private correspondence.[21] "The letters of a master ... escape from their origins as
reservoirs of fact," writes one critic,[22] and I think that this is also
true of letters that do not display the imagination and linguistic
virtuosity of a Sévigné or a Lady Mary Wortley Montague, given the
unending possibilities of affective and discursive complexity in
reading/writing. Equally problematic would be to fail to understand
the historically situated codes that produce both epistolary discourse
and epistolary subjects.[23] The polysemia of the private letter is as
overt as it is unavailable to the kind of analytic excision practiced by
Barthes in *S/Z*. For, as we have seen, the written/read text is always
in the process of being reconstituted, reappropriated, and its codes
reassigned, reinvested, as it moves along its trajectory.

Both these processes of marking/production and reading/writing
can be seen in the practice of *re*reading the other's letters (and copies

of one's own) and coming recursively to understand them as a particular series, touched by, yet distinguishable from, other series. Rereading produces a kind of feedback, a residual effect in addition to the ongoing work of inscribing, attributing, and reattributing meaning through reading/writing. Thus is constituted the epistolary subject, who marks and invests in certain positions of self and other, and continuously revises the codes of the epistolary chain. Every letter, in this sense, is a chain letter.[24] The epistolary subject is "migratory," as Deleuze and Guattari put it, and is not the same in Letter 23 as in Letter 1. Like Foucault's *individu disciplinaire*, the *individu épistolaire* is shaped in and permeated by discursive practice; yet how different a sense one has of the latter's place within the system: written, but writing; reading, but being read; constantly reconfigured or having variant configurations made available to one; existing temporally and therefore subject to change.

Just as one should be wary of reducing epistolary production to "absence," or subjecting reading/writing to a univocal interpretative law, so it would be dangerous to assign any one identity to the epistolary subject. *Les Liaisons dangereuses*, again, offers dramatic examples of the ills that befall readers who only know part of the story. Significantly, the novel's title is uttered on occasions when the speakers are entirely blind to the complexities of the situations in which they find themselves.[25] The most "dangerous" liaisons are apparently the erroneous assignments of meaning in ignorance of the full context. The history of published correspondences offers many such opportunities to the reader. The existence of Diderot's letters only, in the correspondence with Sophie Volland, invites us to efface her altogether, to project our own absence from the scene onto her. One even has a tendency to forget that "Sophie" was the name Diderot gave to Louise-Henriette Volland. The usual portrait of Diderot, presented by himself and others, of the brilliant conversationalist admired by the crowd, both nourishes and is nourished by the one-sided correspondence. Or, to take a different form of readerly partiality, the publication of Julie de Lespinasse's love letters to Guibert has led generations of critics to see in her the incarnation of suffering, passionate femininity, epitomized in the brief, intense, Letter 25:

De tous les instants de ma vie, 1774
Mon ami, je souffre, je vous aime, et je vous attends.[26]

[In every moment of my life, 1774. My friend, I suffer, I love you, and I wait for you.]

The recent re-edition of Lespinasse's letters to Condorcet, on the other hand, reveals another side. Not without emotion, and quite as capable of intimacy without revealing her every secret, she attends conscientiously to her "bon Condorcet" in a range of tones: encouraging, teasing, sympathetic, plaintive, concerned, gossipy, sententious, playful.[27] Lespinasse is perhaps gifted at compartmentalizing; but even these two strains of her complex social and epistolary life exemplify the problems inherent in attempting to identify the subject of a correspondence. Mireille Bossis calls for "a sort of affective asceticism" on the part of the reader of published letters;[28] I would suggest that letters invite many sorts of affective participation, and that such *jouissance* remains part of the reading, but that a certain cognitive asceticism is needed, since, as Bossis says, "We must accept that the writer will always be to some degree opaque as an individual." In this respect we are at only somewhat more of a disadvantage than the intended recipient of a letter. For all her eloquence, Lespinasse remains somehow opaque to Guibert: would not total efficacity be a requirement of total transparency?

As I suggested earlier, this tri-partite description of epistolary discourse corresponds, roughly, to the account Deleuze and Guattari give of a "desiring machine": a system of libidinal ruptures and flows, operating through withdrawal, marking, and investment (*prélèvement*), inscription and distribution (*détachement*), and the residual energy of consumption/consummation (*résidu*).[29] To call on the authors of the *Anti-Œdipe* in this instance, as I did in the prologue to this study, is not to enter into a debate over the universality or cultural specificity of psychoanalytic theory, but instead to take advantage of a vocabulary for describing intense socio-affective interactions and identifications. The three "passive syntheses" are both intrapsychic and social; they are useful in coming to terms with a phenomenon that is libidinal, dynamic, and ultimately irreducible to reifying and mythologizing constructs such as Absence, Law, or what Deleuze and Guattari call "the despotism of the Signifier."

Epistolary networks, with their passions, projections, and permutations, are the constant counterpart to the alternative discourse of systems explored in the previous chapter. Epistolarity exceeds the liberal, conventionally egalitarian, one-man-one-vote accounts that have been given: it is more radical. Epistolary conversation is intensified by the complexity and contingency of the written. It is not an "ideal speech situation," because there is no teleological necessity, no final consensus. The conversation more closely resembles Jean-François Lyotard's concept of the "differend." According to Lyotard, issues from heterogeneous discursive fields are not susceptible to final arbitration or closure (a process he terms "litigation"), but the possibility remains of continuing the deliberation and involving oneself in others' discursive/conceptual categories.[30] In this view, epistolary practice and the *esprit systématique* allow for an apprehension of social (and other) relations as "non-sutured" or "paratactic," to borrow terms from Ernesto Laclau and Chantal Mouffe. For Laclau and Mouffe, such an understanding of the social is the first step toward a program of "radical democracy," in which hegemonic practices are constantly open to subversion and reconfiguration, and in which opposition is no longer constituted in reductive or monological terms.[31] Without overemphasizing a causal relationship between letter writing, philosophy, and political theory, one can conceive of ways in which certain practices permeate and subtly inform consciousness, rather than simply "reflecting" it. As Terry Castle says of the relation of thermometers, barometers, and the construction of gender, "the subliminal charisma of the material world" inflects practice and opens space for thought.[32]

INTERCEPTED MAIL

For the remainder of this chapter, I will take a closer look at moments in three specific correspondences from the 1640s to the 1740s – roughly the same period that saw the rise of *l'esprit systématique*. In each case, I will consider the material parameters of the correspondence and its publication history and focus on one of the epistolary-machinic functions discussed above, with a view to understanding the various constraints that are imposed on the letters' meaning by readerly or editorial practices, as well as the logic governing the particular epistolary exchange. As we shall see, despite internal and external strictures and structures, these letters maintain their capacity for exceeding those limits, producing meaning, and resisting closure.

Marking: Elizabeth of Bohemia and René Descartes

The "Elizabeth-Descartes" correspondence exists at the intersection of two significant epistolary networks. Descartes was a particularly energetic letter-writer, as the five volumes of correspondence in the Adam-Tannery edition of his works testify. That epistolary writing existed for him on a continuum with other sorts of textual production is suggested not only by the importance to him of discussing published works and works-in-progress with Elizabeth and other correspondents, but also by the way in which such exchanges could be incorporated into later published work, of which a vivid example can be seen in the Objections and Replies included with the *Meditations*. Just as he describes himself as abandoning a solitary life for roving "here and there in the world," so too the multiple voices and possibilities of epistolarity infiltrate the most linear ideal of "method."[33]

Elizabeth, the oldest daughter of Frederick V, sometime king of Bohemia, was twenty-five when she first wrote to Descartes in 1643. In later years she would exchange letters with Leibniz and Malebranche; in the 1640s she moved among complicated sets of diplomatic, familial, and social relations as she sought to improve her family's situation.[34] The letters bear witness to such difficult events as her brother's conversion to Catholicism, the execution of her uncle, Charles I of England, and the numerous obligations that call her from city to city, or the interruptions and "impertinent rules of civility" that interrupt her letter-writing.[35]

The complexity and interrelatedness of Descartes's epistolary connections is amply rendered by the Adam-Tannery edition, which offers letters to and from various correspondents in chronological order. The "Descartes-Elizabeth" exchange has taken shape as an entity in various ways. Originally his letters to her appeared alone in the 1657 Clerselier edition of his letters, marking a "place" for her in print culture – as did his dedicatory epistle to the 1644 *Principiae* – even though her own words remained unpublished until 1879.[36] As the titles of several of the editions suggest, the Descartes-Elizabeth exchange is never really a closed binary circuit. The presence of "autres lettres" reminds us that even the most clearly-defined exchange is implicated within others, rendered more complex by intermediaries such as P. Chanut, by redirected mail, by overheard "conversations." Consider, for example, the questions of protocol

that arise when Descartes sends copies of his letters to Elizabeth to
be read by Christina of Sweden:

Ces écrits que j'envoie à Monsieur Chanut, sont les lettres que j'ai eu
l'honneur d'écrire à Votre Altesse touchant le livre de Sénèque *De vita beata*,
jusques à la moitié de la sixième ... et je lui mande que je ne le prie point
de présenter d'abord ces écrits à la Reine, pour ce que j'aurais peur de ne
pas garder assez de respect que je dois à Sa Majesté, si je lui envoyais des
lettres que j'ai faites pour une autre ... mais que, s'il trouve bon de lui en
parler, disant que c'est à lui que je les ai envoyées, et qu'après cela elle
désire de les voir, je serai libre de scrupule ... (Descartes to Elizabeth, Nov.
20, 1647: 194)

[These writings that I am sending to Chanut are the letters that I had the
honor to write to Your Highness on Seneca's *De vita beata*, up through the
middle of the sixth one ... and I ask him not to present them to the Queen
immediately, as I fear not showing sufficient respect to her Majesty if I send
her letters written for someone else ... but if he has occasion to mention
them to her saying that it is to him I have written these, and then she
desires to see them, I have a clear conscience.]

Descartes's numbering system ("jusqu'à la moitié de la sixième")
indicates that for him, not only does the correspondence with
Elizabeth exist as a particular sequence, but also that it contains sub-
sequences within it. The (tactfully engineered) transformation of the
"letters to Elizabeth" into "letters for the eyes of Christina" reveals
the way in which Descartes regards his letters as an extension of his
ongoing projects, another manuscript to be circulated.

The correspondence between Elizabeth and Descartes can be said
to exist as an entity in the eyes of the participants and in the eyes of
subsequent editors, in a way that his voluminous correspondence
with Marin Mersenne cannot. At the same time, even this focussed,
fairly linear (except for a few periods when pairs of letters criss-cross)
epistolary conversation cannot be entirely sealed off from other
chains, other affective, political, strategic links. What then gives this
exchange its specificity and degree of integrity? To answer the
question, let us examine the ways in which the two correspondents
"mark" or define one another as interlocutors, particularly in the
early letters.

The written exchange begins on the occasion of a missed meeting:

Monsieur Descartes,
    J'ai appris, avec beaucoup de joie et de regret, l'intention que vous avez
eue de me voir, passé quelques jours, touchée également de votre charité de

vous vouloir communiquer à une personne ignorante et indocile, et du malheur qui m'a dérobé une conversation si profitable. (May 16, 1643: 3)

[I have learned, with both joy and regret, that you manifested the intention of coming to see me a few days ago; I am touched equally by your charity in wishing to communicate with an ignorant and indocile person, and by the misfortune that kept me from so profitable a conversation.]

While absence, or a missed conversation, occasions the initial letters, for the most part the correspondence is viewed by both as an event in itself, for which the adjunct of conversation remains a rare possibility, but hardly a necessity, a "lack." Others have analyzed the particular philosophical stakes of the exchange, in which Elizabeth's "indocility," her capacity to raise questions, brings her to the heart of one of the most problematic issues in Cartesian philosophy, the relation between soul and body.[37] She avers personal experience in remaining skeptical of the utter separation of the two, as well as of the mind's ability to dominate the body or its "passions": "I cannot rid myself of doubt as to whether or not one can attain the happiness of which you speak, without the aid of things that do not depend entirely on our own will" (Elizabeth, August 16, 1645: 65–66). To satisfy her objections, Descartes develops his ideas beyond his earlier work and the *Principiae* to a commentary on Seneca and ultimately to his treatise *Les Passions de l'âme*. Beset by illness, troubled by her family's fluctuating fortunes, Elizabeth recalls Descartes to the body's materiality and temporality, in much the same way that letters themselves, in their physical trajectories and as records of particular moments of writing, persistently bring other signifying chains within what is sometimes presented as a disembodied flow of ideas.

Elizabeth and Descartes delineate themselves and each other as interlocutors partly through various devices or protocols of "attentiveness"; i.e., responding not only to points raised in the ongoing discussion, but also to concerns such as Elizabeth's health or Descartes's entanglements in various controversies. There is a protocol of "privacy" as well. Beginning with Elizabeth's initial avowal of "shame" at showing "so irregular [*déréglé*] a style," she shows a remarkable confidence in her correspondent's discretion, as, for example, in her avowal that he has prevented her from inclining to skepticism.

Encore que je vous doive cette confession, pour vous en rendre grâce, je la croirais fort imprudente, si je ne connaissais votre bonté et générosité, égale au reste de vos mérites, autant par l'expérience que j'en ai déjà eue, que par réputation. (July 1, 1643: 20)

[Although I owe you this confession out of gratitude, I would think it highly imprudent did I not know, as much from experience as from your reputation, that your goodness and generosity are equal to your other merits.]

By calling her reflection a "confession" and underscoring its significance, Elizabeth further marks the exchange as a privileged one, a gesture repeated when she asks him to burn one of her letters (May 24, 1645: 47) and later when the two consider writing letters in code (October 10, 1646: 156–7).[38]

"Attentiveness" and "privacy" contribute to giving an identity to the correspondence, but there is a significant affective dimension as well, a kind of epistolary euphoria infused throughout the letters. Descartes's expressions of happiness ("un sentiment de joie extra-ordinaire," Nov 3, 1645: 114) and of "zèle" are frequent. Perhaps the term should be epistolary "recognition."

je ne puis m'abstenir d'ajouter que j'ai été aussi ravi de joie, et ai pris la vanité de voir que le calcul, dont se sert Votre Altesse, est entièrement semblable à celui que j'ai proposé dans ma Géométrie. (November, 1643: 29)

[I cannot resist adding that I was filled with joy, and taken with vanity, to see that Your Highness's calculation is entirely similar to the one that I proposed in my Geometry.]

We are accustomed to relegating epistolary passion to our love letters (or the letters section of *TLS*) or to letters that supplement a strong affective relation – as between parent and child – already in existence. But "supplements" do not always complete a lack; instead they may also embark on their own paradoxical modes of production. The Elizabeth-Descartes correspondence produces a friendship-in-writing that becomes a topic for discussion in a couple of their letters from the summer of 1645, to which I now turn.

Descartes writes in response to the letter that Elizabeth had asked him to burn, describing his "ressentiments extrêmes" upon reading about her physical ailments and melancholy. He expands upon his usual recommendations (that she "divert her thoughts" so as to heal in body) to emphasize the importance of certain pleasures, such as watching "the green of the trees, the colors of a flower, the flight of a bird" (May–June, 1645: 50). Elizabeth's reply speaks to another source of *agrément*:

Vos lettres me serviront toujours d'antidote contre la mélancolie, quand elles ne m'enseigneraient pas, détournant mon esprit des objets désagréables qui lui surviennent tous les jours, pour lui faire contempler le bonheur que je possède dans l'amitié d'une personne de votre mérite ... (June 22, 1645: 52)

[Your letters will always afford me an antidote to melancholy, even if they did not also teach me to turn my mind away from the disagreeable objects that accost it every day, in order to contemplate the happiness that I find in the friendship of someone of your merit.]

As ever, however, she finds thoughts and feelings difficult to separate, and philosophical therapy insufficient. Two letters from Descartes follow which answer different aspects of Elizabeth's letter and which, coincidentally, precede and follow a meeting and conversation between the two. There is one textual echo of that conversation, during which Elizabeth apparently mentioned that the letters offered her a pleasant "diversion"(July 21, 1645: 57). It is conversation that serves as ancillary to the letters, not the reverse; in the following paragraph, Descartes pursues topics already broached in the correspondence without a break.

Je m'imagine que la plupart des lettres que vous recevez d'ailleurs, vous donnent de l'émotion, et qu'avant même que de les lire, vous appréhendez d'y trouver quelques nouvelles qui vous déplaisent, à cause que la malignité de la fortune vous a dès longtemps accoutumée à en recevoir souvent de telles; mais pour celles qui viennent d'ici, vous êtes au moins assurée que, si elles ne vous donnent aucun sujet de joie, elles ne vous en donneront point aussi de tristesse ... (57–58)

[I imagine that most of the letters that you receive from elsewhere affect your feelings, and that even before reading them, you fear to find unpleasant news within, given the way in which malicious fortune has accustomed you to receiving such; but as for letters from here, at least you can be assured that, even if they give you no joy, at least they will not occasion sorrow.]

Epistolary therapy is at least as efficacious, it appears, as taking the waters at Spa. Descartes closes his letter with an offer to begin a "slow reading" of Seneca in collaboration with Elizabeth, in what marks a significant new stage in their correspondence.

Descartes's excursus on letters and emotions aptly underlines the capacity of many sorts of letters to produce feeling, but exempts "celles qui viennent d'ici" from the troublesome affective realm ("you may open them at any hour, without fearing to trouble the digestion of the waters," 58). His letters, as he describes them here, are associated with "philosophy," specifically philosophy's ability to show us how to attain the happiness "that vulgar souls expect from fortune, but that we can only find within ourselves." It is but a short, graceful move to the analysis of Seneca's discussion of happiness, but it does not entirely capture the dynamics of the conversation at hand, Descartes's own "joie" or "ressentiments extrêmes." In the course of the reading of *De vita beata*, however, Descartes will offer a revised understanding of Stoic "sovereign felicity," one that allows some place for the passions (September 1, 1645: 84). So too his and Elizabeth's epistolary felicity stems from a subtle and not entirely explicable mutual implication of body and soul. In speaking of the "souveraine félicité ... que nous ne saurions avoir que de nous-mêmes," the *nous* resonates as both singular and plural, evoking not only a descent into the self, but also the collaborative project at hand.

Reading: Marie-Catherine Desjardins and Antoine de Villedieu

Epistolary "felicity" is not the first thing called to mind by the letters Marie-Catherine Desjardins wrote to the man whose name she would adopt following his death, even though in life he had broken their engagement and married someone else. Instead, the ninety-one missives of the *Lettres et billets galants* have been cited as an extreme example of female abjection. As we shall see, however, it is difficult to impose any one narrative here.

The situations alluded to in the letters and the circumstances of their publication are indeed dramatic. For a period of several years in the early 1660s, Desjardins, already a writer of some note (and thus a "notorious woman," as Joan DeJean observes)[39] entered into a liaison with Antoine de Villedieu. In early 1667, he had her sign a document releasing him from any promise of marriage, then married another woman and soon thereafter left for Louis XIV's Flanders campaign. He was killed at the siege of Lille in August of the same year. In May, however, perhaps under the financial pressures of equipping himself for the campaign, he had gathered up the eighty or so love letters Desjardins had written him and sold the entire lot to publisher Claude Barbin. Hearing of the transaction during a trip to the Netherlands, Desjardins protested, but to no avail: Barbin published the slim volume of *Lettres et billets galants* in early 1668.

The work apparently saw two printings, in the second of which Desjardin's name had been removed from the *privilège*. (Since she was one of his authors, Barbin had an interest in respecting her sensibilities at least to some extent.) The lack of contemporary response to the *Billets* is interesting, given Desjardins's social visibility, and suggests that the print runs may have been fairly small. Few copies have survived. In any event, the *Billets* were quickly overshadowed by the appearance of the bestselling *Lettres portugaises* (also chez Barbin, a reliable purveyor of female passion). Desjardins, adopting the name Villedieu, continued her successful – if never truly "respectable" – literary career.

The lack of attention granted the *Billets* in 1668 stands in contrast to the critical scrutiny they have received since Micheline Cuénin's 1975 edition. A number of features of the collection have attracted notice: the relation of the representation of passion in the *Billets* to that of Desjardins/Villedieu's later novels, notably *Les Désordres de l'amour*; the *Billets'* possible influence on *Les Lettres portugaises*; the history of publication of letters by women; the topos of the abandoned, suffering woman in the configuration of early-modern femininity.[40] Then there is also that rather unusual arrangement between Desjardins and her lover that resulted in the letters being written. Unlike the Portuguese Nun, who comes to writing after her lover's desertion; and unlike Heloise, who maintains a relationship despite forced separation, Desjardins has entered into a contract with Villedieu whereby for each stunningly beautiful letter that she writes, he will pay her a visit. The allusions to this agreement in the *Billets* tend to occur when there has been a breakdown of some sort.

Sans doute vous demeurerez d'accord que le manquement de votre parole peut bien me dispenser de tenir la mienne. Aussi n'est-ce pas pour m'acquitter que je vous écris; mais pour me venger de la malicieuse pièce que vous m'avez faite. Il me semble que je me vengeray beaucoup mieux par une lettre qui vous déplaise, que si je vous privois seulement de celle que vous attendez. Je sçay que vous n'y cherchez que l'esprit & non pas l'amour, dont les témoignages vous sont ennuyeux & insupportables. Il ne faut donc que je vous faire la plus sotte lettre qu'il me sera possible. (Billet xv; 39)

[You will agree that your failure to keep your word dispenses me from keeping mine. Thus I write, not to acquit myself of my part, but to avenge the nasty little trick you played on me. I think I will be better avenged by writing a letter displeasing to you, than if I simply deprived you of the sort you expect. I know that you are interested in wit, not love, expressions of which you find tedious. All I need do, then, is to write you the stupidest letter possible.]

As Elizabeth MacArthur observes, the pact between Desjardins and Villedieu posits an unusual equivalence between art and life by "presuming the interchangeability of letters and experiences" (46). Villedieu evidently does write to Desjardins, as we can gather from her complaints regarding his letters' brevity and nonchalance (XXXVII, LX), but the real exchange is to a certain extent *hors-texte*. How does each benefit? Villedieu apparently derives satisfaction for his vanity and presumably shows the letters to his friends (as she seems to be suggesting in Billet XXVII). Already, then, there are "unintended readers" in the epistolary circuit, and already Villedieu is aware that these letters possess a "value" that is not sentimental in the least. Desjardins's pleasure is at least sexual:

Je n'ay pas plutost versé des larmes de regret d'avoir eu trop de bontés pour vous, que je brûle d'impatience de vous les continuer. (Billet I, 33)

[No sooner have I shed tears of regret at having been too generous with you, than I burn with impatience to continue.]

– but rare are the letters in which she expresses emotional satisfaction or the security of feeling loved. The *Billets* express a hundred shades and gradations of unrest: jealousy, anger, yearning, irony, pleading, melancholy...

Desjardins's letters thus delineate a very specific interlocutor/reader in the unreliable Villedieu. It is the specificity of the intimate relation that she presents as her main argument against publication:

Quand on fait un livre qu'on sçait qui doit estre vu de tout le monde, on tâche d'y traiter de matieres generales dont le public puisse estre satisfait. Mais lorsqu'on écrit à ses amis, comme on n'écrit que pour eux, on leur parle dans des termes qui ne sçauroient convenir à nul autre, & qui perdroient toutes leurs graces, si on leur ostoit celles de l'application & de la conjoncture. (letter to an unidentified recipient, May 15, 1667: 91)

[When one writes a book that will be seen by everyone, one strives to treat general matters that will satisfy the public. But when one writes to friends, as one writes to them only, one uses terms that no one else would understand, and that would lose their every grace if one removed those arising from the specific application and circumstances.]

Katherine Ann Jensen has discussed Desjardins's efforts to stop the publication of her letters in terms of a conflict between the desire for privacy and the temptation of allowing herself to be seen in the culturally acceptable guise of suffering lover, a conflict Jensen places in the context of the period's received ideas regarding (male) art and (female) authenticity (Jensen, 37–44). Such tensions do seem evident in Desjardins's letter of May 25, 1667, apparently to Barbin, where she argues that the "best written" of her letters are the least suitable for the public gaze: "such letters belong to my heart alone, and even if my hand had the audacity to steal away a few, no printer should be allowed to take advantage of those thefts" (92). The elegant turn of phrase, of course, only compounds the problem by rendering the letter of protest as publishable as the rest. But in addition to the complex psycho-social dynamics of the event, we should also pay attention to Desjardins's earlier claim that words written for an intimate friend "ne sçauroient convenir à nul autre," that is, that such letters will remain to some degree opaque to anyone other than the intended recipient.

Barbin's implicit reply is that the letters make perfectly good (commercial) sense to him. To what extent, however, does the loss of the actual moment of the letter, *la conjoncture*, result in the loss of the letter itself, or of its ability to produce zones of meaning? I am not arguing that our lack of historical or even experiential knowledge of the Desjardins-Villedieu relation impedes our access to the "ultimate truth" of her letters – supposing that one could conceive of such a thing – but, inversely, that it is precisely that lack of interrelated circumstances that in fact urges critics, beginning with Barbin, to see in the letters one narrative, one truth, only.

For Micheline Cuénin, for example, the key term is "authenticity," a quality which would apparently be damaged, rendering the letters less admirable, were one to impute any sort of authorial conscious-ness to their writer (Introduction to the *Billets*, 20). Instead, she argues, we should grant Desjardins "the benefit of the doubt" and assume total sincerity (14). A later generation of feminist readers would be less eager to give Desjardins the "benefit of the doubt" regarding her sincerity, than regarding her sense of herself as a writer, less likely to put "literature" between deprecating quotation marks. As DeJean and others have noted, it has been precisely the gendered distinction between "life" and "art" that has relegated women's writing to the margins of the literary world. Elizabeth

MacArthur, for example, begins her discussion of the *Billets* by criticizing Cuénin's assertion that "this is life speaking" and by observing that "the letters themselves put into question the belief that language can represent life unambiguously" (MacArthur, 45). MacArthur offers a compelling narrative of Desjardins's struggle with the insufficiency of language to convey her feelings, with her inability to control how Villedieu will read the letters, and ultimately with the realization that the contractual nature of their relationship has siphoned away the authenticity of even the physical experience of love: "If letters and visits are interchangeable, then, it is because both have become artful constructions whose emotional content matters far less than the signifying systems ostensibly in the service of their content" (MacArthur, 59).

Whereas MacArthur reads increasing sophistication and self-awareness in the *Billets*, Katherine Jensen sees therein a woman digging herself deeper and deeper into a trap, the trap of incarnating the cultural ideal of "Epistolary Woman," and thereby limiting herself to "a self-defeating heterosexual plot of seduction and betrayal" (Jensen, 3).[41] Jensen's purpose is ultimately to question the nature of the sexual-political investments that led so many women (and so many "female impersonators" among novelists) to replicate the drama of female seduction, abandonment, and pain. Jensen thus analyzes Desjardins's love letters as primarily masochistic, and then procedes to show how later Desjardins, as Madame de Villedieu, worked through this painful experience by writing *Les Désordres de l'amour*.[42]

Like MacArthur, I see in the *Billets* an urgent interrogation of the desire for transparency and authenticity. Like Jensen, I ask what bearing early modern constructions of the feminine have on the present day. It is dangerous, however, to impose any one narrative or fixed form on these texts. Desjardins's *Billets* are even more intractable, more formless, than most collections of letters. None is dated and there is no guarantee that they are presented in chronological order. If anything, the short sequence of letters that are clearly not addressed to Villedieu (xxviii–xxxv) suggests a carelessly gathered collection. Cuénin argues that Billet I is indeed logically and therefore chronologically the first. This may indeed be the case, but the others offer us no clear sense of temporal progression, but rather a series of postures and disconnected moments.

"Doing 'Epistolary Woman,'" as Jensen puts it, involves performing a large repertory, which I cannot pretend to exhaust here. Billet XII, for example, reads like a prose "petrarchist" sonnet in its depiction of a soul torn by antitheses that are uneasily reconciled in the last two sentences, which form a kind of sestet.

Mon ame est si partagée entre ma douleur & mon amour, qu'elle n'a jamais esté dans de plus grandes agitations. Ma douleur veut que je vous fasse des plaintes & des reproches, ou que je tâche au moins à vous montrer de l'indifference, si je ne puis vous faire paroistre de la haine. Et mon amour me sollicite à vous témoigner plus de bonté que jamais, & à vous dire tout ce qu'elle m'inspire de plus tendre. Mais pour ne donner l'avantage ny à la douleur ny à l'amour, je les laisseray dans le combat jusques à ce que vous les separiez. Je souhaiterois que ce fût bientost & que votre lettre eût le pouvoir de bannir celle qui me fait tant souffrir depuis hier. (Billet XII, 38)

[My soul is so torn between my pain and my love that never has it known greater agitation. My pain incites me to reproach you and complain, or at least to show indifference, if I cannot manifest hatred. And my love solicits me to offer you more generosity than ever, and to say to you all that my tenderness inspires. And so that I may not give the advantage either to pain or to love, I shall leave them in combat until you intervene. I hope that you will do so quickly and that your next letter will have the power to banish the one that so hurt me yesterday.]

Consider the serio-comic list of "imprecations," ending on a note oddly echoed in *Le Misanthrope*:

Oui, je voudrais de tout mon coeur que vous déplusiez à tout le monde, que vous parussiez mal fait, de mauvaise mine, sans esprit, & dépourvu de toutes sortes d'avantages. (Billet XVII, 41)

[Yes, I would with all my heart that you displeased everyone, that you appeared ill made, ill favored, and utterly lacking wit or any other advantage.]

There is dry humor, as when Desjardins (cleverly) sends "the stupidist letter possible" cited earlier, and there are superb lyrical effusions. But there is rarely happy quiet plenitude in a correspondence, and none in the Desjardins–Villedieu couple, dependent as they are on various sorts of performances, whether gestural, social, verbal, sexual, or written.

Desjardins is supremely aware that she is engaging in any number of roles, some of which she chooses for herself, some of which she performs at Villedieu's request. It is fundamentally impossible to know what all this "really means." Are the most elegiac, the most imperious, the most distraught letters all part of some elaborate sex game? Are these scenes of pleasure or scenes of abjection? There are no further clues, no textual winks, no hidden cameras to guide us here. Desjardins argued against publication on the grounds that no one could possibly "understand" her private letters. Indeed. Pleasure and pain, dominance and submission, are part of a labyrinth both affective and writerly, authentic and feigned, with multiple entries, exits, and points of cathexis. There are no "true documents" here, none for us to read.

Feedback: Françoise de Graffigny and François-Antoine Devaux

Given the return to prominence in the literary canon of the author of *Cénie* and *Les Lettres péruviennes*, it is sobering to consider that for a century or more her literary reputation was based solely on a series of thirty-one letters (out of the 2,500 or so known to exist), written during a brief period in 1738–39. These were the letters written while Graffigny went from house guest to house arrest while staying with Emilie du Châtelet and Voltaire at Cirey. Those events themselves hinged on epistolary commerce, when Du Châtelet intercepted a letter from Devaux to Graffigny and read it as evidence that she had been circulating the manuscript of *La Pucelle*. The publication of the "letters from Cirey" in 1820 under the title, *La Vie privée de Voltaire et de Madame Du Châtelet*,[43] bears witness to the practice of reading correspondences (whether of houseguests or long dead literary figures) for various kinds of "evidence," "documentation," or secret truths.[44]

The publication of Graffigny's complete correspondence, begun in 1985, allows for these and many other readings. In the 2,500 letters addressed for the most part to Devaux, nick-named "Panpan," over a period of twenty-five years, certainly there is a wealth of "documentary" material here for social and literary historians. Graffigny's letters, however, not only afford us a sense of a life in all its materiality, but also enable us to become attuned to her particular voice, her eloquently colloquial style and dry wit, as well as to sense some of the compelling energy of epistolary intimacy. Devaux is seventeen years younger than she; having met in the early 1730s, they begin to correspond regularly when she leaves Lunéville in 1738. They write for each departure of the post, about three times a week. They are friends, never lovers. Devaux's most passionate attachments are with men; his sexual involvements with women invariably end unhappily.

Graffigny, as English Showalter has pointed out, evades categorization as either "épistolière" or "auteur épistolaire": her letters sometimes clearly anticipate, or at least imagine, eventual publication; she writes both with an eye to significant models like Sévigné and in keeping with the private language of her long relationship with Devaux. Literary ambitions and practical frustrations, private jokes and plotlines, secret codes, shopping lists, and virtuoso set-pieces, all converge in the familiar letter; in the complex network of relationships and physical contingencies, the letter writer defines an interlocutor and delimits a field. But epistolary writing is already reading: as one writes to be read, anticipating a response, so one also rereads previous letters, even copies of one's own, producing a kind of epistolary feedback, a surplus value in meaning.

It is this last aspect I wish to foreground in the exchange between Graffigny and her friend. The current edition of the letters, being based on manuscripts rather than on early editions (the case with Desjardins's *Billets*) enables us to consider aspects of epistolary reading and writing that are often obscured in the absence of manuscript copies. Large excerpts of Devaux's letters appear in the notes to each of Graffigny's letters, as does a description of the physical state of each. Of particular interest are Devaux's annotations. He numbered each letter and made a note as to its contents. At one point, knowing that his friend Liébault, who had fallen out with Graffigny, was looking at the letters, he apparently mis-numbered several in order to hide others or obscure their sequence. To examine any volume of these letters is to confront a number of important issues in reading/writing and rereading. The work of the editorial team, the careful elucidation of the many references, code names, and popular expressions or words of *patois*, the description of the physical state of many of the letters (unusual folds, annotations, seals, etc), and the inclusion of excerpts from Devaux's letters, all help call attention to important aspects of the dialogue: the changing tenor of the exchange, the intimacy of the shared codes, Devaux's careful disposition of the letters. Of course, the editorial work is also the textual marker of our outsider status, our dependence on such glosses for the interlocutors' shared codes.

We are reading a "slice" without elaborate formal structure. Volume Three (October 1, 1740–November 27, 1742), for example, is bounded at either end by Graffigny's changes of address as she seeks a comfortable living situation in Paris. The period does not present dramatic "plot" episodes such as the sojourn at Cirey or significant moments of literary or social success. Events turn on a smaller scale, are organized according to the parataxis of a life: Graffigny's involvement in her friend's lives, as when Clairon Lebrun comes to Paris to give birth to her illegitimate child; brief visits to friends in the countryside; reports on the literary events in the capital, new plays by Voltaire and La Chaussée, a new translation of Richardson, etc. Unable to afford more comfortable or convenient lodgings, Graffigny complains of her life as a *pensionnaire* in a convent, obliged to put up with strict rules and the dull company of the nuns, "ces vilaines béguines."

The letters from this period foreground the ways in which an epistolary exchange is often about itself; it generates its own momentum, its own meanings, simply by taking place. Graffigny must write, if only about "nothing": "Sans doute je m'amuse de tes riens, et je serois fachée que tu ne m'en écrivisses point. Que dirions-nous la pluspart du tems? Mais il y a rien et rien" ["Doubtless your nothings amuse me, and I should be annoyed if you wrote none at all. What should we say most of the time? But there is nothing and nothing"] (3: 124). Graffigny's "nothings" can become quite writerly:

Je ne sais si je t'ecrirai, quoique je tiene une plume, que je la trempe dans de l'ancre, et que je la traine sur du papier, car ce n'est pas ecrire cela ... Je n'ai point pensé. Je n'ai pas meme vegeté: j'appelle vegeter de rever à rien. Je n'ai rien fait de tout cela" (3: 147).

[I don't know if I'll write to you, although I'm holding the pen, and dipping it in the ink, and dragging it across some paper, because that isn't really writing ... I haven't thought. I haven't even vegetated: vegetating is thinking about nothing. I haven't even done that.]

Many of the events recounted are linked to the material conditions of the correspondence: weather-related delays in the postal service, fears of interceptions and prying eyes, lost letters, letters criss-crossing and arriving out of sequence.

Inevitably, perhaps, the most dramatic event in the letters is a prolonged quarrel, from September 1741 to August 1742, during which the conversation slows and even stops for weeks on end. Epistolary time is gradual, heavy with meaning. As the correspondence is the primary means of conducting the relationship and its

embodiment, the silence speaks, and each epistolary act becomes all
the more self-reflexive as one weighs the implications: "Il y a
longtems que je ne t'ai pas ecrit, mon ami, et je n'en ai pas plus a te
dire, car tu me fais enrager. Je te le rend. Voila notre histoire" ["My
friend, I haven't written for a long time, and I have no more to say
than I did, because you antagonize me. And I you. So there."] (3:
252). The paradox of needing to say to someone, "I'm not talking to
you," reveals the self-generating qualities of the exchange.

The twelve-month quarrel highlights the autonomy and recur-
sivity of epistolary writing. Numerous irritations divide the two
friends, but at the heart are questions that mainly concern other
people: Devaux's host and friend Liébault suspects Graffigny of
having favored a liaison between his mistress Clairon and another
friend, Alliot. Graffigny is offended by Devaux's readiness to listen to
Liébault, and so on. At one point, Devaux complains glumly of "the
disadvantage of letters: we hardly ever understand each other"
(3:294 n.3). The problem is not just one of "absence," but rather the
superabundance of epistolary "presence": the letters furnish all too
much material for the deciphering eyes of the two readers, each hurt
by and suspicious of the other. Every detail in the contents, the
physical appearance, and the frequency of the exchange provides
grounds for resentment. Graffigny slows the pace of her replies,
writing one letter in response to four or five from Devaux. Devaux
works himself into a passion and writes a long letter over a period of
several days, replying point by point to one of hers (3: 293 n.1).
Graffigny graphically renders her emotion when she closes a letter
with a request to be left alone, and draws a line ("une courte ligne
vigoureuse," according to the editors) as if to "draw the line," "tirer
un trait" on their friendship (December 8, 1741, 3: 293).

Other letters, other acts of (re)reading, impart further emotional
intensity into the Graffigny-Devaux quarrel. At one point, for
example, Liébault sends a furious letter to Graffigny, after having
shown it to Devaux, who writes to beg her "on his knees" not to
read it (3:282 n. 2). Graffigny refuses to follow the advice, and
further opens the circuit by responding to Liébault in her next letter
to Devaux (November 19, 1741, 3: 280). On another occasion,
Graffigny is appalled to learn that her friend has turned over to
Liébault the letters that Clairon had written to Alliot and that the
latter had entrusted to Devaux (January 14, 1742). These exchanges
and crossovers among apparently "separate" correspondences

bespeak the openness and availability of epistolary circuits to infusions of energy from other sources, other circuits, and multiple readers in the constantly changing network.

Their falling-out is clearly marked by Graffigny's shift to *vous* beginning September 13, 1741, in a letter annotated "bouderie" by Devaux, but Graffigny nevertheless tends to deny for several weeks that anything is truly amiss: "Je ne laisserai pas de vous écrire. Vous croiez bien que je ne vous hais pas" [I won't stop writing to you. You know that I don't hate you.] (October 8, 1741, 3: 262). Even so, both correspondents quickly become aware of a new periodization of their relationship, now dating everything from before and since "la brouille." Devaux pleads for a return to their former situation (August 13, 1742, 3: 330 n.1), and, at last, Graffigny relents:

Alons, n'en parlons plus. Je vais tacher de redevenir ce que j'etois, car je vois clairement que je ne tirerais pas de toi les sentiments que tu me dois. Il faut finir nos disputes, car tu es aussi opiniatre a m'aimer qu'a m'aimer mal. (August 19, 1742, 3: 329)

[All right, let's not talk about it any more. I will try to be as I was before, since I see clearly that you'll never have the feelings that you ought. Let's put an end to the disputes, since you're as determined to be a friend as you are to go about it the wrong way.]

The point here is to emphasize the extent to which multiple readings of their own and others' letters inflect the relationship between the two friends, both in their perceptions of each other and in their self-representations. The durability of the exchange is also worth meditating on. Despite the slowdowns and all threats to the contrary notwithstanding, the two never really cease communicating. Graffigny's use of *vous* and her recourse to a clipped, journalistic chit-chat mode mark her coolness, and at one point she refuses to answer any "personal questions" regarding her health or her relationship with her lover Demarest (February 13, 1742, 3: 303). And yet, throughout the months of the *brouille*, she continues reporting, however drily, on her activities. She looks after Devaux's interests as she endeavors to interest the actors of the Comédie-Française in a play of his.

A few weeks after the rather grudging cessation of hostilities cited above, Graffigny offers a more euphoric reflection on what it means to have resumed the friendship.

Comme tu crie pour une pauvre petite fois que j'ai manqué a [t'écrire]! Tu m'aime donc bien, mon Pamp[ichon]. Eh bien, je t'aime bien aussi car je serois furieuse si je manquois de lettre une seule fois. Je ne veux pas que tu croye que c'est seulement depuis que nous sommes raccom[o]dés. Je t'assure qu'elles m'ont toujours fait bien du plaisir, qu'il me manquoit quelques choses quand je n'en avois point ... Tiens, vois-tu, c'est notre coucherie, cela, c'est cette confiance qui equivaut la lieson intime de l'amour, et qui rend notre amitié unique. (September 27, 1742, 3: 374)

[How you carry on over the one little time that I didn't write! Pampichon, you are a real friend. And I love you too, because I'd be furious if I missed a single letter from you. Don't think that it's only since we made up. I assure you that they always pleased me, and I always missed them when they didn't come ... There, you know, that's our little roll in the sack, it's a closeness that equals the intimate ties of love, and makes our friendship unique.]

The Graffigny-Devaux exchange reveals the power of "idle" chit-chat. The enumeration and recitation of small events, the production of *lettres sur rien*, create a space for intimacy, for a dialogue that exceeds the need for plots or "content."[45] The letter that is written even in the absence of anything "real" to say becomes an enactment, a material confirmation of a relationship whose very formlessness helps to insure its survival. Graffigny and Panpan are subjects-in-writing, in a form of writing that allows them mobility, multiplicity, and self-invention, re-creation. "I'm waiting for your letters three hours before they arrive. I devour them" (3: 375). They read, reread, write, and figure themselves as part of this ongoing process of production, transformation, and immersion in the labyrinthine possibilities of language.

In his essay-cum-epistolary novel *Envois*, Derrida announces the end of "the letter" and of "literature" as a classical institution ensuring the intact transmission of meaning: "letters are always postcards: neither legible nor illegible, open and radically unintelligible ... offered to all the transfers of collectors ... "[46] It would however seem that "the age of the postcard" began some time ago, in the searching, self-conscious constructions of meaning and agency from "the great age of letter writing."[47] Despite affliction of body and mind, mail misdirected or misunderstood, senders and receivers persisted in the hazardous task of reading, writing, and recognition. And although the character "J.D." in *Envois* declares that the letter is "always lost," its destination "immediately multiple, anonymous, and the sender, as they say, and the addressee, you yourself, my beloved angel" – he still persists as they do – "and yet how I miss you." In the individual studies that make up the remaining chapters, we shall see that the loss of the "letter" and the complexity of the system, if anything, increase the possibilities for engagement, dialogue, and change.

As a practice, letter-writing offers parallels to the divergent accounts of Enlightenment that we have already seen: on the one hand, the optimistic view that correspondents are able to speak and write in their own voices, carrying out conversations that cement new social and political alliances. On the other hand, letter-writing can be seen more dimly as partaking of the modernizing process, the complexification and partitioning of various spheres of existence, a simultaneous definition and entanglement of public and private, an insertion into "disciplinary" forms of self-production. As we have seen in the correspondences discussed here, however, there is no one mode of epistolary being, no total closure, whatever the genre, the reliance on prior models, the appeal to protocol, the degree of self-consciousness on the part of the correspondents, the tendency towards narratives and plots. A correspondence takes place in time, but is not bound to linear temporal sequences. I can always reread your letters from last year and come to new conclusions regarding you, regarding me, what we have been, and who we are becoming.

CHAPTER 3

Physics and figuration in Du Châtelet's 'Institutions de physique'

For philosophers and scientists as well as the non-specialist reading public, Newtonian science presented a model of conceptual clarity and methodological purity. Even if Newton's prestige was not enough to save the word "système" from its negative connotations, for d'Alembert, Newton "gave Philosophy the form it should preserve." To the notion that Newton had brought philosophy to definitive perfection one can frame several sorts of replies, and for a number of commentators, aspects of his method and textual practice are problematic, especially as they intersect with specific historical circumstances and institutions. Margaret C. Jacobs goes so far as to assert that "the Newtonian version of the Enlightenment looks increasingly like a vast holding operation against a far more dangerous rendering of Enlightenment ideals."[1] In France, Newton's experimentalism achieved high prestige, but other emphases shifted. French thinkers tended to adopt Newton's insights in mechanics and optics, but tried to fit them into other conceptual frameworks. One can find the effect of what I. B. Cohen calls "the Newtonian style," or mathematicization of the natural world, in Condillac and d'Alembert, but the lingering influence of Descartes, among other factors, prompted a greater tolerance for hypothetical thinking and a continuing concern with explanatory principles in natural philosophy, as opposed to an acceptance of the inexplicable functioning of phenomena.[2] There are few philosophical "purists" in eighteenth-century France. Instead, a number of writers engage in various sorts of projects integrating the aims and insights of Descartes, Newton, and Leibniz, and through such integration, find new vectors and potentials within their work.

Such a project is Emilie du Châtelet's *Institutions de physique* of 1740. As she explains in the *Avant-propos*, one of her goals is to "make Newton's system known, to show you the extent of its consistency

and verisimilitude, and how phenomena can be explained by the
hypothesis of attraction."[3] The association of Newton's name with
"hypothesis" is a mark of Du Châtelet's revisionism, which becomes
further evident in an entire section defending hypothesis, but the
extent to which her version of Newton's system varies from the
canonical becomes evident a few pages later when she offers
Leibnizian metaphysics as an introduction to Newtonian physics,
calling the principle of sufficient reason "a compass capable of
leading us through the quicksand" of metaphysics (13). It is not my
purpose here to decide whether or not Du Châtelet was successful
in reconciling such bitter antagonists as Newton and Leibniz. Nor
shall I go very far in establishing her intellectual genealogy by
sorting out which threads of her argument lead to Leibniz, Wolff,
Newton, Clarke, Descartes, or Maupertuis.[4] Du Châtelet presents
herself at the outset as a kind of cartographer, one of those who
"draw the blueprints" of physics (12). Her cartography involves
more than simply outlining the shapes of things already known,
however. Just as map-making has always been fraught with semiolo-
gical and ideological difficulties, so too Du Châtelet's particular way
of charting the borderlands between physics and metaphysics is
highly significant.

My interest in the *Institutions* lies in seeing how Du Châtelet comes
to terms with a number of the issues that we have seen arising within
the discourse on and of systematicity, inasmuch as both its physics
and metaphysics are geared to explicating *relations*, both logical and
phenomenal. In her project, the split between sequential or discursive and synoptic order that plagued d'Alembert is reconfigured: the
terms retain their separateness, but no longer appear incommensurable. The *Institutions* offer relationality as a conceptual mode adequate to the demands of both science and philosophy, and, it is
implied, other areas as well. Despite a stringent official program of
authorial self-effacement, part of the work's agenda is to construct its
author as a member of the scientific community, and to give her a
significant voice in dialogue with other voices. Thus simultaneity
and sequence, motion, force, and relation, and the institution of a
dialogue create sectors of textual activity which mutually reinforce
one another.

The term I use for these multiple, yet interrelated, activities is
"figuration," understood in its etymological, rhetorical, and philosophical senses. The earliest meanings of *figura* concern a shape

imposed on substance, plastic form; gradually the meaning shifted from the substantial to the abstract: shape, model, image.[5] In ordinary French, *figure* can refer to the geometric illustrations accompanying the text; it can also mean "face." To a great extent, I see the motor behind Du Châtelet's enterprise to be an active self-fashioning or self-configuration, in which both materials taken from elsewhere and her own insights are woven together in a double project of self-education and self-presentation. *"Se figurer"* means to imagine or picture something, and is a common enough expression in Du Châtelet's French as well as in contemporary usage. Du Châtelet se figure, or (con)figures herself, however, in a particularly literal way through this text, where she imposes a shape, attributes an identity, and situates herself in a system of relationships.

I will explore this process by looking at specific passages in the *Institutions*, organizing the reading in terms of a series of general issues: the question of authorial self-presentation and its relation to the tension between abstract and concrete language; the larger question of abstraction with respect to space and time; and the role of divisibility and porosity in the concept of matter and "figure." In the final section of the chapter, we will consider Du Châtelet's foray into the public scientific debate over *vis viva* at the end of the *Institutions*, and her subsequent pamphlet exchange with Dortous de Mairan.

Many of these issues are already implicit in the opening pages of the *Institutions*. In the *Avant-propos*, the relation between pedagogy, interlocution, and self-fashioning is already apparent. Indeed, the pedagogical bent of the work is evoked in the slightly antiquated use of *institutions* in the title. Dedicating the work to her young son Louis-Marie, Du Châtelet begins by instituting a discourse aimed at a specific interlocutor, defining a *je* and a *vous* whose identities remain constant throughout the twenty chapters of the treatise. Her simultaneous inaugural gesture is to situate the text in time, even in several time-frames at once.

J'ai toujours pensé que le devoir le plus sacré des Hommes étoit de donner à leurs Enfans une éducation qui les empêchât dans un âge plus avancé de regreter leur jeunesse ... (1)

[I have always thought that Men's most sacred duty was to give their children an education that would prevent them at a later age from regretting their youth ...]

Du Châtelet elaborates the anticipatory retrospection by imagining possibilities for the way in which her son will look back on his childhood and youth; the project begins almost on a note of *carpe diem.* There are other temporal frameworks: the material time required for Du Châtelet to write the treatise (5), the specifics of past developments in the lives of her son and herself.[6] She also evokes the historical context in which she writes, both microscopically – no one has attempted to write a work of basic physics in French since Rouhault's 1671 *Traité de physique* – and macroscopically, in the larger intellectual renewal that she traces from Descartes to Huyghens, Newton, and Leibniz (5–7). The preface exists simultaneously in these different temporal sequences, from the *longue durée* of intellectual history, to the ephemeral existence in Louis-Marie's memory of conversations at Cirey, to the several possibilities his future may hold. This is already a textual instantiation of her (Leibnizian) opposition to (Newtonian) absolute time. Time, like space, is relational and ideal.

In addition to weaving the time of her work, and her son's and her own *vécu* into the progress of intellectual and scientific achievement, Du Châtelet begins to define herself in other ways. Her descriptions of her project are, however, overtly self-effacing:

> ... je n'ai point chargé ce livre de citations, je n'ai point voulu vous séduire par des autorités; & de plus, il y en auroit trop eu; je suis bien loin de me croire capable d'écrire un Livre de Physique sans consulter aucun livre ... (11–12)

> [... I have not burdened this book with quotations as I did not want to persuade you with authorities; and in any case, there would have been too many; I am far from considering myself capable of writing a book on physics without consulting a single book ...]

Increasingly, the references to what Du Châtelet is not writing become assertions regarding what she *is* writing. The question of authorship skirts the issue of originality in a way typical of the period: the *Institutions* is an assemblage of sorts, but is nevertheless new, and fills a gap in knowledge. Du Châtelet may not be a "physicist," but her role is indispensable to the shared intellectual project.[7]

Du Châtelet reins in her style. "I have not sought to be witty [*avoir de l'esprit*], but to be right [*avoir raison*]" (12), she states, and goes on to eschew the "foreign flowers" [*fleurs étrangères*] of rhetoric. The *Institu-*

tions explicitly abstains from the usual devices of vulgarization –
dialogue, anecdote, lively writing. While the norms of scientific
writing currently in force were still coming into usage in Du
Châtelet's day, this self-imposed restriction is one of the strongest
assertions of authorial "seriousness" in the *Avant-propos*. Du Châtelet
maintains tighter control on her style and presentation than does
Voltaire in a comparable, if less scientifically thorough or rigorous,
work, his *Elémens de la philosophie de Neuton*,[8] or even, as we shall see,
Condillac in his eminently serious *Traité des systèmes*.

There cannot be, of course, any entirely successful exclusion of
rhetoric or metaphor from scientific or philosophical discourse. Du
Châtelet's exclusion offers itself in a metaphor and, as I have
suggested, rhetorical figuration is an integral part of the *Institutions'*
structure. The denial of the figurative in the *Avant-propos* is a
necessary performance that is part of the identification of the writer
as a philosopher; another part of that performance, initially, is
identifying the writer as male, or at least effacing any overt suggestion to the contrary. The jealousy of a former mathematics tutor,
Koenig, had led him to spread rumors prior to publication that she
had plagiarized his work, thus destroying her anonymity. Her name
appeared on the title page of the second edition, an edition which
furthermore included the exchange with Mairan, in which gender
became a not-so-subtle issue. Nevertheless, the effort to erase gender
as a category for interpreting the work occurred early on. In the
manuscript version of the *Avant-propos*, the first sentence reads, "Jai
toujours pensé que le devoir le plus sacré des mères et pères étoit de
donner à leurs Enfants une éducation . . . " ["I have always believed
that the most sacred duty of mothers and fathers was to give their
children an education . . . "].[9] The substitution of *Hommes* for *mères et
pères* removes not only the woman, but also the affectivity of all
parental relationships, from view.

The retreat of the author from the preface, the restrictions placed
on her presence, underscore the paradox of the *Institutions'* task: Du
Châtelet's attempt to gain a voice, to show her face in the scientific
community, is predicated on a kind of dissolution of the identifiable
woman. Two striking analogies for this evaporation occur in Chapter
7, "Des Elemens de la matiere," where she is primarily concerned
with elucidating the relations between the phenomenal world and
"simple substances" or monads. In the first, Du Châtelet performs a
striking dispersion of the here-and-now of her own act of writing.

Qu'une infinité de représentations obscures accompagnent nos idées les plus claires, c'est ce dont nous ne pouvons disconvenir, si nous faisons un peu d'attention sur nous-mêmes. J'ai une idée claire, par exemple, de ce papier, sur lequel j'écris, & de la Plume dont je me sers: cependant, combien de représentations obscures sont enveloppées & cachées, pour ainsi dire, dans cette idée claire; car il y a une infinité des choses dans la tissure de ce papier, dans l'arrangement des fibres qui le composent, dans la différence & la ressemblance de ces fibres que je ne distingue point, & dont j'ai cependant une représentation obscure ... (153)

[That an infinity of obscure representations accompany our clearest ideas cannot be denied, if we heed ourselves. For example, I have a clear idea of this paper on which I write, and of this pen that I use; and yet so many obscure representations are enveloped and hidden, so to speak, in this clear idea; for there is an infinity of things in the make of this paper, in the arrangement of the fibers of which it is composed, in the differences and resemblances among fibers that I do not distinguish individually, yet of which I have an obscure representation.]

As she also says in her chapter on time, Du Châtelet here explains that the condition of our continued orderly perception of reality is obscurity, inattention, or forgetfulness. A few pages later, she explains that extension exists in the blurred perception of certain relations as a form of abstraction: "la même confusion, qui est dans mes organes, & qui fait que la ressemblance d'un visage humain resulte de l'assemblage de plusieurs portions de matiere différemment mues, dont aucune n'a de rapport au Phénomène ... " ["the same confusion that is in my organs, and that causes the resemblance of a human face to result from the assemblage of various, differently prompted portions of matter, none of which has a direct connection with the phenomenon"] (157). Displaced into a passing analogy and subjected to a solvent that equates perception with "confusion," the recognizable human face loses contact with reality. Under the analytic lens in each of these examples, that which is the most present, the most personal, dissipates into obscurity. Such is the odd poetry of analogy in the most rhetorically restrained forms of philosophic writing.[10] This is the other side of the paradox as well, of course, in that the images of dissipation maintain our sense of the writer's inventiveness and control.

Her situation as author parallels the analogy of the face, where the resemblance results, not from internal identity, but from disparity. While the effect of Du Châtelet's syntax is to disperse the known into the unknown, unlike, and incommensurable ("ressem-

blance" to "aucun . . . rapport au Phénomène"), it remains nevertheless the case that the "phenomenon" thus produced is a recognizable
face. Du Châtelet uses the word "visage," but "figure" hovers as a
usable synonym. Disparity, anonymity, and the obligations of
abstraction will not curtail the conversation that she envisages. It is
instructive to consider Du Châtelet's strategies of figuration in the
light of the analysis of "faciality," *visagéité*, in Deleuze and Guattari's
Mille Plateaux, where the face and the voice emanating from it
provide a focussing, exclusionary device that works to impede open
signifying processes.[11] There is in Du Châtelet's text a tension
between infinite dissipation, both in such mathematical problems as
the labyrinth of the continuum and in the implications of philosophical abstraction that we have seen, and the necessity to arrest such
dissipation. To what extent do such limitations imply a curtailment
of the play of meaning in her system? The question is significant, for
although there is clearly a strategic need for Du Châtelet to gain a
voice by constructing certain arguments within the scientific conversation, her victory is hollow if she only succeeds in replicating the
dominating gestures that have repressed her. I hope to show through
the analysis of the *Institutions'* internal arguments and in the subsequent exchange with Mairan, that this is not the case.

Let us consider the equilibrium between abstraction and materiality at the level of Du Châtelet's language. Despite moments of
stylistic aridity that remind one of current norms for "scientifically
neutral" writing, where the *je/vous* relation of the *Avant-propos*
becomes occulted by impersonal constructions and passive voice, the
concrete specificity of the examples (carriages, ships, objects dropped
from a tower, etc) nonetheless anchors the sentence. Significantly, it
is in the final chapters of the *Institutions* on Newtonian mechanics,
where the examples are the most abstract (line A–B, body C,
inclined plane D, etc), that the rhetorical relation between Du
Châtelet and her son comes the most frequently into the text: "as I
told you," "as you have seen," "as I am showing you," etc. Or in a
more explicit reference to their shared experience:

Vous avez vu l'explication de cette loi dans les Elémens de la philosophie de
Newton, que nous avons lus ensemble . . . (305)

[You have already seen the explanation of this law in the Elements of the
Philosophy of Newton, which we read together . . .]

The conscious staging of the text's communicative and pedagogical functions, the evocation of life at Cirey, the virtual presence of Voltaire, recuperate the abstraction of the text. Even the most unrelievedly abstract demonstrations are granted materiality, through *figures*, both the traditional schematic line drawings representing bodies, planes, vectors, and so forth, as well as the "figurative" headpieces, allegorical engravings at the beginning of each chapter. Chapter 9, "De la divisibilité de la Matière," for example, offers a Mediterranean countryside where Achilles pursues the Tortoise in the foreground. Chapter 18, "De l'Oscillation des Pendules," describes "Corps P suspendu à un fil BP," but its illustration shows an eighteenth-century French interior, and a large ornate clock on one wall; the pendulum is not visible, but among the clock's embellishments is the figure of a nude, semi-reclining woman, who offers herself to the gaze of a male geometer and gives form to the uncertain and searching expression of both scientific inquiry and male desire.

The connection between abstraction and the phenomenal world is at the heart of Du Châtelet's discussion in the chapters on space and time, of "how we come to form our ideas of extension, space, and continuity" (101). Like Locke, she believes that we arrive at the idea of space from our experience of extension. The path taken is different, however. Locke touches on the notion of space in the context of his discussion of solidity (*Essay* Book 1, Chapter 4); and as he summarizes the simple process in a later chapter, "we get the *Idea* of Space, both by our Sight, and Touch" (*Essay*, Book 2, Chapter 13, § 2). Du Châtelet's intricate construction of the process starts from perceptions of difference and exteriority; the frequent repetition of the verb *se représenter* underscores the mediated, even fictive, quality of experience.

Du Châtelet argues against the existence of absolute space by showing its derivation from the notion of extension through the process of abstraction. She further shows that the notion of extension, taken to the requisite level of abstraction, enters into conflict with the principle of the identity of indiscernibles (103). She pauses, however, over the question of abstraction itself. We imagine ("nous nous figurons," 104) that ideal entities such as space, extension, etc, have a real existence because we are able to strip qualities away from certain entities and apply them to others.

... il nous semble que nous portons toutes ces choses dans cet Etre idéal, que nous les y logeons, & que l'étendue les reçoit & les contient, comme un vase reçoit la liqueur qu'on y verse. (104)

[... it appears to us that we carry all these things into an ideal entity, that we lodge them there, and that the extended substance receives and contains them as a vase receives the liquid one pours into it.]

The prominent features of the process are the stripping away of qualities, *dépouillement*, and their transportation and relocation within the new structure (*porter, transporter, loger*). As Paul de Man commented on similar passages in Condillac's 1746 *Essai sur l'origine des connaissances humaines* and Rousseau's Second Discourse, abstraction is here constructed as metaphor, or more broadly, as the process of figuration itself.[12] In Du Châtelet's other "figurations," the process involves both substitution and definition. The simultaneity and indeterminacy of experience can be given a repeatable structure, and that structure in turn offers form to experience and makes it available to reflection. Du Châtelet constantly reminds us, however, that this is a mental activity, a function of thought and perception in their interaction with the world, not the world as brute fact. Her analysis pursues the reasons why space must *appear* to be, as the Newtonians argue, empty, penetrable, immutable, and infinite – but also why it is not so.

Like Condillac, Du Châtelet uses her epistemological genealogies as a critical weapon: "Cette explication, de la façon dont nous formons l'idée de l'espace et de ces prétendues propriétés, fait tomber tous les raisonnemens que l'on a coutume d'en tirer pour prouver la possibilité du vuide" (110). Genealogy unmasks error. Despite its potential for spurious uses, however, abstraction's necessity is also clear in this part of the discussion. Du Châtelet will go on in the final pages of the chapter to a series of definitions of related abstract concepts (*Lieu, Place, Situation*), whose status she indicates by concluding the abstraction with explicit reflections on the links between abstraction in mathematics and science and other works of the imagination: "ces sortes de fictions, qui sont un des plus grands secrets de l'art d'inventer ..." (111). Figuration/fiction, once recognized for what it is, is not to be abolished from science or philosophy; like hypothesis, this is a necessary constituent of knowledge, although it is not to be taken from the actual physical world. She thus situates her concluding definitions within the conceptual sphere by which the world is made intelligible to us. They also mark the transformation of the subject at hand from the title, "space," to a discussion of *relation*.

Du Châtelet defines space in Leibniz's terms, as the "order of coexistents" (105). These beings coexist in total continuity, since there is no empty space, no vacuum, "de façon qu'il n'est pas possible de mettre rien de nouveau dans l'Univers" (107). There is no "in between" or *entre-deux*; the coexisting beings surpass mere contiguity inasmuch as they "cohere" or are held in place by relationships of force (106). This definition explains the importance of the debate on force that Du Châtelet will take up in her final chapters; it also shows the necessity of the careful definitions of the nuances of "place" with which the chapter ends. Within the plenum, *relation* is the key to perception and reason.

Du Châtelet's basic terms, and her argument from the principles of sufficient reason, indiscernibles, and continuity, are clear reminders of the extent to which the *Institutions* is intended as an exposition of Leibniz's thought. A reading of the source she foregrounds in Chapter 5, the Leibniz-Clarke correspondence, however, is an equal reminder that her work has its own vectors and zones of intensity. The examination of abstraction is one such area, indicating interests in interiority and the psychology of perception and ideation that have roots in the Cartesian intellectual tradition, and furthering the process by which her text actively constructs a thinking subject engaged in dialogue with the world.[13]

As Du Châtelet points out at the beginning of Chapter 6, "Du Tems," Leibniz's definition of time has "beaucoup d'analogies" with his account of space. As space is the order of coexistents, so time is the "order of successions." So thorough is the analogy that she proceeds to demonstrate in parallel manner to the previous chapter why, through the process of abstraction, time must appear to be uniform, independent of objects, and eternal, and why, nonetheless, it should be understood as none of those things. Stylistically, the organization of the chapter on space foregrounds narrative linearity; that on time, repetition, as the basic definition occurs in a series of contexts, each with slightly different analogies and emphases. Repetition, accompanied by change, produces the effect of temporality. Yet, as Du Châtelet indicates, spatial and temporal representations – for abstraction is representation – function analogously. In Leibnizian thought, temporality and simultaneity are projected onto one another through their parallel structure of relationality. In the

Monadology, each simple substance mirrors the totality, just as the totality exists in terms of its relation to each monad, the resulting labyrinth of relations is both spatial and temporal: "every body responds to all that happens in the universe, so that he who saw all, could read in each one what is happening everywhere, and even what has happened and what will happen" (*Monadology*, § 61, p. 265).[14]

The Leibnizian model is a powerful one, not merely because of its role in physics, as historically influential as that was, but also because it responds to a problem we have seen elsewhere, notably in d'Alembert's *Discours préliminaire*, the problem of reconciling two apparently disparate and incommensurable orders of knowledge, the synoptic or systematic – "coexistent" – and the discursive or "successive." The Leibnizian chiasmus rearticulates the orders by foregrounding the spatial aspect of the discursive, and the temporal dimension (through repetition) of the synoptic. Du Châtelet circumvents d'Alembert's problem by showing both orders to be construals of relationships, and by arguing for the usefulness of different constructions or explanatory schemes in different contexts. Her guiding figure is the non-canonical trope of analogy (rather than metaphor or metonymy). Analogy enables multi-directional correspondences based on shifting points of resemblance and contiguity, and providing not a single model, but instead a series of connections. The ability to see the correspondence between space and time parallels the overall work of the *Institutions*, which is to see connections and intersections of metaphysics and physics.[15]

Thus on several fronts, we see how Du Châtelet arrests the dissipative effects of abstraction through connections and "figurations" of various sorts. The question comes to the fore in the chapters that serve to explicate the Leibnizian view of matter. Here, Du Châtelet examines the potential for infinite regress lurking within the Leibnizian principle of continuity (because of matter's theoretically infinite divisibility into "imperceptible gradations"). Leibniz himself referred to this problem as the "labyrinth of the continuum." His arguments against the Newtonian vacuum invoke the continuity of the plenum as one of the implications of the principle of sufficient reason: "what reason can anyone assign for confining nature in the progression of subdivision? There are fictions merely arbitrary, and unworthy of true philosophy."[16] That "progression of division" led to other problems, however. As Du Châtelet explains:

nous sommes naturellement portés à croire que si nous pouvions étendre nos divisions jusqu'à l'infini, nous trouverions toujours de quoi diviser, ce qui entraine nécessairement dans ce labirinte de la composition, & de la division infinie du continu dans lequel on ne peut jamais trouver, ni le dernier terme de la division, ni le premier terme de la composition, & dont les Etres simples peuvent seuls nous tirer ... (194–95)

[we are naturally led to believe that if we could extend our divisions infinitely, we would always have more to divide, thus bringing us into the labyrinth of the composition and infinite divisibility of the continuum, in which we can never find either division's final term, nor composition's first term. Only simple substances can lead us out ...]

Her distinction between the (infinitely divisible) geometrical body and the (composite, finite) physical body simplifies Leibniz's distinctions among the geometrical, the physical, and the phenomenal.[17] Du Châtelet also tends to emphasize the extent to which the infinite underscores the ultimate unknowability of the world. Speaking of recent experiments with the microscope, she asserts that an infinity of smaller entities (*corpuscules*) escape our senses (197), rendering indispensable the simple substances which stand as the limit of divisibility. A marginal note in the manuscript puts it well:

... il devient tous les jours plus vraisemblable que la nature nagit que par developmens, or si chaque grain de bled contient le germe de tous les bleds qu'il doit produire il faut necessairement que les divisions actuelles de la matiere ayent des bornes, quoique ces bornes soyent imaginables pour nous. (ms 158 verso, marginal addition)

[... every day it appears more likely that nature works developmentally, so, if each grain of wheat contains the germ of all the wheat it will produce, it follows necessarily that the actual divisions of matter must have limits, although these limits are (only) imaginable for us.]

The manuscript passage does not appear in the 1742 edition of the *Institutions*, where Du Châtelet emphasizes that our powerlessness to perceive and know the mechanical causes of phenomena does not hamper our ability to offer different schemas of explanation that enable us to function in the world. Du Châtelet is not persuaded that in order for science to proceed it is necessary to close off questions with over-hasty answers. Even though certitude is not available, careful hypotheses and delimiting of the needed explanatory register offer sufficient material "to satisfy our desire to know, when we know how to regulate it" (205).[18] Du Châtelet negotiates a path between knowledge and skepticism, the endless proliferation and infinite divisibility of phenomena, and a term at which one can begin to construct an account of the world. Despite the limitations on what we may know, knowledge is still possible within the labyrinth of the continuum.

Thus, while the labyrinth continues to be an emblem of the insoluble, it no longer presents the kind of menace it holds for d'Alembert or others. Du Châtelet's Leibnizian universe of dynamic complexity and connectivity has its labyrinthine aspects, but is not overwhelmed by them. Du Châtelet uses the word in a conventional sense, but still gives it a different twist, when in Chapter 1 she affirms that the principle of sufficient reason preserves us from "ces labirinthes d'erreur que l'esprit humain s'est bâtis pour avoir le plaisir de s'y perdre" (27). Certainly the potential for pleasure in the vertiginous proliferation of possibilities has not been particularly remarked on before. There is no total dissolution of structure or meaning, needless to say. The dissipative tendencies of the labyrinthine are balanced by the shapes in which inquiry, identity, perception, and desire may be channelled or "figured." The universe is infinitely complex, but absolutely harmonious.

Du Châtelet follows her discussion on infinite divisibility with a chapter that shows its relation to the qualities of matter: porosity, solidity, and of course "figure." Here she defines figure, not simply as an attribute of finite extended bodies, their "configuration," but rather as having "sa raison suffisante dans les Corps environans" ["its sufficient reason in the surrounding bodies"] (207). "Figure" is thus neither imposed from without nor perfectly innate; it is a function of dynamic relations among particles.[19] In this chapter, which provides part of the transition between the "metaphysics" and "physics" halves of the *Institutions*, Du Châtelet considers the labyrinthine potential of matter itself, asserting that all bodies are penetrable and that they contain "une infinité de pores," and remarking that our senses belie their appearance of unity and correspondence by a real incommensurability: "la main ne jugera jamais des sons, ni l'oreille des couleurs" ["the hand will never judge sounds, nor the ear colors"] (212). The schism among the senses suggests a kind of unanchored multiplicity in the reality they communicate; Du Châtelet's image of a being with only one sense at a time contrasts with the progressive accumulation of sensory and mental faculties in Condillac's well-known statue. One finds a kindred intuition in Walter Benjamin's essay on Naples, where

"porosity is the inexhaustible law of the city, reappearing everywhere."[20]

The stamp of the definite is avoided. No situation appears intended forever,
no figure asserts its "thus and not otherwise." (166)

Although similarly destabilizing, neither the "separateness" of the
senses, however, nor the permeable universe of objects shot through
with "matiere étrangere" provokes quite the sense of unease that we
find in Benjamin. This is a world of relations and movement, of
infinite penetrability without loss of identity, of disparate phenomena
and substance, in which all that appears solid would melt into air but
for the constant dynamic forces in matter which enable us to
perceive cohesion in mere contiguity.

  Universal harmony maintains balance within the system; hypotheticalism allows for knowledge within contingency; simple substances
make the physical world finite and graspable within an endless
network of relations. Yet even as she recognizes throughout her
exposition the interdependence of the various components of Leibniz's system – the principles of contradiction and sufficient reason,
continuity and the plenum – her awareness of the system's complexity is accompanied, especially in the manuscripts, by the occasional desire to speculate beyond the system.[21] In the chapter on
divisibility, for example, she returns to the principle of the identity of
indiscernibles; i.e., that no two entities are ever identical. Her earlier
discussion of this notion in Chapter 1 included the oft-cited anecdote
of Leibniz's stroll through the gardens of Herrenhausen with
Princess Sophia, to whom he explained that amidst the myriad of
leaves around them, no two would ever be alike. In the margins of
her discussion on divisibility and indiscernibles, Du Châtelet
wonders aloud: "pourroit il y avoir quelquun entierement semblable
a moi dans un autre monde" ["could there be someone exactly like
me in another world"] (ms 180 verso). The answer is obvious, within
the Leibnizian scheme wherein the possibility of two entities
differing in number only is resolutely denied, and so the published
text affirms ("personne ne doute que la suite des idées d'une Ame
quelconque, ne soit différente de la suite des idées de toutes les
autres Ames qui existent" ["no one doubts that the sequence of
ideas of any person are different from the sequence of ideas of all
other existing persons"], 145).[22] The question's poignancy, however,
remains. It suggests, among other things, that there is no such

similar being in *this* world. The momentary marginal reflection
hovers as a ghostly presence in the printed version. There is no one
quite like Emilie du Châtelet; the *Institutions de physique* give her
solitude a deeper meaning and lend it a purpose. Hence the vital
importance of establishing a voice.

"Voice," as we usually conceive of it, is related to identity, and as
we have seen, the problem of preventing "identity" from dissolving
into the continuum is of prime importance. On the one hand,
everything in the plenum coheres along the cognitively infinite
gradations of the *labyrinthus continui*, and is held in place by the
harmony of sufficient reason. Like metaphor, such relations suggest a
stable, ahistorical identity. On the other hand, the dynamic forces at
work within the system, the metonymic insistence on the relations of
each to all and all to each, leave a space for contingency and
constant change.[23] And our perception, Du Châtelet explains,
contains elements of both. As we saw earlier in the discussion of
divisibility, the totality of objects, relations, and gradations is not
available to perception – if it were, phenomena would dissipate into
unintelligibility. We perceive continuity, but only because of gaps,
memory loss.

... rien ne peut nous assûrer qu'entre deux perceptions qui paroissent se
suivre immédiatement, il ne s'en est pas écoulé une infinité dont nous avons
perdu le souvenir, & que des temps immenses séparent. (131)

[... nothing can assure us that between two perceptions that appear to be
in immediate succession, there has not flowed an infinity that we have
forgotten, separated by immense periods of time.]

It is the work of analogy that constitutes our experience, a kind of
cognitive *bricolage* weaving resemblance, contiguity, identity, and
change into the constant narrative of perception. Such is the work of
hypothesis.

Furthermore, as I have been arguing all along, this *bricolage* is
emblematic of the textual work of authorial self-construction, or
figuration, that provides a large measure of the impetus for the
Institutions de physique. As she explains in the chapter on "figure,"
form finds its sufficient reason in its environment, *les Corps environans*,
just as, in later chapters, she will discuss gravity in relation to its
effect on the shape of the earth ("la figure de la terre," 322–8), and
explain force in terms of its effects among elastic bodies.[24] The
elasticity of form is crucial to the understanding of *vis viva* or *force vive*

(now understood as kinetic energy), since force is legible only in "restitution," reaction, and re-configuration (475). Textually, Du Châtelet herself takes shape, first, through the encounter with two bodies of work, Leibniz's and Newton's, and in the search for points of coordination; second, as she finds herself narrating, and eventually being drawn into, the scientific debate – becoming a voice.

The place of the *Institutions* in intellectual history is due to a large extent to its twenty-first chapter, "De la force des Corps," which marks Du Châtelet's foray into the controversy over *force vive* or *vis viva*. The significance of that debate is still subject to discussion, but twentieth-century commentators have generally moved away from d'Alembert's pronouncement (in his 1743 *Traité de dynamique*) that the entire debate was a mere dispute over words. Both the Leibnizian and Newtonian notions of force have become part of modern physics.[25] Du Châtelet comes down squarely on Leibniz's side. In so doing, she criticizes various other accounts of force, among them that of Jean-Jacques Dortous de Mairan, Perpetual Secretary of the Academy of Sciences. The ensuing exchange in many ways realizes the authorial trajectory of the *Institutions*; the impression that it functions as a continuation of Du Châtelet's text is heightened by her decision to include both Mairan's reply and her rejoinder in the 1742 edition.

Du Châtelet's chapter on force begins with a strategic footnote:

Quoique l'Auteur des Institutions ait fait beaucoup de changemens à son Ouvrage pour cette seconde Edition, elle n'en a fait aucun à ce Chapitre XXI (on a seulement ajouté quelques mots au §582 pour l'éclaircir), afin que le Lecteur le trouve ici tel qu'il étoit, lorsque la dispute publique qu'elle a eue avec Mr. de Mairan, au sujet des Forces Vives, a commencé. On joint à cette Edition la Lettre de Mr. de Mairan à l'Auteur des Institutions, & la Réponse qu'elle lui a faite, ce sont jusqu'à présent les deux seules pièces que cette dispute ait produites. (435–6n.)

[Although the author of the *Institutions* has made a number of changes for this second edition, she has made none to this Chapter 21 (other than adding a few words to §582 for the sake of clarity), in order that the reader may find it as it was when the public dispute with M. de Mairan on the subject of *vis viva* began. We have included M. de Mairan's Letter to the Author of the Institutions, as well as her reply. To date these are the only pieces produced by the dispute.]

This note retrospectively illuminates the care taken earlier by Du Châtelet in various footnotes (for example, 373n) to show her willingness to listen to new arguments and modify her views. The note will also be revealed some pages later to be a reply to Mairan's remark – chronologically anterior, but necessarily later in its placement in the book – that he has made no changes in the reprinting of his 1728 work on *force motrice* that she attacked in her chapter 21 (477).[26] The proliferation of reprints indicates the hardening of the opponents' positions. Judgements have varied as to the relative effectiveness of Du Châtelet's and Mairan's arguments,[27] and contemporary reactions, while generally favorable to the marquise, were sometimes marked by personal allegiances or a reluctance to become involved. In certain respects, however, the simple fact of Mairan's public reply achieved an important aim of the *Institutions*. As Du Châtelet wrote to Argental, "I am very honored to have such an adversary. Even to fail at this juncture would be fine, but I hope not to fail" (March 22, 1741).[28]

   The tone of Chapter 21 is quite different from the preceding ones. Du Châtelet begins with an expansive recapitulation that both situates the argument in a direct line from her basic principles and recalls its discursive location: "Vous avez vu dans le Chapitre prémier, que le principe de continuité, fondé sur celui de la raison suffisante, ne souffre point de saut dans la nature ... " ["You saw in the first chapter that the principle of continuity, founded on that of sufficient reason, tolerates no leaps in nature ... "] (435). The renewed foregrounding of the I-you relation between the writer and her son sets the stage for an increasingly prominent use of the first person pronoun as she inserts herself more and more into the debate. Du Châtelet recalls to her son the work by Mairan that they have read together and that she now proposes to examine in some detail in order to refute it. This is the most extended piece of close reading and criticism in the *Institutions*; its significance is underlined at the outset by another sign-posting footnote:

Voiez à la suite de ce Chapitre la Lettre de Mr. de Mairan à l'Auteur des *Institutions*, & la Réponse de l'Auteur à cette Lettre. (453n.)

[See following this chapter the Letter from M. de Mairan to the author of the *Institutions*, and the author's response.]

The readers – since "voiez" and the third person suddenly evoke an audience other than young Louis-Marie – are thus enjoined to observe the debate, a debate in which they will be called upon as judges by both sides.

The citations from Mairan's treatise that Du Châtelet first comments on reveal much of the fundamental differences between their positions.

Mr. de Mairan dit, No 38 & 40 de son Memoire: "Qu'il ne faut pas estimer la force des corps par les espaces parcourus par le mobile dans le mouvement retardé, ni par les obstacles surmontés, les ressorts fermés, &c mais par les espaces non parcourus, par les parties de matières non déplacées, les ressorts non fermés, ou non aplatis: or dit-il, ces espaces, ces parties de matière, & ces ressorts sont comme la simple vitesse." (453)

[M. de Mairan says in parts 38 and 40 of his book: "That a body's force cannot be estimated by the space traversed by a moving object in retarded motion, nor by obstacles overcome or springs closed, etc; but by the spaces not traversed, by the particles of matter not disturbed, the springs not closed or flattened; for, he says, these spaces, these particles of matter, and these springs are like simple velocity."]

As Carolyn Iltis observes, "Mairan was analyzing nature not as it was, but as it was not."[29] The passage chosen by Du Châtelet to begin her refutation underscores this problem by its remarkable insistence on negation and non-engagement. As we have already seen, the position Du Châtelet espouses demands connection, activity, and reciprocity, through "restitution" and elasticity.[30] The Newtonian Mairan instead viewed matter as inert, acted on from without, devoid of internal activity or force.

In a sense, the two models inform the textual activity of the ensuing exchange. In her reading of Mairan in Chapter 21, Du Châtelet quotes extensively and couches her comments in the first person. Her remarks do not spare Mairan, whose work she presents as "the most ingenious attack on *vis viva* to date" (453), and she is clearly aiming at provocation in the final lines of her commentary, where she assumes the role of protective mother guarding her impressionable young son against the "seductions" of bad physics. To have his arguments described as *séduisans* (457) rankled with Mairan in the extreme and would haunt his reply, as if it had exerted its etymological power to divert his argument off course, away from the technical weight of Du Châtelet's analysis and onto her rhetorical model. There are dangers in his approach. Although he will score a few points on form, his irritation causes him to neglect much of the substance of the argument, leaving her the last word.

Mairan's reply is in the form of a letter – a typical gesture in many public "quarrels" of the period – which, typographically and textually, has the effect of foregrounding his institutional position and her gender and class.

LETTRE
DE
MR. DE MAIRAN,
Secrétaire Perpetuel de l'Académie Royale
des Sciences, &c. A Madame la Marquise
DU CHATELET.

With Mairan's opening words, "the Public shall judge," several things happen. The *Institutions* shifts onto an entirely new communicational plane: *je* and *vous* are re-identified, Du Châtelet's son disappears, and both interlocutors will call upon *le Public* as arbiter of their debate. The act of publication becomes significant; Mairan calls attention to the new (but emphatically *un*revised) edition of his *Dissertation*, which he "includes" with his letter, although Du Châtelet does not reprint it in her 1742 edition; she thanks him ceremoniously (505) and marks her mastery of his text by citing pages from both his 1728 edition and the new one.

Mairan's header underlines their respective social status: his important function in the nation's primary scientific institution, and her role as "society lady," however influential or singled-out for note by the very fact of his acknowledgment. Much of Du Châtelet's dilemma as an intellectual is present in these lines: she may have been able to help her male friends achieve election to the Academy which remained closed to her, but she must spend her life distinguishing herself from the various amateur marquises who inhabit the popularizing scientific works of Algarotti and Fontenelle.[31]

Mairan's main line of attack – and his error – is to accuse her of not having read his work. He is at pains to cast her in the light of a gullible amateur, given to whims, easily influenced, and not disciplined enough to read primary texts. He refers to Leibniz as her "hero," on whose "altar" he, Mairan, has been sacrificed. This is the language of sexual intrigue, not science. His flattering references to Du Châtelet's native intelligence are offered only so that he may claim that she is no more than the tool, or dupe, of "the Partisans of *vis viva*" (478–9). The assumption is that Du Châtelet's intelligence exists purely as "natural light," *vos propres lumières*, incapable of withstanding corrupting outside influences. Most of his reply is couched in similarly condescending terms. Had she only "reflected a little," she would have better understood the weakness of the arguments she put forth; had she read him at all, she would not have attacked him. Mairan's letter is shot through with requests to be read, for an "attentive and disinterested reading" (480). He claims that her quotations are wrong, and insinuates that she is not responsible for them.

C'est, Madame, que vous y paroissez toujours citer mes propres paroles, & que ce ne sont pourtant que les vôtres, ou celles d'un autre que vous avez citées, ou de simples résumés que vous y avez transcrits. (483)

[You appear, Madam, always to cite my own words, and yet they are your own, or those of someone else whom you are quoting, or simple paraphrases that you have transcribed.]

Mairan's bitterness shows through in his italicized borrowings of words and phrases from the *Institutions* ("séduisans" and "subterfuge" for example), and in his constant insinuations that Du Châtelet has neither done her reading nor intended what she wrote (498).

Mairan both protects himself and shows his non-engagement with his interlocutor, by repeatedly emphasizing that his reply is a schematic one, neither "a complete Treatise" nor "a formal Refutation" (485). Tellingly, it is after having ironically qualified one of her arguments as *ad hominem* (by which he apparently means, unanswerable) that he permits himself one of his most brutal dismissals, but without addressing his criticisms to her directly.

Mais que diroit-on d'un homme, ... dans la fausse persuasion que le double de tout nombre entier, ou rompu, est égal à son quarré ... ? Ne lui répondroit-on point sur le champ, que 3 & 3 font 6, & que le quarré de 3 est pourtant 9; ... ou plutôt se donneroit-on la peine de lui répondre? (486–7)

[But what would one say of a man ... under the false impression that the double of any whole number or fraction is equal to its square ... ? Wouldn't one simply say that 3 and 3 are 6, and that the square of 3 is 9; ... or would one even bother to respond?]

Although Mairan has referred to the proof in question as having come from Du Châtelet's acknowledged source, Herman, the passage still has the effect of achieving the sleight-of-hand (and truly *ad hominem!*) transformation of Du Châtelet into "un homme" just long enough for Mairan to gesture toward "his" foolishness and unworthiness as an interlocutor; even as he suggests that he cannot permit himself this level of boorishness with Madame la Marquise, he nevertheless succeeds in passing the message through rhetorical deflection.

Even when he does not claim to correct her argument, Mairan belittles her examples as "fortuitous" and "equivocal." In his final paragraphs, he enlarges his perspective and situates the *vis viva* controversy in the contexts of the struggle between *lumière* and *obscurité*, unreflective nationalism, and the misfortunes brought about by "presuppositions, prejudice, recourse to authorities, and bias" (500). Having gone to at least some trouble to respond to them, he then claims that Du Châtelet's arguments contain nothing new (500), and recapitulates and enlarges his earlier insinuations that Leibniz is no more than a fad, a "hero" to "les Partisans des Forces Vives" in general, and to one would-be woman intellectual in particular. His final words politely tell us just what he thinks of her.

Je me flat[t]e, Madame, que vous regarderez toutes ces réflexions comme une preuve du cas que je fais de vos lumières, & de ce bon esprit qui ne sauroit vous permettre de résister au Vrai, quand il se présentera à vous sans nuage. (504)

[I flatter myself, Madam, that you will regard these reflections as proof of my high opinion of your insight, and of the excellent mind that will not allow you to resist Truth when it is presented to you clearly.]

Whatever her philosophic allegiance may be or become, the marquise remains in Mairan's discourse an unresisting female awaiting revelation from beyond, from his own incarnation of the Truth.

Truth, Du Châtelet points out in the final pages of her reply, is certainly more important than the *nouveauté* or originality that he sees lacking in the *Institutions*, but it is not necessarily in his possession for all that.

... je me flatte, du moins, d'y avoir démontré, que votre façon d'estimer la force des corps, n'a pas l'avantage de la *vérité*, & je ne cherche pas à vous disputer celui de la *nouveauté*. (541)

[... I flatter myself, at least, that I have demonstrated that your manner of calculating the force of bodies does not have the advantage of *truth*; I do not seek to dispute you that of *novelty*.]

As the italicized terms from Mairan's text suggest, Du Châtelet makes extensive use of his technique of ironic quotation. As he had shown himself to be nettled by her use of *séduisans*, she rises to the challenge of his injunction that she should *lire et relire*: "but I can assure you that the more I read and reread, the more I am confirmed in my opinion" (508).

"Reading" is in some ways at the heart of the matter. As Du

Châtelet said in her preface, one could hardly write such a work as the *Institutions* without consulting others. Thus what is at stake is not her originality as such, but rather her ability to read, to comprehend, and to judge. Her first step in the demonstration of her abilities is to provide a scathing close reading of Mairan's letter, in which no indirect insult or insinuation goes unnoticed, any more than do the challenges to her proofs. Just as Mairan was pleased to paint himself as the purveyor of truth and the voice of Enlightenment, so Du Châtelet, having called attention to his tactics by echoing him, casts herself as the defender of scientific neutrality and seriousness (513, 516, 526, etc.). She calls attention to her procedure by affecting to abandon it, noting that "it is in spite of myself, and only to follow you, that I depart from the severe style" of philosophic debate (529–30). She subtly casts Mairan as the non-serious, unengaged dilettante, a role that his assertions that he was not offering a "full" reply only reaffirm.

Part of Du Châtelet's defense includes maintaining her position as someone who is open to new ideas, without appearing to be driven by whim. In effect she goes between the horns of the dilemma posed by Mairan, who criticized her for having changed her mind regarding his work, on the one hand; and for being subject to prejudice and authority, on the other: she would thus be both vacillating and obstinate, and in either case incapable of rational judgement. As we have seen in her use of footnotes, Du Châtelet presents herself as open to new ideas and hardly inflexible. But in her reply to his account of the writing and printing of the *Institutions*, she emphasizes the fact that her ideas on *vis viva* are not as recent, or as sudden, as he implies. As she narrates it, her work thus bears the mark of the successive stages in her ongoing process of self-education and figuration. It remains for her to indicate that she has correctly understood Mairan, and has not "tronqué et défiguré" his text as he claims.

To what extent has she "truncated and disfigured" Mairan? Here it is she who calls on the reader to judge the evidence presented in the double columns where she compares her Chapter 21 quotations and Mairan's 1728 text (510). It is in fact the case, as Mairan had said, that she has offered her readers a paraphrase, not a quotation. The paraphrase is syntactically marked as such by the use of indirect discourse, but the use of quotation marks (which appear on every line in the original) gives the passage the visual appearance of direct citation. Mairan protests that such "resumés" are not the same as his text (484). Unlike Mairan – or Leibniz, for that matter – Du Châtelet believes in synonymy, and she defends her paraphrases (which are, in fact, extremely close) by identifying them as his own words, "your very own" (513), as he would have recognized, she adds ironically, had he only "read closely."[32] The real issue is the question of authority, not authorship, although Mairan would like for the two to coincide.

Mairan's actual words, however, are not his personal property. Du Châtelet demonstrates this both by pointing out the adequacy of her paraphrases and, more insidiously, by adopting his technique of ironic italicized quotation. She had made it clear in her *Avant-propos* that she had no particular stake in "original authorship" as such. Her inaugural gesture of dispossession renders possible the authorial *bricolage* throughout the *Institutions*, gives her a place to stand, and makes the public debate possible. She appropriates or puts to use texts, without possessing them. As she observes in the opening lines of her reply, the significance of a text derives to a certain extent from its circulation in the world and its interaction with other texts:

je commence à croire véritablement les Institutions de Physique un Livre *d'importance*, depuis qu'elles ont procuré au Public la Lettre à laquelle je vais repondre ... (505)

[I have begun to believe the *Institutions* to be a truly important work ever since it procured the Public the letter to which I am about to reply ...]

The exchange between Du Châtelet and Mairan offers two models of knowledge, each of which shows parallels with the philosophical positions of the two interlocutors. In Mairan's account, Du Châtelet's mind is like matter in Newtonian theory: inert and subject to external agency (Mairan's identification with *le vrai* puts him in the structurally same position with respect to Du Châtelet as God is in with respect to the world). He furthermore attempts to reassert control over a text that has slipped from his hands, both by reprinting his 1728 thesis without changes, and by claiming that any refutation of Du Châtelet's must be based on a misreading.

Du Châtelet's model for knowledge is the process I have been referring to as "figuration." While denying herself absolute authority, she is free to pursue connections and variously structured analogies among texts, and to construct an intellectual position in which relations and encounters determine significance, and in which every element contains its possibilities for change: a mental monadology. As Steven Shapin has observed, if Newtonian matter-theory suggests a "hierarchy-justifying" model, then a hylozoist, intrinsically active model offers a position "available to groups resisting domination by a hierarchy."[33] Despite the privileges of her social position, it is not difficult to see why such a model might appeal to Du Châtelet, who was keenly aware of the restrictions imposed by her sex. Du Châtelet is also part of a larger movement of integrative work in natural philosophy, as was Mairan himself. But her work on Leibniz and Newton goes beyond a simple catalog of useful concepts from either; it gives form, or "figure," to those insights. The face-off with Mairan and the figurative strategies of the entire treatise enable us to understand how she can find a voice and face her public, without being liable to the critique Deleuze and Guattari level at *visagéité*. The figures of her discourse are not coercive impositions of a single name or interpretation on malleable and indeterminate reality, but instead negotiations based on the mutual interaction of "les Corps environans." This same mobility and adaptability allows her to see the analogy between temporal/sequential and spatial/synoptic orders, where others, less able to maintain an equilibrium among differing interpretive schemas, founder on the shoals of incommensurability.

There is a sense in which Du Châtelet's Chapter 4 on hypothesis best represents this equilibrium in her writing. The chapter explicitly counters the Newtonian dictum, *hypotheses non fingo*.[34] Instead, Du Châtelet argues for the usefulness of hypothesis, which she examines in terms that emphasize its in-between status: between past and future, as it articulates what we know and what we don't yet know; between *a priori* and *a posteriori* truths, as it weaves existing schemas together with the potential changes wrought by experience. Du Châtelet acknowledges the danger of overextending one's hypotheses, but, like Descartes, she likens the technique to "the pathway leading to truth" (79).

By properly gauging their degree of probability, Du Châtelet asserts, one can prevent hypothesis from falling into "une fiction indigne d'un Philosophe" ("a fiction unworthy of a Philosopher") (92). One might turn the phrase around to say that, properly used, hypothesis can provide *une fiction digne d'un(e) Philosophe*. As I.B. Cohen and others have noticed, the *fingo* of Newton's famous phrase can be rendered by either "frame," as Andrew Motte translated it, or "feign," which was Newton's usage. "Feign" brings out the etymological relation to "fiction," a path provided by the common stem of *fingere* and *figura*. "Framing" is "feigning"; the hypothetical or "figurative" act posits, ultimately, that we construct reality in order to understand it in the dialogic process of perception. "Je me figure ..." as Du Châtelet often says, is a common enough equivalent for "je pense," but in her implicit version of the *cogito*, "thinking" has become a tool for framing – or feigning – a self and projecting it into the world. Even if there is only a negative answer to her marginal question,

Could there be someone just like me in another world?

the task of self-creation has produced results, through change and the apprehension of relations. In that act of apprehension, Du Châtelet finds her voice.

CHAPTER 4

Condillac and the identity of the Other

In 1749, the year of Du Châtelet's death, the year Buffon published the first three volumes of *L'Histoire naturelle*, Etienne Bonnot, abbé de Condillac, delivered what many considered the final blow to the activity of "systematizers," his *Traité des systèmes*. The *Traité* became an important reference point for d'Alembert in the *Discours prélimi-naire* and would furnish the substance for two of the *Encyclopédie*'s articles in the series "Système" (rubrics *Métaphysique* and *Philosophie*). In the twentieth century, despite strong interest in his approach to Lockean empiricism, his linguistic theories, and his logic, there has been relatively little analysis of the *Traité* per se.[1] In this chapter, I shall look first at some general issues in Condillac's language theory and logic, in particular at his form of genealogical critique and his understanding of the key notions of analogy and identity, before turning to the *Traité des systèmes*. From Buffon and d'Alembert to Du Châtelet, we have been made aware of the degree to which the split between analysis and synthesis, the linear and the simultaneous, method and system, constitutes a founding problematic in Enlight-enment thought. It is no less so in Condillac and, as we shall see in the following chapter, in Diderot. Certainly one aspect of Condillac's thought that makes him interesting in this context is what Foucault called his "hesitation" between the two.[2]

For Condillac as for his contemporaries, the issue of origins and derivations is of prime importance, in the *Traité des systèmes* just as surely as in his better-known *Traité des sensations* (1754) or the *Essai* (1746), where he studied the origin of ideas. In the *Traité des systèmes*, Condillac's object is the geneology of error. "Error" has in Condillac vocabulary the full force of both its epistemological and spatial etymons *error, errare*: error and erring, straying from the path. Having examined each false direction, he tells us, "Peut-être qu'alors ... on en verroit un autre où commence l'unique chemin qui conduit à la

vérité" ["Perhaps then ... we will see another from whence begins
the single path that leads to the truth."] (*Essai*, 101).[3] The familiar
vocabulary of paths that may lead one to either truth or error is
accompanied in the *Traité des systêmes* by a terminology entirely in
keeping with a Foucaltian genesis. Both the etymological siblings
génération, générer, engendrer, and their semantic cousins *germe, concevoir,
enfanter*, and *fécond* constantly recur in his philosophical explication
and critique. The terms imply continuity and organic/biological
links, but their etymological network (genus, gender, gentle [noble])
suggests difference, distinction, and hierarchy. Similarly, Condillac's
genealogy of error, although wrought within the context of a
philosophy built on identity, analogy, and resemblance, finds itself
principally concerned with gaps in what should be the natural *liaison
des idées*, difference instead of identity. That is as it should be, you
may point out, since the *Traité* is intended as a gallery of failures.
True. However, given the critical importance for the abbé of
establishing an identity of the other with which he can engage – to
render his analysis something other than solipsistic or as he might
put it, "frivole" – such incommensurability presents a problem. At
the same time, while it is not without its elements of blindness and
coercive logic, the *Traité*, like the other works thus far examined, has
its own zones of mobility, its own possibilities for dialogue.

The questions of origins and generation, the degree to which
language is natural or arbitrary, the function of analogy in language
and cognition, and the possibility of naming and constructing
identities, all intersect throughout Condillac's work, from the *Essai*
to the posthumous *Langue des calculs*, and are worth considering
briefly here in order to illuminate what is at stake in the *Traité des
systêmes. Genèse* – origin and generation – remains a common term in
all these areas. In the *Essai*, Condillac follows a path traced by
Arnauld and Nicole in distinguishing signs as "natural," "acci-
dental," or "instituted" (i.e., signs "that we have chosen, and that
have but an arbitrary relationship with our ideas," *Essai*, 128). The
etymological resonance of *arbitraire* reinforces a notion of the use of
arbitrary signs as an indication of will or mastery. Condillac sees the
choice of signs as a measure, on the one hand, of control over one's
own imagination ["se disposer par lui-même de son imagination"]
and, on the other, of human superiority over other natural creatures
(*Essai*, 131). Thus *arbitraire* takes on a very different ring from
d'Alembert's use: there it suggests our domination by something

alien and unknowable, here it affirms our ability to rule. Nevertheless, the more disruptive possibilities in the term appear to lead to its
replacement in his later work, with "artificial." Whether he termed
them "artificial" or "arbitrary," Condillac always intended to root
signs in some motivating, generative experience, in the successive
stylizations and abbreviations of the originary, gestural *langage
d'action*.[4] Thus, in *La Langue des calculs*, he banishes arbitrariness by
setting it in opposition to analogy, the source of true connections
among ideas and in the production of signs – their "sufficient
reason," one might almost say.

Les langues ne sont pas un ramas d'expressions prises au hasard, ou dont
on ne se sert que parce qu'on est convenu de s'en servir. Si l'usage de
chaque mot suppose une convention, la convention suppose une raison qui
fait adopter chaque mot, et l'analogie, qui donne la loi, et sans laquelle il
seroit impossible de s'entendre, ne permet pas un choix absolument
arbitraire. Mais, parce que différentes analogies conduisent à des expressions différentes, nous croyons choisir, et c'est une erreur: car plus nous
nous jugeons maîtres du choix, plus nous choisissons arbitrairement, et
nous en choisissons plus mal.[5]

[Languages are not a collection of expressions taken at random or used
simply by convention. If the use of each word presupposes a convention,
that convention presupposes a reason that leads to the adoption of each
word, and analogy, which governs and without which no understanding
would be possible, does not allow an absolutely arbitrary choice. But,
because different analogies lead to different expressions, we think that we
are making a choice, and this is an error: for the more that we believe
ourselves masters of the choice, the more arbitrarily we choose, and the
worse we choose.]

Arbitrariness is still linked to the exercise of will, *liber arbiter*,
although, almost perversely, it here implies a fall into error rather
than an affirmation of human mastery.[6]

    Analogy moves into the legislating place.[7] It carries the legiti-
mating mark of exteriority, the sensuous world which is the origin of
all ideas, and thus preserves Condillac from assenting to a rationalist,
innate basis for true judgment. At the same time, as Auroux points
out, language's arbitrariness or artificiality offers Condillac a solution to the empiricists' problem of explaining how, if language and
ideas are born of sensation, they frequently fail to correspond
directly to it or to each other. Condillac makes no direct link
between the structure of propositions and the structure of facts; he

mitigates this disjuncture by claiming that the degree to which language relies on analogy is proportional to the degree to which it escapes arbitrariness and becomes *une langue bien faite.*[8] The well-made language is not a "universal language." Real language will always remain to some degree equivocal, subject to repetition, distortion, unevenly overlapping shades of meaning, but it can become *bien faite* insofar as certain criteria of choice are applied: exactitude, simplicity, and especially analogy.[9] Analogy also drives the "relations of ideas" [*liaison des idées*] constitutive of thought; it is part of the reason why Condillac can escape the dilemma fore-grounded by the "inversion debate" of the grammarian-philoso-phers, on whether discursive successivity or experiential simultaneity governs the "natural order" of language.[10] Still, the emphasis on resemblance and analogy – and thereby identity – does not imply a quest for a univocal discourse. Analogy acts as a restraint on arbitrariness and tempers the intractability of the equivocal through chains of resemblance that permit us to choose "the best" expression in a universe of sliding shades of meaning,[11] but it also assumes and maintains some degree of difference at the heart of the *liaison des idées.* That which is "analogous to" cannot be "the same as." It will be important to consider this nuance as we examine Condillac's notion of identity.

In the *Discours préliminaire*, d'Alembert presented the universe as "une vérité unique" and knowledge as a series of algebraic transla-tions of that truth, an idea which surfaces in a number of Condillac's works. Analysis, the only legitimate philosophical tool in his view, involves the "decomposition" of complex ideas into simple ones, followed by their reordering in chains of identical propositions A=B, B=C, C=D, etc. Condillac is consistent in this view throughout his works, shifting only his emphasis at times from underscoring the work of "translation" to that of the ideational "chain": "Tout système peut n'être qu'une seule et même idée" ["A system can be only a single idea"].[12] Translation, abbreviation, and recognition permit the "identification" toward which strives Condillac's logic. Condillac is at pains to correct what he sees as the error in Locke's *Essay Concerning Human Understanding* on so-called "trifling proposi-tions" ("propositions frivoles" in Condillac). Locke classifies as trifling those propositions "that though they be certainly true, yet they add no Light to our Understanding, bring no increase to our Knowledge": identical propositions of the form "an A is an A"; a part of the definition predicated of the word defined, or a genus of the species (ex. "lead is a metal"); a simple idea affirmed of a complex to which it belongs ("All gold is fusible").[13]

In upholding analysis – i.e., the decomposition and recomposition of simple ideas – as the ideal philosophic method, Condillac admits that "we make identical propositions only, whenever we make true propositions" (*Langue des calculs*, 60). He seems to recognize the danger of falling into what continues to be called the "paradox of analysis": if an analyzed expression is synonymous with its analyzing expression, then the analysis conveys nothing and is indeed "trifling." If the two are not synonymous, however, then the analysis is false. All analysis would thus be either trifling or false.[14] Condillac argues that "just because it is identical does not make a proposition frivolous" (*Langue des calculs*, 61). He distinguishes between a simple identity or repetition of terms, which he does see as trivial, and the identity of ideas, which is not, since it is through such identity that we extend our understanding as we progress from the known to the unknown: "you have progressed from the known to the unknown only because what you did not know is the same thing as what you knew" (*Langue des calculs*, 122).

The question of what constitutes *la même chose* is problematic, however, as Derrida points out, inasmuch as for Condillac the discovery or "remarking" of a new object or proposition is inevitably the recombination, re-marking, and retracing of pre-existent propositions. Thus the passage "from the known to the unknown," while it presents itself, on the one hand, as filling a need or lack, remains, on the other hand, a frivolous surplus. One might invoke Condillac's rejection of absolute synonymy as a possible entry into this problem. The contention that A is never entirely synonymous with A may be a radical version of Condillac's position, but we do find something of the sort in Leibniz's critique of Locke's discussion of trifling propositions, where (in conformity with the principle of the identity of indiscernibles) he denies that identical propositions or what he calls semi-identities are necessarily trivial.

In addition to what I have said about completely identical propositions, these semi-identicals will be found to be useful in their own special way. For example:
A wise man is still a man lets one know that he is not infallible, that he is mortal, and so on.[15]

Even more for Condillac than for Leibniz, repetition carries semantic weight; what Condillac would call "verbal identity" [*l'identité dans les mots*] is rendered meaningful, and not frivolous, by a shift in the ideas produced by the sequence of propositions and our reconsideration of them over time.[16]

The identity of an object and our ability to know and understand it are inextricably bound up with the notion of analysis. Condillac's definition of analysis is more sophisticated than the razor-like shearing away of qualities discussed by d'Alembert, since it involves the dual procedure of dismantling the object and reordering its constituents in a cognitively expressive way. In the *Traité* he speaks of a man coming to understand the functioning of a clock by taking it apart, and then arranging the pieces in a logical order (*Traité des systèmes*, 202). Here too he and others unconsciously participate in what some have called the "Leibnizianism" of the Enlightenment, inasmuch as Leibniz also construes identity in terms of the predicates contained within a given notion.[17] "Thus the content of the subject must always include that of the predicate in such a way that if one understands perfectly the concept of the subject, he will know that the predicate appertains to it."[18]

The resulting proposition – hotly debated in Leibniz's correspondence with Arnauld because of its implications for human and divine liberty – that "as the individual concept of each person includes once and for all everything which can ever happen to him, in it can be seen, *a priori*, the evidence or the reasons for the reality of each event, and why one happened sooner than the other" (*Discourse on metaphysics* §13: 19),[19] is compellingly echoed in Condillac's meditation at the end of the *Essai* on the concept of "Corneille's first play."

Je finis par poser un problème au lecteur. *L'ouvrage d'un homme étant donné, déterminer le caractère et l'étendue de son esprit, et dire en conséquence non seulement quels sont les talens dont il donne des preuves, mais encore quels sont ceux qu'il peut acquérir: prendre par exemple, la première pièce de Corneille, et démontrer que, quand ce poëte la composait, il avoit déjà, ou du moins auroit bientôt tout le génie qui lui a mérité ce grand succès.* Il n'y a que l'analyse de l'ouvrage qui puisse faire connoître quelles opérations y ont contribué, et jusqu'à quel degré elles ont eu de l'exercice; et il n'y a que l'analyse de ces opérations qui puisse faire distinguer les qualités qui sont compatibles dans le même homme, de celles qui ne le sont pas, et par-là donner la solution du problème. Je doute qu'il y ait beaucoup de problèmes plus difficiles que celui-là. (original emphasis, *Essai*, 289)

[I conclude with a question for the reader]. *Given a man's work, determine the character and extent of his mind, and consequently say not only what abilities he demonstrates, but also what abilities he might yet acquire: take, for example, Corneille's first play, and show that when the poet composed it, he already had, or at least would soon possess the genius that brought him his great success.* Only the analysis of the work can reveal the operations that contributed to it, and the degree to which they were put to use; and only the analysis of these operations can enable us to distinguish those qualities that are compatible within one man from those which are not, and give thereby the answer to the problem. I doubt that there are many problems more difficult than this one.]

Already, in Leibniz's view, understanding the notions "Caesar" and "Adam" in the total multiplicity of their respective predicates, could only be accomplished in the mind of God; Condillac's problem, with its additional requirement of constructing not only the mind of the playwright, but also his subsequent works, from an early text, points to a confidence equal to Leibniz's in the fundamental harmony of the metaphysical relationships constituting existence, as well as to a supreme confidence in the power of reading. Condillac has not often been thought of as a New Critic, intently focussed on textual analysis, and yet, as we shall see, this is precisely his method in the *Traité des systêmes*, in which close readings of selected texts are intended to put him in contact with Malebranche, Leibniz, and Spinoza, thus enabling him to formulate a genealogical understanding of the systematizers. Nevertheless, the concentration on analysis, even if pursued to the point of banishing all indiscernibles, does not entirely free Condillac's search for clear and distinct *propositions identiques* from the threat of the frivolous or trifling.

Condillac's analysis remains somewhat precariously balanced between the *utile* and the *futile*, as Derrida puts it, as he strives on the one hand to delineate an unbroken chain of identical propositions and on the other to establish an identity, a partner for dialogue, in a text – not Corneille in this case, but instead Malebranche, Leibniz, or Spinoza. The confluence of these efforts, in their premises and in their procedures, renders Condillac liable to Adorno's critique of what he called identity-logic or identitarian thought, which forces resemblance on the dissimilar. Adorno's proposed remedy, "negative dialectics," does not however eschew the notion of identity, which Adorno does not think wholly possible. Neither does it attempt simply to propose its contradiction, which would be identity in a different form. The negative dialectic is understood rather as "the consistent sense of nonidentity" (5), constantly maintained and thought in relation to identity, through ongoing internal or immanent critique. In Condillac, the place of "nonidentity" is the place of the other. In the *Traité*, when Condillac constructs the identity of the other – interlocutor or reader – he cannot entirely come to terms with the other. As we shall see, his encounters emphasize difference and non-continuity, but his argument is similar to identity-logic, making unlikes alike. The systematizers, Descartes and Co., are alike in their deviance, their failure to apply Condillac's standards and definitions. This is the *Traité*'s coercive side.

Condillac's task here is a delicate one. He needs to show that, despite certain formal similarities, true and false systems must be distinguished. He must therefore establish his interlocutors as distinct from himself. His strategy is to let the other speak within his text, even to play the role of the other and to speak in his name. He enacts a number of different techniques for "being" or engaging the other: thus, for example, Leibniz comes alive and says *je* in this variant on the classical *dialogue des morts*. Condillac's purpose – to denounce visualist, falsely analogical, metaphorical, and affective elements in his opponents – is carried out by both close reading and a kind of ventriloquism. As he suspected on the final page of the *Essai*, deducing or creating an other from a text is a most difficult problem. The interlocutors are uniformly guilty of the charge that they "rely on words alone" [*ne roulent que sur des mots*] and he accuses them of making payments in "tokens," *jetons*, rather than good, hard philosophical currency. To the extent that the *Traité* more closely resembles a dialogue of the deaf than a dialogue of the dead, one may wonder whether the entire exercise is not to some degree frivolous.

And yet, explicating or characterizing the other remains an imperative. The uneasy, impossible dialogue must be maintained. Thus even the *Traité*, for all the sharpness of its categorizations and the apparent strength of its allegiance to identitarian logic, reasserts difference, dialogue, and change. The final sentence anticipates a new beginning, a new interlocutor, in the reader/learner: "Commencez par apprendre votre langue" ["Begin by learning your language"].

THE PATHOS OF READING

Having considered Condillac up until now in a synthesizing mode, I will now take up the points of the *Traité* roughly in the order in which they occur. Without attempting to reduce the arguments to a perfectly structured chain of identical propositions, it is possible to appreciate the formal qualities of the work and the strength of its indictment against so-called abstract systems, even as there accumulates in the discursive background an increasingly loud murmur that renders the overall programme problematic.

Structurally, the eighteen chapters of the *Traité* follow a fairly simple plan: having defined three basic types of systems – abstract, hypothetical, and "true" – Condillac proceeds first to demolish any claims to validity of the first type, then to weigh the ambiguities of the second, and last to expound upon the virtues and fields of application of the third. The equilibrium of the plan is offset, however, by its disproportionate distribution. Following an introductory chapter setting up Condillac's classification of systems, the next twelve are devoted to the attack on abstract systems: a series of numbered "examples," first of a general sort, then focussed in individual readings of Malebranche, Leibniz, Boursier, and Spinoza, and followed by a chapter on hypothesis and another in which Condillac takes up the challenge he had posed at the end of the *Essai*, explicating the "génie" of the abstract systematizers. The next four chapters, less than a quarter of the total work, discuss the usefulness of true systems. The chapters that stage Condillac's engagement with other philosophers offer a useful perspective from which to consider the place of identity and otherness within the "system," and it is on those that I will concentrate, after a look at the introduction.

The first chapter not only sets up the issues the *Traité* is to confront, but also exemplifies some of its textual difficulties.

Un systême n'est autre chose que la disposition des différentes parties d'un art ou d'une science dans un ordre où elles se soutiennent toutes mutuellement, et où les dernières s'expliquent par les premières. (121)

[A system is nothing other than the disposition of the various parts of an art or a science in an order in which they are mutually supported and in which the last are explained by the first.]

Although he epitomized for his generation the *esprit systématique*, Condillac's definition suggests less the "freely moving" philosophic energy eulogized by Cassirer, than the structured form ostensibly characteristic of the *esprit de système*. (Despite d'Alembert's indebtedness to the *Traité*, it should be noted that this pair of terms is never used by Condillac.) Condillac wants to simplify and demystify philosophy, as suggested by the phrase "nothing other than" as well as to insist on greater rigor in methods of proof. As we have seen in other writers, a kind of hesitation between the means of apprehending or expressing order wanders into his definition. That the parts of a system "are mutually supported" recalls *système*'s etymological sense as an aggregate, and points to, for example, a Diderotian understanding of system as network. On the other hand, the sentence promptly recasts this formula by imposing a notion of succession from "first" to "last." Given Condillac's emphasis in his other logical and philosophical writings on the necessity of establishing a linear chain of propositions, the shift in emphasis seems to redirect the definition onto his usual path. Perception of an occasionally non-directional, complex reality will, however, continue to haunt the text.

Almost immediately, the abbé begins to develop his argument by means of quotation and commentary, citing as an example of an "abstract principle" the Port-Royal logicians' definition of what constitutes an adequate first principle.

Tout le monde demeure d'accord qu'il est important d'avoir dans l'esprit plusieurs axiômes et principes, qui, étant clairs et indubitables, puissent nous servir de fondement pour connoître les choses les plus cachées. Mais ceux que l'on donne ordinairement, sont de si peu d'usage, qu'il est assez inutile de les savoir. Car, ce qu'ils appellent le premier principe de la connoissance, *il est impossible que la même chose soit et ne soit pas*, est très-clair et très certain; mais je ne vois point de rencontre où il puisse jamais servir à nous donner aucune connoissance. (Original emphasis, 121)

[Everyone agrees that it is important to have in mind several axioms and principles that, being clear and indubitable, can serve as a foundation to discover the most hidden things. But those that are ordinarily given are of so little use that it is rather pointless to know them. For what they call the first principle of knowledge, *that it is impossible that a thing both be and not be*, is very clear and very certain; but I cannot imagine any instance in which it might help us learn anything.]

I cite the passage at length because of the way in which Condillac promptly begins to insert himself into Arnauld and Nicole's vocabulary and to turn it against the original. Blithely quoting their second "first principle," as well as a few which follow it, he announces that although there are eleven altogether, it is pointless, *inutile*, to report them all and that the examples given must suffice. Lest the reader miss the irony, he continues:

La vertu que les philosophes attribuent à ces sortes de principes, est si grande, qu'il étoit naturel qu'on travaillât à les multiplier. Les métaphysiciens se sont en cela distingués. Descartes, Mallebranche, Leibnitz, etc., chacun à l'envi nous en a prodigué, et nous ne devons plus nous en prendre qu'à nous-mêmes, si nous ne pénétrons pas *les choses les plus cachées*. (121)

[The virtue attributed by philosophers to such principles is so great that it was natural for them to work to increase their number. Metaphysicians have distinguished themselves at this. Descartes, Malebranche, Leibniz, etc, have poured them out, and so we should only blame ourselves if we do not penetrate *the most hidden things*.]

The reader could have already caught a glimpse of Condillac's irony in his third paragraph, where he claims to put abstract principles first as being "à la mode." Within the first pages, the tone is established and irony stands out as one of the primary tropes of the *Traité des systèmes*.

In his treatise on the tropes – a work much admired by Condillac– Du Marsais classifies irony as one of the tropes of 'opposition, contrariety, and difference' (1: 249–50) and makes the observation that since it involves saying the opposite of what one means, then of all the tropes it relies the most heavily on "accessory ideas" in order to be understood: "the tone of voice, and to an even greater extent our knowledge of the personal merit demerit of someone, and of the manner of thinking of the person speaking, help make the irony evident more than the words being used" (1: 199). Just as irony comes close to exceeding Du Marsais's definition of what constitutes a trope (tropes are a subset of "figures de mots" dependent on word choice and thus distinct from "figures de pensée," 1: 16), it also infuses a kind of excessiveness or redundancy into Condillac's text. If our understanding of his meaning depends on "accessory ideas," that is, on our foreknowledge of Condillac's thought and the "démérite" of his subjects, then the *Traité* comes dangerously close to being unanchored in any real need, repeating what is already known, trifling with the reader.

Groundlessness also haunts Condillac's later narrative account of the birth of science, which takes place as a kind of immaculate conception, independent of human need, or human desire, or indeed human agency.

... les systêmes se seroient achevés, en quelque sorte, tout seuls, parce que les faits se seroient arrangés d'eux-mêmes dans l'ordre où ils s'expliquent successivement les uns les autres. (123)

[... systems appear to have arisen, after a fashion, all by themselves, because the facts arranged themselves in the order in which they explained each other.]

Elsewhere, when we saw d'Alembert at a similar juncture, he linked the pursuit of knowledge with pleasure and feeling. Having just made a connection between self-gratification and the sort of false philosophizing he condemns, Condillac has no such option. Such passions and desires will rather intrude upon this edenic scene as the source of ill-begotten abstract systematizing. Thus the narrative apparently intended to show the naturalness of true systems shows them as products of spontaneous generation, or as downright mystical. The account of the event itself is invaded by the language of conjecture. This description does nevertheless achieve an important goal: that of removing true systems as far as possible from the vagaries of human error. For, as Condillac explains in the chapter's remaining paragraphs, we are incapable of judging, or "seeing" what we have thought: thus we confuse unfounded and unproved suppositions with legitimate, factual first principles, and we fail to understand that, since abstractions are merely convenient devices for classifying phenomena, they are unsuited for use as "principles." As important as these distinctions are to the construction of Condillac's argument, it is also problematic for him that his plea for empirically-based reason should so emphasize the imperfection of perception.

Later, as Condillac explains how systems either are or aren't rooted in the real, he also begins to give us a more complete idea of what, in his view, the real is.

Que des hommes, au sortir d'un profound sommeil, se voyant au milieu d'un labyrinthe, posent des principes généraux pour en découvrir l'issue; quoi de plus ridicule? Nous naissons au milieu d'un labyrinthe, où mille détours ne sont tracés que pour nous conduire à l'erreur: s'il y a un chemin qui mène à la vérité, il ne se montre pas d'abord; souvent c'est celui qui paroit mériter le moins notre confiance. Nous ne saurions donc prendre trop de précaution. Avançons lentement, examinons soigneusement tous les lieux par où nous passons, et connoissons-les si bien, que nous soyons en état de revenir sur nos pas. Il est plus important de ne nous trouver qu'où nous étions d'abord, que de nous croire trop légèrement hors du labyrinthe. (127)

[That men, emerging from a profound sleep and finding themselves in the middle of a labyrinth, should begin by stating general principles in order to find the exit – what could be more absurd? We are born in the middle of a labyrinth, where a thousand turns have been traced only to lead us into error; if there is a path that leads to the truth, it is not evident at first; often it is the one that seems the least worthy of our confidence. We cannot take too many precautions. Let us advance slowly, carefully examining each place we pass, and let us come to know them so well that we will always be able to retrace our steps. It is more important to return to where we were before, than to believe ourselves too easily out of the labyrinth.]

The image of the labyrinth here does not seem to convey the sense of radical undecidability that we saw earlier in d'Alembert, but the notion that there seems to be no escape from it, or that one might not be able to judge whether one is in or out of it, gives one pause. Here it functions as an emblem of both complexity and fixity: although not readily apprehendable, it can nevertheless be mapped, gradually. Thus certain cartographic projections are right while others are wrong, and knowledge can be accumulated. A few pages later, however, Condillac gives in as many sentences two slightly different constructions of reality. Having ascribed certain erroneous explanations of natural phenomena to the power of the imagination willfully to suppose "a relation between things," he goes on to observe that "everything is related in the universe ... what we take for the action of a single part is the result of the combined action of all" (134). The maze of causal connections is more mobile than the labyrinth in which the philosopher earlier awoke, and the emphasis on our inability to perceive it leads one to question by what criteria the relationships previously denounced could be definitively said to be a product of the imagination.

As I have mentioned, the attack on abstract systems gathers momentum through the opening chapters of the *Traité*, becoming progressively more concrete, more focussed on specific philosophers. There is one significant figure who is treated differently from the others, however: Descartes. Unlike the other major philosophers, he does not have a chapter specifically devoted to his work, remaining instead a spectral presence in such passages as Condillac's treatment of the "prejudice" of innate ideas. This pivotal chapter connects the vaguely *ad hominem* approach of the preceding chapters to the more properly philosophical case studies which follow. Now, although there can be little doubt as to whose name would most immediately come to mind, in France in 1749, upon the utterance of the words "innate ideas," the chapter begins by denying them any legitimate paternity ("I don't know whether the system of innate ideas belongs more to the people [*peuple*] or to the philosophers" 141). Condillac reduces the "system" to a matter of prejudice and popular tradition, no more intellectually respectable than divination by bird entrails. Throughout the chapter, Descartes is never mentioned, although a footnoted reference to "les Cartésiens *mêmes*" (141n.; my emphasis) underscores his unvoiced importance. Between this analysis of origins and effects, there is no discussion of the theory itself – only a footnote sending the reader to Book 1 of Locke's *Essay* for a fuller treatment of the issue. It is as though there were nothing innate in the doctrine of innate ideas, and nothing innate in Descartes either, that either should be subjected to Condillac's usual textual analysis. Instead, Descartes shades off into "des Cartésiens," the Port-Royal logicians, or Malebranche.

Similarly, and predictably, Condillac turns his skeptical eye to the concept of a clear and distinct idea, taking as his text the statement, "Tout ce qui est renfermé dans l'idée claire et distincte d'une chose, en peut être affirmé avec vérité" ["All that is enclosed in the clear and distinct idea of a thing can be truthfully affirmed of it"] (144). Now, Condillac, as we have seen, does for certain purposes maintain the truth, and usefulness, of analytic propositions. Here, however, his emphasis is on the difficulty – potentially the impossibility – of claiming that an idea can ever be perceived as a simple self-enclosed entity: "We have many ideas that are only partial" [*qui ne sont que partielles*] (144). It is the same problem that arose in the passage on our inability to know all the causal ramifications of an event: in the labyrinth of relations that constitute the universe, how often can any phenomenon or construct be said to exist "clearly and distinctly"?[20] Interestingly, Condillac concedes that Descartes made one justifiable use of this concept, the first time that he invoked it: in the clear and distinct perception of mental activity that followed his purgation by radical doubt: the *cogito*. Beyond this, however, "les Cartésiens" have made indefensible applications, and clear and distinct ideas are a mere "je ne sais quoi" (145). The text thus only allows Descartes to exist as something other than as the vaguest of reference points, at the moment he affirms his existence as a thinking entity. Condillac will return to this formidable figure only after having disposed of a series of others, but will never engage with his work as he does with theirs.[21] Let us turn to the series of case studies.

Malebranche comes first. Condillac's critical technique operates in this chapter with its most laser-like efficiency. Malebranche is for him an elegant writer, given to brilliant insight, but all too frequently led astray by the seduction of the imagination and by *le verbe* (151). "Qu'auroit fait Mallebranche, si cette belle expression métaphorique, *des inclinations droites*, n'avoit pas été française?" ["What would Malebranche have done, had this fine metaphorical expression, straight inclinations, not been French?"]. Condillac's account of the Oratorian is thus less committed to the paraphrase and discussion of the principal ideas of the work in question, *La Recherche de la vérité*, than the close reading and scrutiny of linguistic interstices, where unfulfilled promises to the reader, forgotten metaphors, and casual concessions erode the overall framework. That framework is less important to Condillac as having "few partisans" in 1749.[22] The *Recherche* is thus chosen to provide a very specific kind of case study.

Malebranche is in many ways an interesting figure with respect to Condillac. His particular blend of Cartesianism and Augustianism won him no great support from either the Church or other Cartesians (he engaged in a passionate and prolonged polemic with Arnauld), but his assessment that we can never form an entirely adequate or distinct idea of either the self or the outside world continued to reverberate in Hume and Berkeley. As with Bayle, Condillac acknowledges Malebranche's critical insight even as he proposes to turn it against him.

Il semble que les Cartésiens soient faits pour remarquer l'inexactitude des idées des autres, ils ne réussissent pas également à s'en faire eux-mêmes d'exacts. (145–6)

[It appears that although the Cartesians are able to observe the inexactitude of others' ideas, they are not as successful in forming exact ideas of their own]

What follows is Condillac's close reading of a few paragraphs from the first chapter of the *Recherche*. He disputes certain theses on conceptual grounds, as when he argues that Malebranche's view of the effects of the soul's internal configuration suggests a force or action that does not stem from God, thus contradicting his basic occasionalist contention that all causality resides in God (148), or that he mistakenly conflates an impulse toward "le bien en général" with an impulse toward God (150). For most of his treatment, however, he is at pains to demonstrate the process by which

Malebranche proffers an analogy between mind and matter originally as a heuristic device, and then makes it part of the substance of
his argument. Malebranche performs this operation, Condillac
enjoys pointing out, while repeatedly conceding that the comparison
is neither absolute nor exact. "Malebranche is mistaken [*s'y est trompé
lui-même*]" (146). Condillac cites brief portions of text, then comments
on them, teasing out a contradiction, a juxtaposition of terms, a
revealing revision in successive editions of the work. Malebranche's
remarks on the generation of ideas brings him into Condillac's
territory and provoke a more general discussion, although at least
one of his comments tells us more about his own system's configuration than Malebranche's. This is the point at which Condillac,
having just previously denounced Malebranche's exaggerated
distinction between ideas and sensations (Malebranche failing to
recognize that the former arise in the latter), makes the opposite
criticism, offering the following paraphrase from the *Recherche* as
though it represented in itself the height of absurdity and required
no further comment.

L'âme change autant par le passage d'une ignorance parfaite à une
véritable science, que par celui du plaisir à la douleur. (148)

[The soul changes as much in the passage from perfect ignorance to true
science, as it does in passing from pleasure to pain.]

Condillac's indignation here requires an *idée accessoire* for clarifica-
tion: not only is Malebranche's nascent idealism offensive, but also
his failure to distinguish and appropriately hierarchize disembodied
wisdom from sensate pleasure.

Accessory ideas are present as well in Condillac's persistent irony.
His use of sarcasm throughout the *Traité* has already impelled him to
call attention to it himself, apologizing for his teasing (*badinage*, 133),
or wondering if readers will "suspect" him of deliberately ridiculing
the philosophers (145). These cautionary glances at the reader do not
prevent him, however, from concluding his discussion of Malebranche with an elaborate parody of the geometrical demonstration,
complete with definitions and axioms, of a proposition that he
qualifies as patently absurd: "L'amour et la haine ne sont qu'une
même chose" ["Love and hate are one and the same thing"] (150).
The satirical proof is promptly followed by a citation from Malebranche to much the same effect, although – Condillac notes soberly
– Malebranche does allow that hate "feels" different from love.

Parody, like certain forms of critical exegesis, involves establishing a relationship with the other which is unequal and, by some standards, "unfair." Du Marsais's discussion of parody speaks of the liberty of the parodist and of the act itself as one of *détournemenmt* and difference (*Des Tropes*, 1: 317). The etymon *para-* further suggests a counter-action or defensive measure (as in "parasol" or "parachute"). Condillac's close reading constitutes such a detour away from the conventionally understood intent of the text, as much for its concentration on Malebranche's sins of analogism as for its almost total refusal to look beyond the introductory chapter of a two-volume work for an account of its "system." Condillac's exegetical perspicacity does not completely defend him, cannot parry an application of similar procedures to his own text – none can. The *Traité des systêmes* does not question its own methods, however. Malebranche speaks for himself up to a point, but his presence is carefully circumscribed. His text remains a site of difference – different from Locke, with whose praise the chapter ends; different from itself in its contradictions and unfulfilled promises, as well as by virtue of the detouring and parodic doubling initiated by reading. But, as the succeeding chapters show, no two readings are quite the same either.

The opening statement in the following chapter, "Sixième exemple, des monades," may lead one to think that its procedures will be similar to those of the chapter on Malebranche, because of the emphasis on the difficulties of interpreting the language of Leibniz.

... craignant de choquer les opinions reçues, il se rapproche des façons de parler ordinaires, et de faire entendre le contraire de ce qu'il veut dire. Peut-être aussi que, pour avoir traité les différentes parties de son système, à diverses reprises, il a été contraint de varier son langage à mesure qu'il a développé ses idées. (151)

[Fearing conflict with received opinions, he makes use of ordinary speech and suggests the opposite of what he means. Perhaps as well, because he took up the various parts of his system at different times, he was constrained to vary his language as he was developing his ideas.]

The problem with Leibniz is that there is no single reliable text on which to base an analysis, given the scattered and incomplete publication of his works at that time. Condillac notes that he can only speak to the works in Latin, although he presumably knew Du Châtelet's work and was evidently familiar with Christian Wolff's exposition (which Condillac describes as burdened with abstractions and *longueurs)*. He would have known the *Theodicy* published in French in 1710, and have been aware of the correspondence with Samuel Clarke, published in English and French in London in 1717, and in French in Amsterdam in 1720 (and referred to by Du Châtelet).

The *Monadology* appeared in Latin in 1720 and is the main target of the attack in the *Traité*. Whatever Condillac may have known of the early logical writings in the *Journal des sçavans* and *Acta eruditorum* – *short* articles that seem to have been generally overlooked during the eighteenth century – was, as he says, probably of too piecemeal a nature to allow for much of an idea of Leibniz's logic.

So, having deconstructed Malebranche, Condillac now proposes to reconstruct Leibniz: "je vais présenter par quelle suite d'idées j'imagine qu[e le système des monades] s'est formé dans la tête de Leibnitz ... je ferais parler ce philosophe" ["I will present the sequence of ideas by which I imagine that the system of monads was formed in Leibniz's head ... I will make this philosopher speak"] (151). The first expository section of the chapter is thus composed of ten "articles" expounding the theories of monads, of the plenum, of pre-established harmony, etc. The language is marked by a first-person pronoun representing Leibniz/Condillac, and by an un-accustomed number of logical terms such as *donc, car, or, ainsi*, etc. Without an apparent intent to parody, Condillac seems to have produced a Leibniz who sounds more like Pangloss.

Il y a des composés: donc, il y a des êtres simples; car il n'y a rien sans raison suffisante. Or la raison de la composition d'un être ne peut pas se trouver dans d'autres etres composés, parce qu'on demanderoit encore d'où vient la composition de ceux-ci: cette raison se trouve donc ailleurs, et par conséquent elle ne peut être que dans des etres simples.[23] (152)

[There are composites: therefore, there are simple substances; for nothing exists without a sufficient reason. Now, the reason for the composition of a being cannot be in other composites, because we would ask what caused their composition; therefore the reason must be elsewhere, and conse-quently it can only be in simple substances.]

Rather than becoming enmeshed in the question of Condillac's sources for his account, or indeed in that of its adequation to its subject, let us look instead at the way he situates Leibniz in his text.

Part II of the chapter, the refutation, treats Leibniz as an adversary worthy of respect. Condillac begins, for example, by refuting a recent refutation of Leibniz, the paper by J.H.G. Justi that had won the Berlin Academy prize in 1748 (an event generally seen as marking the decline of Leibniz/Wolffism in Germany). Condillac claims that Justi misrepresents Leibniz's arguments through an incomplete understanding of his views: "the longer I study the system of monads, the more I realize that everything is related. There are errors, but they are in places that M. Justi has not pointed out" (160n.).[24]

Condillac begins his critique by observing that there are two things to avoid in establishing a workable system: begging the question and explaining phenomena with principles that are as incomprehensible as the phenomena. He takes a passing shot at the Cartesians by claiming that they are guilty of the former error, then examines why the Leibnizians commit the latter. The question is one of "des mots qui n'offrent rien à l'esprit" ("words that tell us nothing"), rendering Leibniz's system *frivole* (160). Condillac suggests that one test terms to be sure that they remain "close" to their referents.

Pour juger si nous avons l'idée d'une chose, il ne faut souvent que consulter le nom que nous lui donnons. Le nom d'une cause connue la désigne toujours directement: tels sont les mots de *balancier, roue*, etc. Mais, quand une cause est inconnue, la dénomination qu'on lui donne, n'indique jamais qu'une cause quelconque avec un rapport à l'effet produit, et elle se forme toujours avec des noms qui marquent l'effet. C'est ainsi qu'on a imaginé les termes de force centrifuge, centripète, vive, morte, de gravitation, d'attraction, d'impulsion, etc. (161)

[In order to judge whether we have the idea of a thing, often we need only consult the name we give it. The name of a known cause always designates it directly: such are the terms *pendulum, wheel*, etc. But when a cause is unknown, its denomination can only indicate a cause that has some relation to the effect produced, and we form it with a noun that indicates the effect. Thus were created terms regarding force as centrifugal, centripetal, inertial, kinetic (*vis viva*), gravitational, attractional, impulsive, etc.]

Condillac asks a great deal of words here. From the suggestion that they should "offer" something other than "nothing," to the requirement that they should furnish, not simply the "idea" of something, but rather an understanding of its cause, the passage places the brunt of Condillac's critique on the conceptual difficulty of the "force" of the monads. Afterwards, his emphasis on the connectedness of Leibniz's system enables him to "reject everything" all the more easily. In addition, the series of examples – centrifugal, centripetal, gravitational force, etc. – evokes Newtonian physics as a subliminal counter-example to the theory of monads. Even Newton is perfectible, however: a term such as "gravitation" gives less of a true idea of its referent than a noun like "pendulum." The physicality of Condillac's *langage d'action* sends its tendrils throughout the linguistic system, rendering certain forms of relationality problematic. What this passage and the discussion that follows show most vividly is that the relational dynamism of Leibniz's thought is incommensurate with Condillac's requirements, partly because it was incompletely understood in 1749, and partly because it does not depend on the same kind of groundedness that Condillac demands. Condillac's reading of the German philosopher constantly returns to demands for intelligibility, de-metaphorization, words taken "dans le propre." They do not speak the same language. A ≠ A.

At the same time, the rhetoric of the analysis underscores speech, dialogue, and exchange. Having taken on the role of Leibniz earlier, in the second section Condillac frames his critique as a sort of virtual dialogue, stressing indirect discourse and the verbs *dire, parler, demander*, etc. The virtual interlocutor is for the most part an anonymous *on*, but is personified near the end: "But, Leibniz will say ..." (163). The identity of this "Leibniz" comes however into question in the chapter's concluding lines:

> C'est ainsi qu'en voulant raisonner sur des objets qui ne sont pas a notre portée, on se trouve, après bien des détours, au même point d'où on étoit parti. [Parce que j'ai réfuté le système de Leibnitz, quelques Leibnitiens ont dit que je ne l'ai pas entendu. Si cela est, le système des monades, tel que je l'ai exposé, est donc de moi. Je ne le désavouerai pas; mais il n'en prouvera pas moins l'abus des systêmes abstraits.] (164; bracketed section added in 1771)

> [Thus in attempting to reason on issues that are beyond our reach, we find ourselves, after many a detour, back where we began. (Because I refuted the system of Leibniz, some Leibnizians have said that I did not understand him. If that is the case, then the system of monades, as I have explained it here, is my invention. I will not disavow it; but it furnishes no less a proof of the abuse of abstract systems.)]

As the addition in the revised edition indicates, the virtual dialogue sparked a real one. Condillac's defiant assumption of the authorship of his version of the *Monadology* has the double effect of completing the exchange of identities sketched in the chapter, as well as of conceding that the Leibnizians may not be wrong. But if Leibniz was not "à notre portée" in the *Traité*, then the chapter is liable to the same criticism that it levels at others – and we find ourselves "back where we began." If the monadology critiqued here is imaginary, then surely part of the point of Condillac's proof is abstract, groundless – the very problem he finds in Leibniz.

The inability of the dialogue effectively to take place in the absence of an authentic textual interlocutor may explain why, after looking at the major intellectual figures, Malebranche and Leibniz, and before taking on the formidable adversary Spinoza, Condillac devotes an entire chapter to a work, which although controversial in its day, has not the scope of the others, Père Boursier's treatise on grace and "la prémotion physique."[25] Tellingly, the chapter is by far the shortest in the group of case studies; here Condillac feels at liberty to indulge in ironic asides without apology.

The basic technique is similar to the Malebranche chapter. Condillac underscores its "partial" nature: "I will not follow these principles through all of their consequences; I will examine them only to see whether they have the usual defects of abstract principles" (165). Boursier's arguments are presented through paraphrase and quotation; increasingly, as in the Leibniz chapter, Condillac couches the discussion in the form of a debate, punctuating the text with *dis-je, répondrez-vous*, etc. A new element, however, is an emphasis on Condillac's own experience as a reader, recounting his reactions both somewhat humorously:

Quand je suis bien rempli de ce systême, je me fais un vrai plaisir d'ouvrir, de fermer et de rouvrir sans cesse les yeux. D'un clin d'oeil, je produis, j'anéantis, et je reproduis des êtres sans nombre. Il semble encore qu'à tout ce que j'entends, je sente grossir mon être ... (165)

[When I am imbued with this system, I take real pleasure in opening, closing, and reopening my eyes. In a single blink, I produce, I annihilate, and I reproduce countless beings. It further seems that with all that I understand, I feel my own being enlarged ...]

and more prosaically in detailing his train of thought. Unlike the conversational present of the "dialogued" sections, here the account is cast as narrative: "The first time that I studied this system ... I applied ... I concluded ... I realized ... I worked ... I sought the cause" (166). Alternating between dialogue and *récit*, Condillac spends most of his time in search of definitions: "Let me point out the language that your imagination is imposing on you" (169).

As it happens, the "language" in question at this juncture involves Boursier's postulate that there exist "commerce" and "communication" between the entities (perceptions and successive states of mind) of his study. In successive states, where one produces the next, there is neither "real commerce" nor "veritable and substantial communication," replies Condillac. Condillac's criticism strikes Boursier's argument at a particularly weak spot; he soon after closes the book and declares that it is better to admit to ignorance than to claim knowledge by such a system. His chapter, however, suggests a possible alternative to Boursier. Between Boursier and Condillac there is no *commerce réel*; certainly not "dans le propre." Boursier's name does not appear in the work and is never mentioned by Condillac, adding to the lack of "dialogue" in this chapter. Communication, such as it is, is only achieved through successive texts, Boursier's treatise and Condillac's Chapter 9, the second of which does not pretend to give a full (im-partial) account of the first. There is no question of "identity" between the two: Condillac does not equal Boursier, and even Condillac's Boursier does not entirely equal Boursier, either. One could not speak of Boursier as having influenced Condillac; like the other portraits in the gallery, he is present as a negative example. And yet, something is produced, something gained, something communicated in the encounter of the two texts. Boursier exists in Condillac, even if in a way not foreseen by his own text. The emphasis on dialogue and on the act of reading, the way that both stimulate ideas, holds out a model of conversation/commentary/reflection as an alternative to the absolute of "véritable et substantielle communication" which Condillac would like either to affirm or to deny in Boursier.

Condillac's chapter ends with a paradox on identification and distinction. He blames Boursier and other theologians for having ventured outside their domain: "If only theologians could limit themselves to the teachings of faith, and philosophers to those of experience!" (169).[26] Boursier and those like him, in Condillac's view, are responsible for the divisions in the Church. Crossing certain boundaries – whether those between faith and reason or simply stepping outside the circumference of each is not clear – is productive of rifts. The remedy, the *Traité* appears to say, is in its own salutary philosophy, practiced well within the faith (but in such a manner that questions of faith do not arise) by an *abbé philosophe*.

Having affirmed his position of mastery, Condillac begins Chapter 10 ("Huitième et dernier exemple, le spinosisme réfuté") with a statement suggesting a large-scale attack: "A unique, indivisible, necessary substance, from whose nature all things necessarily follow like modifications that express its essence each in its own way: this is the universe according to Spinoza" (169). Once past the generalizing overtones of this first sentence, however, Condillac quickly informs us that he will offer no résumé, but instead a more painstaking and restrictive approach, by way of a literal translation, with commentary, of Part 1 of the *Ethics*. He informs us that the *Ethics* represents more than any other work the vices of abstract systems, and indicates one direction that his critique will take by promising to see whether Spinoza has fulfilled the two prime conditions for "geometrical" demonstrations, "la clarté des idées" and "la précision des signes." Given his earlier satire of such proofs in the discussion of Malebranche, one may suppose that here, too, the intended target is not Spinoza's work alone.

Paradoxically, despite the greater textual presence of the *Ethics* in the *Traité* compared with the other case studies, its author is further removed from the possibilities of dialogue than were Malebranche, Boursier, or even Leibniz. Spinoza is almost invariably referred to in the third person, and there is less of the virtual debate that characterized the preceding chapters. In one of the few such passages, the exchange is displaced or distanced via an intermediary. Imagining what Spinoza "would say" to one criticism, for example, Condillac responds indirectly with what he "would say to such a philosopher" (175).[27] The acidity of Condillac's tone and his greater willingness to dispense with reasoned commentary in favor of abuse – referring to Spinoza's *scholia* as "verbiage" for example – stem no doubt in part from Spinoza's low philosophic stock in 1749 and the general tendency to equate "le spinosisme" with morally abhorrent determinism and atheism, but Condillac's rising tone of condemnation is also motivated by the fact that this final example represents the *summa* of the abstract systems and that by attacking it, he attacks them all.

One can see this shift of attention away from the individual Spinoza, despite the meticulous attention to his text, in the first pages of the chapter. Responding to the crucial Definition 3 on substance, Condillac notes as usual that this definition leads to no clear idea, and then shifts to a more general perspective: "I need only the language of the philosophers to prove our ignorance in this respect" (170). To the series of examples which follows, Condillac gives footnotes referring us to Descartes, Malebranche, Wolff, and

Leibniz; when a debate errupts in the main text, it is not Spinoza but another who speaks ("But, Monsieur Wolff will reply ..." 171). Throughout the chapter Condillac emphasizes the extent to which his comments apply not only to Spinoza alone: "Tel est l'aveugle-ment des philosophes, quand ils se contentent de notions vagues" (179) ["Such is the blindness of philosophers, when they let them-selves be satisfied with vague notions"].

There is a similar shift, as the chapter proceeds, from literal translation and attention to textual detail, to paraphrase, abridge-ment, *renvoi*, and outright dismissal. While leaving Spinoza's proposi-tions intact, Condillac abridges a number of the scholia, and even certain demonstrations, reducing as many as seven pages of discus-sion to a few sentences. He also relies more and more heavily on sending the reader back to earlier parts of his critique ("Voyez ce qui a été dit ..." 181, etc). Clearly, there is a certain logic to Condillac's *renvois*, insofar as the stages of the geometrical proof are considered to be contingent on previous definitions, axioms, etc. However, contemporary spinozists would argue that such a reductive under-standing of the method fails to allow for the more fluid relations among the arguments' constituent parts.[28] The abridgements begin at a telling moment. Having worked his way through the series of definitions and axioms of Articles I and II off the *Ethics*, I, Condillac begins to paraphrase about halfway through the scholium that follows the demonstration of Proposition II. Proposition II, which culminates the series presenting Spinoza's version of the Ontological Argument (in which God's existence is seen as a necessary part of his essence) presents a particularly apt case for viewing the incompat-ibility of Condillac's thought with that of the rationalists.

The history of objections to various forms of the Ontological Argument, from Guanilo's reply to Saint Anselm to the present, involves questioning first whether or not God is the only being of which existence can be said to be a necessary predicate, and later, whether or not existence can be said to function as a predicate at all.[29] Thus Kant's classic critique of the argument denies that existence is a real predicate; all assertions of existence are synthetic statements, and as such must be submitted to the test of experience: none can be proved analytically.

In his reading of the *Ethics*, although he does not venture into a formal logical refutation of the argument, we can see Condillac's aversion to it as being based on a similar stance.

Spinosa devroit démontrer qu'il y a, dans la nature, un objet qui répond à l'idée qu'il se fait de Dieu. Autrement ses démonstrations, vraies tout au plus par rapport à sa façon de concevoir, ne prouvent rien pour la chose même. (182–3)

[Spinoza should demonstrate that there is one object in nature that corresponds to his idea of God. Otherwise, his demonstrations, at the most true within his way of conceiving things, prove nothing with respect to reality.]

Or, more brutally:

Falloit-il tant de discours pour conclure d'une définition arbitraire l'existence d'une chimère? (180)

[Did we need so much talk to conclude from an arbitrary definition the existence of an illusion?]

Given Condillac's undeniable strengths as a logician, it is perhaps surprising not to see him trying his hand more systematically at a problem of such enduring philosophic interest. As far as Condillac is concerned, however, Spinoza's argument relies on a definition of "substance" which is itself incomprehensible, and is therefore itself "frivole." The problem with the Ontological Argument – in any version – is that it requires a much more unwavering certitude in the commensurability of logical and linguistic constructs with the nature of things. Thus what I have dubbed Condillac's "skepticism" leads him to withhold assent to any such construct. Speaking of substance as "a Proteus who takes pleasure in presenting himself to me in a thousand different forms," he goes on to postulate its unknowability. "Aucun philosophe ne le sauroit fixer, et montrer la détermination essentielle d'une substance quelconque" ["No philosopher can fix or show the essential determination of any substance whatsoever"] (171). What can be known with certitude must be known otherwise, through the senses: the scholia to the demonstration of Proposition 8 ("All substance is necessarily infinite") inspire an empiricist credo and overwhelming rejection of "the blindness of philosophers" (179).

As previously indicated, the other main line of Condillac's attack is to see whether or not Spinoza truly lives up to the requirements of the geometrical method. The merit of exposition through definitions, axioms, and propositions, as opposed to a discursive exposition – the *méthode de composition* or *synthèse* as opposed to the *méthode d'invention* or *analyse*, in Port Royal's terms – was said to be the most persuasive, "celle qu'on a toujours jugée la plus propre pour persuader la vérité,

& en convaincre entièrement l'esprit,"[30] since if readers accepted as self-evidently true the opening definitions and axioms, they would be compelled to assent to the truth of the demonstrations.[31] Although Arnauld and Nicole suggested that analysis was more suited to discovery and synthesis to the presentation of results, Condillac had already disputed this division in the final pages of the *Essai*, where he also redefined analysis, replacing deduction with induction (*Essai*, 281, 288).

In his comments on Spinoza's method, Condillac disputes both "the precision of the signs" (*la précision des signes*), by claiming that key terms such as "substance" are never satisfactorily explicated, and the "clarity of the ideas" (*la clarté des idées*), by contending that Spinoza's argument begs the question. This may seem a fairly pointless – even "frivolous" – accusation to make of a technique that by definition is based on the meticulous explication or "unfolding" of the consequences of self-evident statements. The model of the unsympathetic reader, Condillac refuses the self-evidence of the definitions and axioms, and furthermore holds their elaboration to a much more strictly linearist model than Spinoza demands. The logic of the *Ethics* is more recursive and the interrelationships among its parts more mutable, than Condillac will accept.[32] This particular form of rigor needs to be imposed, as we have seen elsewhere, to prevent confusion between any element of Condillac's own project and that which he criticizes. For despite the obvious differences in outlook and approach between the abbé and the author of the *Ethics*, there is in the former's understanding of "tout système" as "une seule et même idée" expoundable through successive translations of identical propositions, a distant sympathetic vibration to the note struck by the self-completeness of Spinoza's logically unfolding universe. That which might be similar must be denied; the utterance which is the *Traité* aims at delimiting and dismissing that which it most conscientiously renders present within itself. The question of "fairness" is lost in the polemical and self-assertive needs of the text.

In his story, "Kierkegaard Unfair to Schlegel," Donald Barthelme wryly seizes upon the projections and personal engagements that can suddenly reach out and break the frame of the most abstract discussion. In the schematic sequence of questions and answers that constitutes the short story, the answerer's erudite discussion of philosophical theories of irony takes an unexpected turn.

A: We have to do here with my own irony. Because of course Kierkegaard
was "fair" to Schlegel. In making a statement to the contrary I am
attempting to ... I might have several purposes – simply being
provocative, for example. But mostly I am trying to annihilate
Kierkegaard in order to deal with his disapproval.

Q: Of Schlegel?

A: Of me.[33]

The discussion is doubly or triply ironic. The answerer has just
offered a technical disquisition on distanciation and alienation, but
he ends by positing an impossible link between Kierkegaard and
himself; this momentary cadence, or dénouement, is however followed by a real "untying" as the dialogue moves on to disparate
subjects and the two voices express increasing dissatisfaction with
one another.

Condillac's irony operates effortlessly, even maliciously, in his
discussion of Spinoza:

Les expressions *nature naturée* et *nature naturante* sont si heureuses et si
énergiques, qu'il eût été dommage que Spinosa ne les eût pas employées.
(191)

[The expressions *natura naturata* and *natura naturans* are so felicitous and so
energetic that it would have been a shame had Spinoza not employed
them.]

Operating under the trope of division, he reduces two of the
founding terms of the *Ethics* to the status of gratuitous stylistic
embellishments, just as he excludes the logically organic as merely
circular and denies any relationship between Spinoza's verbal
construct and the world.

And yet, despite division and exclusion, the *Traité* also functions
through replication. That replication, weak in the chapter on innate
ideas, gains momentum and fills more and more textual space in the
chapters which follow. Some forms – the selected quotation of
Malebranche, the account of the experience of reading Boursier, the
translation of Spinoza – appear more successful from Condillac's
point of view than his synthesis of Leibniz, which he is forced to
admit is to a certain degree his own invention. The *Traité* is a
profoundly ambivalent work. Geared toward ironizing, revealing the
logical fissures and internal disparities of the texts it examines,
making them "say" something other than they intend, it seeks to
accomplish this goal by giving the others a voice, by assuming the

role of the other. Condillac's tactics of reading for the elusive detail, the fateful metaphor – reading against the grain – resemble in certain respects those protocols of reading often dubbed "postmodern." Yet Condillac's readings place themselves in the service of an empiricism that postmodernism rejects.

A further irony: for Condillac, as for Leibniz and Descartes, a preferred category for the kind of philosophy he sees as opposed to his own is Scholasticism. Yet surely there is a certain medieval quality to his own writing. In order for the *Traité* to operate smoothly, it requires another text, to which the act of commentary must lend a kind of privilege. True, Condillac's line-by-line approach to Spinoza does not match the intertextual intricacy of Abelard's gloss on Boethius's comments on Porphyry's introduction to Aristotle's *Categories*, nor are his aims the same: the scholastics sought the unfolding of an ultimate meaning, whereas Condillac is searching for fault lines. A better parallel might be found in the quadrivium, in what the medievals called a trope. Neither flower nor figure, but rather a line of music. A trope is an insertion of text, and eventually of music, into the line of an existing plainchant. The original technique is one of repetition with modification. The trope is a feature of monophony, and provides the means by which a single musical line could gain in complexity. The growth of such complexity and the advent of a usable notation system permitted the development of the juxtaposition of musical voices, polyphony. In Condillac, too, there is an incipient conversation, a multi-voiced texture, despite the linearist frame.

The remaining chapters of the *Traité* explore the sort of thought that is possible once one has escaped the errors of abstractionism and achieved "une vue assez nette et assez précise" ["a rather clear and rather precise view"]. The phrase marks a significant revision of the *idée claire et distincte*: the substitution of the sensorial for the cerebral and the approximative qualifier *assez* indicate important features of the new program. After lending a limited support to the use of hypothesis – the term *tâtonnement* suggests the need for physical proximity and quick verification or rejection – Condillac explores the fields of application of what he calls true systems, i.e., those based on empirically verified premises and constructed from identical propositions. The argument tends to perpetuate itself by means of juxtaposing pairs of terms, thus maintaining something of the dialogic structure of the preceding chapters. In the chapter "Du génie ... '' the pairs are oppositional and elaborate the division between "imagination" and "analysis" and their corresponding activities *imaginer* and *concevoir*. *Concevoir* belongs to the semantic field of *génération, engendrer, germe*, etc., which allows it to be recuperated from the ironic *fécondité* that continues to characterize wrong systems, the productions of the imagination. Divisiveness functions even more intimately at this level, however: the term *génie* as it appears in the title as indicating both the character (and cause) of the abstractionists; it also refers, in its modern sense, to "the greatest degree of perfection to which the human mind can attain" (205), a quality entirely lacking in the abstractionists. Although the final sections of the *Traité* encourage the reader to look to physics and the mechanical arts for positive avenues of exploration, the earlier divisiveness shades into bleaker tensions and contradictions when Condillac considers the application of his critique of false systems in politics (Chapter 15). And in the chapter on hypothesis, the moral enlightenment that Condillac nearly despairs of at the end of the chapter on politics, seems no less difficult than our scientific enlightenment when he reflects on our place in the order of things.

Placés, comme nous le sommes, sur un atome qui roule dans un coin de l'univers, qui croiroit que les philosophes se fussent proposés de démontrer en physique les premiers élémens des choses, d'expliquer la génération de tous les phénomènes, et de développer le mécanisme du monde entier? C'est trop augurer des progrès de la physique que de s'imaginer qu'on puisse jamais avoir assez d'observations pour faire un système général ... Car, tout étant lié, l'explication des choses que nous observons, dépend d'une infinité d'autres, qu'il ne nous sera jamais permis d'observer. (197)

[Placed as we are on an atom rolling in a corner of the universe, who would believe that philosophers proposed to give the physical demonstration of the first elements of things, to explain the generation of all phenomena, and to explain the mechanism of the entire world? It would be auguring too much of the progress of physics to imagine that one could ever have enough observations to construct a general system ... For, all things being related, the explication of the things we observe depends on an infinity of others that we will never be permitted to observe.]

For Condillac, the most poignant example of our ignorance is the human body itself, fundamentally unobservable in all its immediacy, since death, although rendering a body materially available for our utmost scrutiny, simultaneously absconds with the ultimate purpose of our study: "la mort en cache tout le jeu" ["Death hides all of its action"] (198).

The concluding chapters never entirely respond to this acknowledgement of ultimate unknowability; rather, they sketch limits within which a kind of certitude can be reached. Condillac suggests that systems of all sorts are defenses against that unknown, but that those constructed within the limits of empirical evidence offer (provisional) truth, whereas those constructed without are based only on fear, emotion, and ignorance, offering nothing. Nevertheless, "Bad systems are made no differently than good ones" (216). Structurally the same, they are responses to real human needs, as the chapter "Du génie . . ." makes clear; thus they are naturalized by the very genealogical critique that was meant to unseat them. The false remains an inescapable simulacrum of the true: "frivolous" perhaps, but no less present.

The nearest thing Condillac can offer as a solution is not a hope for the perfection of experimental method, but instead the model of the *Traité* – an act of reading. Speaking of the tendency to read the great philosophers under the influence of their intellectual prestige, he suggests that it might be better "pour nous et pour la vérité, de les lire dans une disposition d'esprit tout opposée" (206) ["for us and for the truth, to read them from an opposite mental disposition"]. Oppositional reading or reading against the grain has clearly been the feature of Condillac's readings of his predecessors (as it has been of my reading of him) and it comes to bear in a literary example which he gives to make his point.

Le pauvre en sa cabane, où le chaume le couvre,
    Est sujet à ses lois;
Et la garde qui veille aux barrières du Louvre,
    N'en défend pas nos rois.

[The pauper in his hut covered by thatch is subject to his laws, and the guards at the gates of the Louvre cannot defend our kings from him.]

Condillac claims that the lines from Malherbe illustrate the difference between *imaginer* and *concevoir*; it is absurd to "conceive" that the guards could protect the king from death, he declares, but we might "imagine" it (206). His momentary, against-the-grain literalizing of the text produces some odd echoes a paragraph later, when we are told to be "en garde" and take "précautions" against abstract systems, and the remarks elide Malherbe's main point: that death renders unequals equal, unlikes alike. Distinctions are life.

Thus, even as the *Traité* proceeds on one level in its identitarian program, convicting Malebranche, Leibniz, and the others on similar charges, it also strives to keep them apart, give them separate textual identities. Condillac's relation with each text is different; there is no textual repetition of the same. Instead, there is the "negative dialectic," the integrated heterogeneous other, whose presence gives the text a productive tension. Reading oppositionally produces a new text, and different philosophical points. The final injunction to the reader, "Commencez par apprendre votre langue" (217), while it relates on the one hand to Condillac's normative program, clearing the air of systems where "les mots ... tiendroient lieu d'idées" ["words ... take the place of ideas"], it is on the other a call to attend to those same *mots* by recursion and communication. One must return to the language, to the system, to the text, that one already has, and learn it anew, yet differently.

CHAPTER 5

Diderot – changing the system

As we have seen, within the early-modern and Enlightenment preoccupation with systematization, mathematicization, and natural order, the tension between linear, sequential, or temporally-oriented modes of thought or presentation, and synoptic or analytic modes takes on many forms. While they can be offered as alternatives, as when Arnauld and Nicole consider the narrativizing "order of invention" alongside the systematizing "order of analysis" in the *Logique de Port-Royal*, as we move into the eighteenth century there is more often a clear opposition between the two, as when Buffon challenges Linnaeus's "system" in the name of his own "method." Sometimes they produce significant disruptions in textual continuity and logic, as when d'Alembert tries to integrate "encyclopedic order" and "genealogical order" in the *Discours préliminaire* of the *Encyclopédie*. We have seen how Du Châtelet and Condillac, despite what appear to be very different programs, both engage the notion of the "philosophical system" in ways that can be problematic and contradictory, but which are also richly productive.

I have been arguing that to the extent to which systematization can be shown to be heterogeneous and mutable, rather than monolithic, the severe view offered by the radical critique of Enlightenment should be called into question. The work of Denis Diderot is a crucial reference point in this process. Diderot shares with Buffon an intuition of the radical contingency of the connections that we map onto the world; both mistrust totalizing categories and classifications. Unlike Buffon, Diderot does not always attack this approach head on, nor does he have any qualms about appropriating the term "system," although, as various critics have shown, his understanding of the term is not always that of his contemporaries.[1] Much recent scholarship points to his revision of Enlightenment systematicity in his assumption of a mobile, labyrinthine version of events.[2] Much of the emphasis on Diderot's sense of complexity – and his affinities with contemporary reflections on complex systems – has relied on his scientific writings. Thus Ilya Prigogine and Isabelle Stengers cite *Le Rêve de d'Alembert* and look to Diderot's reflections on chemistry and life science to counter "l'impérialisme abstrait des newtoniens."[3] In this chapter, I want to extend this thinking to other texts and other issues. Just as I have argued that the complexity of systematic reason can be traced not only in scientific discourse but also in the social-affective logics of epistolary writing, so here I want to show Diderot's revisionary approach operating in his fiction and criticism, as well as in the philosophical texts.

For example, in two works that I have explored elsewhere, the "Promenade Vernet" sequence of the *Salon de 1767* and the *Leçons de clavecin* of 1771, Diderot's unorthodox practice of linearity revises the notions of both discursivity and systematicity, and overcomes what many had perceived to be an unresolvable dichotomy. This revision is complex and paradoxical, taking a discursive, readerly approach to painting and a structural, synoptic approach to music, even as it evokes the immediacy and simultaneity of the visual, and the sequential temporality of the musical.[4] Indeed, Diderot's writings abound in passages exploring, on the one hand, the dialogic nature or multiplicity of the singular line, and, on the other, the linear linking or *enchaînement* of the seemingly disparate. At the same time, his style and approach have also earned him the title of "philosophe du décousu," master of a parataxic "style coupé."[5] There are indeed various "lines" in Diderot: the broken lines of parataxis, the irregular swerve of not-quite patrilinear descent (Diderot imagines posterity as *neveux*); the split, shared, oppositional or proleptic line of "dialogism"; the contorted, knotted and frayed narrative line of *Jacques le fataliste*; the impossible narrative line of *La Religieuse*, where analepsis inexorably leads to aporia. Another line is the *ligne de beauté* evoked at the beginning of the *Salon de 1767*, in which the Promenade Vernet occurs. Diderot had an ongoing fascination with the Hogarthian "line of grace."[6] Here his reflections move beyond the line as drawn as he replaces the Platonic Form or *modèle premier* with a "model" constituted by and constantly changing under the influence of observation, experience, touch and "taste" (both physical and aesthetic): "Through long observation, through a consummate experiment [*une expérience consommée*], through exquisite tact, through taste, instinct, a sort of inspiration."[7] The passage itself is rendered lyrical and undulating through the repetitive, but syntactically mobile refrain, "modèle idéal de la beauté, ligne vraie" ["ideal model of beauty, true line"]. Assimilated with the *modèle idéal*, the *ligne vraie* moves beyond figural complexity to incessantly mutable virtuality: inspiring, compelling, and calling forth artistic activity. Constituted in the act by which it is apprehended, the line is both paradigm and principle of change and non-identity.[8]

In this chapter I will trace the development of this logic through language theory on the one hand and a reflection on textual (and other) appropriations on the other, moving from Diderot's revisionary considerations of the "line" to his exploration of complex systems in linguistic and social relations. I want to show that his gestures, when seen within the discursive context I have been elaborating, signify a profound and sustained engagement with the logical, ontological, and ethical issues that beset his contemporaries. Perhaps "exploring the system" is as important as "changing" it. Nevertheless, while some of Diderot's pronouncements sound resolutely anti-systematic (as in the *Supplément*, "Don't trust him who wants to put things in order"), he is intensely interested in multiplying and strengthening alternative connections, *rapports* that produce meaning rather than abolishing it. Like Foucault, Diderot wants to avoid the "blackmail" of Enlightenment, the twin traps of either facile celebration or thoughtless dismissal of the *esprit systématique*. Rather he wants to see what possibilities for thought and action arise when orders are multiplied and categories transgressed in language and in the world.

HIEROGLYPH AND HYPERTEXT

The reverberations and crossed categories of the linear and the simultaneous find a source at the heart of linguistic communication, within language itself. In the *Lettre sur les aveugles* (1749), the *Lettre sur les sourds et les muets* (1751), the article "Encyclopédie" (1755), and the *Plan d'une université pour le gouvernement de Russie* (1776), the meditation on language is carried out in various domains and on several levels. The formal qualities of the works actively seek to produce nonsequential readings with multiple points of entry: the *Encyclopédie* is of course exemplary in this regard. The issue of the relation of language to thought, its categories and sequential structure, is central to the two *Lettres*. Finally, the question of translation, a recurring subcurrent in many Diderotian texts, takes us to his preoccupation with communication and textual transmission (to a specific reader, or to posterity), as well as his sense of language's own problematic inner relations, identities, and differences.

This non-linear understanding of language takes as point of departure a requirement for a collaborator, a reader. Diderot's interpellation, through a variety of techniques, of a reader or partner in dialogue, calls forth and gives form to an active, thinking interlocutor; many critics have commented on his implied pedagogical strategy.[9] Here parataxis, at the level of the sentence, and digression, at the organizational level, play a role.[10] Large-scale organizing principles are absent, leaving readers the possibility of (and the responsibility for) construing connections, "making" (literally, producing) sense. The works examined in this chapter not only all present significant meditations on the place of language's internal structures in the transmission and production of meaning, but also offer a range of formal qualities that contribute to the production of the enlightened reader.

The *Encyclopédie*, of course, comes immediately to mind as a text that all but prohibits a linear reading.[11] Encyclopedias fascinate from their very "unreadability," both because of their physical proportions and typography, and because of the mental challenge of imagining the "circle of knowledge" enclosed within a single work. Readers may turn to the maze of articles and plates of the Diderot-d'Alembert project either in quest of specific documentary information, whether on the state of eighteenth-century technology or *mentalité*.[12] Or, they may follow Jacques Proust's injunction to read the *Encyclopédie* "non plus comme un recueil de documents, mais comme un ensemble de textes ... dans leur contenu non manifeste," finding therein a rich source for analyses of classical discursive strategies, questions of authorship, uses of the visual, etc.[13] Mindful of the sheer volume of the whole, the echoing of cross-references that lead from one article to another and, ultimately, to the "système général des connaissances" where everything is related to everything else, each reader seeks the apprehendable fragment that gestures meaningfully toward the whole without pretending to recapitulate or stand as a microcosm of that whole. Whatever kind of a reading one performs on the *Encyclopédie*, one is never allowed the luxury of a comfortable fusion with or absorption in the text, which constantly reminds us of our reading strategies, and compels us to pay attention to our choices and selections.[14] It is the text's non-coincidence with itself, its ability to play figurative against literal, precision against indeterminacy, essence against matter, that produces a space "most compatible with freedom of thought and most inimical to literal-minded assimilation."[15]

In the passage of "Encyclopédie" where he proclaims the necessity of arbitrariness in the encyclopedic order, Diderot evokes the complexity of the phenomenal world and necessity of choosing a point from which to begin any account of it. The first two elements of the project's triple charge of the collection, exposition, and transmission of knowledge are actively constructed by the editors, and available for active participation on the part of the readers.[16] Although, as we saw in the earlier discussion of d'Alembert, the tree of the "système raisonné," for all its professed abstraction, is perfectly capable of carrying a complex ideological load of hierarchically determined relations. Once one steps into the net of articles and cross-references, the relations are less clearly spelled out. Not that the references are a homogeneous structure devoid of meaning – far from it, as Diderot makes clear in his famous passage on the different functions of the *Encyclopédie*'s *renvois* (221–4), where every connection between parts of the text is endowed with and productive of meaning.[17] No connection is "merely formal," but all are essential to the success of the whole and the progress of human knowledge.

Par le moyen de l'ordre encyclopédique, de l'universalité des connaissances & de la fréquence des renvois, les rapports augmentent, les liaisons se portent en tout sens, la force de la démonstration s'accroît, la nomenclature se complète, les connaissances se rapprochent & se fortifient; on aperçoit ou la continuité, ou les vides de notre système, ses côtés faibles, ses endroits forts, & d'un coup d'oeil quels sont les objets auxquels il importe de travailler pour sa propre gloire, & pour la plus grande utilité du genre humain. (227–8)

[By means of encyclopedic order, the universality of knowledge, and the frequency of the cross-references, relationships are augmented, connections are made in every direction, areas of knowledge come together and are strengthened; the continuities or the gaps of our system, its weaknesses and strengths, become apparent, and in a glance one can see the objects to work on for one's own glory, and for the greater utility of the human race.]

While certainly Diderot's article distinguishes between enlightened readers and "nos ennemis," the *Encyclopédie*'s interpellation of an ideal reader leaves open the possibility that any reader may become the ideal reader.[18] There is no pre-determined path that the reader must take: one may begin with a given article (deliberately sought out in the performance of some task or chosen at random in browsing) and follow its connections at different levels: through the *renvois*, the rubrics at its head attaching it to the *système général*, its connections to the volumes of plates, or simply the articles preceding or following, particularly if it happens to fall into one of the (sometimes) multi-authored sequences of articles such as "Caractère," "Femme," or "Système." One might pursue an alphabetical series, or attempt to pick out pieces by a particular author – this last relational principle, while available, is significantly the most difficult to put into practice (owing to the use of sigla to designate authorship and the problematic issue of assessing Diderot's contributions)[19] and is not discussed at all in "Encyclopédie," although the editors call attention to certain contributors in the *avertissements* to the early volumes.

Diderot's complexly connected machine corresponds closely to Michel Serres's model of productive communication, the multilinear network, *réseau*, in which multiple connections and temporal mutations allow for experiencing and experimenting with any number of local "sub-groups" or meaningful moments which are not dependent on a whole.[20] Serres's point about temporality ("momentary and local associations") is important as we consider the potential for the *Encyclopédie*'s reader to change. While the Heraklitan argument can be made that no two readings of any text would ever be quite the same, given the vagaries of the circumstances attendant on one's readings and rereadings, the *Encyclopédie* compounds the situation through a formal/physical structure offering so many possibilities for distraction and rerouting that the chances increase that any two textual consultations will take different directions, bring different objects and relations to one's attention.[21]

The development of hypertext in recent years has also enabled scholars to reflect more acutely on the aesthetic, cognitive, and political stakes of work that functions more as a *réseau de communication* than as a unilinear and univocal set structure, a rhizome rather than a tree, a text rather than a book. While I do not believe that these dreams of a new (Borgesian?) Total Document invalidate the emancipatory potential of bound books or earlier forms of reproducing[22] – not only the historical role of the printing press comes to mind, of course, but also that of the photocopy machine in the diffusion of *samizdat* literature in the Soviet Union – the new technology is remarkably effective in helping us see the issues afresh; certainly, the claims made for the possibilities for pluralism, critique, and empowerment of the reader through hypertext cast the power of the *Encyclopédie* into sharp relief.[23] Connection and communication are at the heart of Diderot's social program and give the *Encyclopédie* its "character" – "de changer la façon commune de penser" ["Changing ordinary ways of thinking"] (222). Or in another passage: "One must examine everything, disturb everything without exception and unsparingly" (223). Diderot's materialist poetics echoes here: the proliferation of actual conjunctions, encounters, sympathetic vibrations and "arrangements bizarres" (217) produce all features of social, material, aesthetic, and cognitive existence. Comparisons have been drawn between the *Encyclopédie* and others of Diderot's works that invoke complex interrelations and bifurcations,[24] but no other work could be literally so open-ended or put so many paths at its reader's disposition. Yet even in smaller-scale, less overtly experimental, works, Diderot complicates his genres and suggests multiple patterns and dimensions of reading.

The *Plan d'une université*, while presenting itself as a systematic treatise with a carefully reasoned division into historical and practical aspects of its proposed curriculum, poses many of the same problems of selection and sequencing as did the *Encyclopédie*. Unlike the *Encyclopédie*, the proposed curriculum is unilinear and students must begin at a certain point and proceed through carefully ordered courses, although, as scholars have pointed out, the institutional requirements for an order of "decreasing utility" of courses, and the conceptual interrelations among the subjects create significant tensions within the text.[25] Furthermore, the text itself blurs the outlines of its formal divisions through a constant tendency to shift to dialogue form, and a general hovering incertitude or openness as to his interlocutor: Catherine of Russia, to whom the work is dedicated? the "Aigle de l'Université de Paris" (educator Charles Rollin) whom Diderot apostrophizes? Any reader, of course, can fill the role, and reflect upon the proposal for the Russian university, not as one expected to fall in synch with its linear order, but as an outsider free to think between Russia and France, pondering which reforms in the one might be useful to the other.

Similar redirections and complications occur in the *Lettre sur les aveugles* and the *Lettre sur les sourds et les muets*.[26] "Still more gaps [écarts], you'll say. Yes, Madame, it's the condition for our treatise" (*Aveugles*, 66). Diderot's "Additions à la Lettre sur les aveugles," written near the end of his life, begin with a disclaimer similar to the opening lines of *De l'interprétation de la nature* from thirty years earlier. Having earlier "let the thoughts follow one another under my pen, just as they offered themselves to my reflection" (*De l'interprétation de la nature*, DPV 9: 27), he now proposes to set down his ideas "without order" ("Additions," 95). Both these introductions point to a continuing fascination in Diderot with the central issue of the *Lettre sur les sourds et les muets*, that of coordinating language with the patterns of thought. The rhetorical *écarts* and labyrinthine detours of these texts with their repetitions, chiasmic redoublings, and refrains, do much to divert any single argumentative *chemin*. Like the *Encyclopédie*, both *Lettres* ask us to interpret images and texts together. Of particular interest is the plate in the *Lettre sur les sourds et les muets* that accompanies citations from Virgil and Lucretius. Diderot "amuses himself," he tells us, by presenting the same subject imitated in poetry, painting, and music: "This object of imitation is a dying woman ..." (*Sourds*, 183). Several things happen here at this intersection of multiple textual and visual relations. To begin with, the two Latin texts do not strictly coincide; the passage from the *Aeneid* is indeed the description of Dido's final agony –

> And Dido tried
> In vain to raise her heavy eyes, fell back,
> And her wound made a gurgling hissing sound.
> Three times she tried to lift herself; three times
> Fell back; her rolling eyes went searching heaven
> And the light hurt when she found it, and she moaned.[27]

– but the lines from Lucretius describe impersonal, biological death:

> [And unless dry food and gentle water
> sustained us, we'd lose flesh, and] life would be
> dissolved from every muscle, every bone.[28]

This passage is however part of the famous section on the combination and recombination of atoms in both animate and inanimate life that concludes with a parallel between the material collision of atoms and the recombination of letters as they form words.

In the very verse I write, you see
dozens of letters shared by dozens of words,
and yet you must admit that words and verses
differ from one another in sound and meaning.
Such power have letters when order alone is changed.

(Book 1, lines 823–7)

Like atoms in the Lucretian swerve, the various passages play off each other in complex and interesting ways: the tragedy of Dido's death is reabsorbed into the flux of matter, to which is further assimilated the flux of language.

. . . atoms of many kinds, combined
in many ways, are present in many things.
Thus things are nourished by things unlike themselves.

(Book 1, lines 814–16)

Diderot's atomic letters and "material words" also vibrate with the potential of all their possible recombinations and relations: a theory Diderot elaborates on, as we shall see, in describing the "hieroglyph."

There is a further connection between Virgil and Lucretius here, made explicit if one skips back to the *Lettre sur les sourds et les muets*'s liminal "Lettre de l'auteur à son libraire," where he describes what he wants for the plate depicting the dying woman:

Vous trouverez dans la planche du dernier livre de Lucrèce, de la belle édition d'Avercamp, la figure qui me convient; il faut seulement en écarter un enfant qui la cache à moitié, lui supposer une blessure au-dessous du sein, et en faire prendre le trait. (*Sourds*, 133)

[In the plate from the last book of Lucretius, in that fine Havercamp edition, you'll find the figure I want; you need only take out the child that hides her by half, imagine a wound below the breast, and take the outline.]

Diderot's instructions were followed closely.[29] The dead or dying mother, the central figure in an illustration supposedly evoking the force of natural disasters, has become Dido expiring.

The pictorial Dido and the poetic Dido are accompanied by a musical Dido, unidentified by the DPV editors, although Diderot knew at least one, and perhaps other, musical renderings of the scene.[30] Here the musical example is dissected by an analysis, its segments indicated by letters corresponding to the textual commentary, which further weaves together musical, textual, and visual by advancing correspondences between the Latin texts, thereby greatly extending the music's textual "reach" beyond the words indicated in the plate that actually correspond to the notes: "Je me meurs; à mes yeux le jour cesse de luire." The juxtaposed pages thus offer a complex network of visual signs in the letters, engraving, musical notes, and their various interrelations.

To an even greater degree than the *Lettre sur les aveugles*, whose form it consciously echoes, the *Lettre sur les sourds et les muets* is a complicated machine. In the "Lettre à son libraire," Diderot defends his approach as appropriate to a "letter," where "the last word of a sentence is transition enough" (*Sourds*, 133). What he calls his textual "leaping" involves not only labyrinthine digressions, but also significant segmentation, large-scale parataxis; the *Lettre sur les sourds et les muets* is not one "letter," but several. The modes of the segments vary: retraction, defense, questions and answers, an outline recapitulating the main *Lettre* (which already contains its own resumé in its final pages), and the gentle provocation of the "Avis à plusieurs hommes," announcing that there are numerous women capable of sustaining a philosophic conversation. The recipient of the "Lettre à Mademoiselle ... " will later be identified in Diderot's story "Ceci n'est pas un conte" as one Mlle de la Chaux (whose fate bears a certain resemblance to Dido's). The texts point in all directions.[31]

The fusion is introduced by an epigraph from Virgil, which, despite a warning to the publisher "not to let a single error slip into the examples" (*Sourds* 133), Diderot *misquotes*, giving

> ... Versisque viarum
> Indiciis raptos; pedibus vestigia rectis
> Ne qua forent ... (*Sourds* 129)[32]

rather than,

> Atque hos, ne qua forent pedibus vestigia rectis,
> Cauda in speluncam tractos versisque viarum,
> Indiciis raptos saxo occultabat.

Truncated and syntactically reversed, the reference to theft, reversal, and covered tracks provides a stunning "hieroglyphic" sign for Diderot's meditation on "inversion."[33]

Having explored the formal and material ways in which these texts thwart straightforward readings, let us consider their theoretical proposals. Here are further forms of multidirectionality. In both *Lettres*, when faced with a topic of intellectual debate, whether the Molyneux problem or the inversion controversy, Diderot performs similar moves, first restaging the discussion through recourse to an "other," blind or deaf-mute, then dividing and dissolving the question. Language is the central object of analysis, the solvent in which dichotomies dissipate.

The *Lettre sur les aveugles* turns on a set of interconnected questions on blindness, (in)sight, dialogue, and representation; the text is a manifesto for conversation, material interaction, and a strategy of "écart."[34] "Philosophy" is more properly understood as a verb than as a noun: "Je me suis mis à philosopher avec mes amis" ["I started philosophizing with my friends"] (*Aveugles*, 17). We are warned to expect reversals and paradoxes from the moment of the epigraph, another misquotation from Virgil (in this case, typographically marked as deliberate). The line from the Book v description of the funeral games for Anchises "should" read, "Possunt, quia posse videntur" (in the Humphries translation, "They can because they think they can"). Diderot gives, "Possunt, *nec* posse videntur" (Diderot's emphasis; "They can; [but] they are *not* thought able to"]. This departure from the original (which is nonetheless attributed, straightfacedly, to Virgil by both Diderot and the DPV editors) marks a first *écart*, or redirection, and repositioning, of Diderot with respect to both his sources and his audience.

Language drives the dizzying, destabilizing process. Although he begins by asserting the divergence in world-systems among those whose senses are differently configured (*Aveugles*, 26), the questions turn more acutely on issues of language. There are fault lines and gaps even within the language of those who share a common physical experience of the world; when shared experience is lacking, so too is any hope of a common language. As evinced by the accounts of various characters – the blind man of Puiseaux, Saunderson the blind Cambridge mathematics professor – the blind are hardly lacking in what the sighted should perceive as a novel and creative understanding of the world. When the blind man from Puiseaux explains what he understands by the word "mirror," Diderot experiences the object anew. The experience is probably a familiar one to all who have mastered a foreign language, and felt the shiver of newness that occurs when a word in the new language crystallizes a perception not previously available through one's native tongue. Here, Diderot encounters, within his native French, a foreign language: French. Not surprisingly, the discussion turns on an analogy with foreign languages, in which we see that what might have been thought to be an imperfect or incomplete understanding of the world is instead productive and creative:

Mais toute langue en général étant pauvre de mots propres pour les écrivains qui ont l'imagination vive, ils sont dans le même cas que les étrangers qui ont beaucoup d'esprit, les situations qu'ils inventent, les nuances délicates qu'ils aperçoivent dans les caractères, la naïveté des peintures qu'ils ont à faire, les écartent à tout moment des façons de parler ordinaires, et leur font adopter des tours de phrases qui sont admirables ... (*Aveugles*, 42)

[But all languages in general lacking precise words for writers with lively imaginations, they find themselves in the same situation as clever foreigners, (and) the situations that they invent, the delicate nuances that they perceive in characters, the freshness of their depictions, constantly remove them from ordinary ways of speaking and make them adopt admirable turns of phrase.]

The unexpected grouping of the blind, writers of genius, and clever foreigners trying to make their way in a strange language alerts us both to language's richness and to its poverty, neither of which is quite where one might have expected it.

There is no simple, linear relation between the experiential world and our ideas, through language. Limpid parallels such as Arnauld and Nicole's "Concevoir, c'est voir" ["To conceive is to see"], no longer function.[35] Diderot offers a complex world where varying configurations of the senses, language, and understanding all interact. We encounter this approach most vividly in his handling of the Molyneux problem. Responding to the puzzle that had attracted philosophers from Locke to Berkeley, Condillac, and others, Diderot argues on the one hand, that sight and speech interact over *time*, and that the hypothetical newly-sighted patient would need to learn to distinguish and organize visual information, and then to verbalize that knowledge, with or without the aid of touch; and, on the other, that there are no "hypothetical" subjects, but rather individuals whose different abilities and capacities for discernment would affect the outcome of any experiment. Diderot's logic here is typical, redrawing the parameters of the debate rather than allowing himself to be caught within a single affirmative or denial.

The *Lettre sur les sourds et les muets* proceeds along an argumentative structure similar to that of the *Lettre sur les aveugles*. In the debate over linguistic inversion,[36] when called upon to decide whether French did or did not correspond to the natural order of thought, Diderot again dissolved the question, first by spinning proliferation of "orders" that one should take into account, then by observing that individual temperaments and perceptions vary ("what is inversion for one will not be for another," 155), and by asserting that no syntax, no linear order, truly renders the simultaneity of thought:

Autre chose est l'état de notre âme; autre chose le compte que nous en rendons soit à nous-mêmes, soit aux autres: autre chose la sensation totale et instantanée de cet état; autre chose l'attention successive et détaillée que nous sommes forcés d'y donner pour l'analyser, la manifester et nous faire entendre. (161)

[Our state of mind is one thing; the account of it that we give to ourselves or others is another; another still is the total and instantaneous sensation of this state; another, the successive and detailed attention that we are forced to give in order to analyze it, manifest it, and make ourselves understood.]

Language is always already "analytic" as it breaks thought down into linearized segments, organized according to the varying perceptual systems and the immediate, contingent needs of individuals. It always arrives "too late" ("la langue se traîne sans cesse après l'esprit" ["language endlessly crawls behind the mind"], 158) to be an authentic manifestation of experience.[37] What in some writers has been viewed as a split between (temporal) linearity and (simultaneous) analyticity is now displaced, as the interconnection of the linear and the analytic is cast into relief. In Diderot, here as elsewhere, the "line," the thread unravels into countless filaments that, far from indicating only one way out of the maze, recreate and creatively transform the labyrinth itself. For Diderot, the object here will be to elaborate a theory of language from which the immediacy and simultaneity of perception/experience is not excluded: the hieroglyph.

Something happens in poetry.

Il passe alors dans le discours du poète un esprit qui en meut et vivifie toutes les syllabes. Qu'est-ce que cet esprit? j'en ai quelquefois senti la présence; mais tout ce que j'en sais, c'est que c'est lui qui fait que les choses sont dites et représentées tout à la fois; que dans le même temps que l'entendement les saisit, l'âme en est émue, l'imagination les voit, et l'oreille les entend; et que le discours n'est plus seulement un enchaînement de termes énergiques qui exposent la pensée avec force et noblesse, mais que c'est encore un tissu d'hiéroglyphes entassés les uns sur les autres qui la peignent. (169)

[In the poet's discourse there passes a spirit that moves and enlivens all syllables. What is this spirit? I have sometimes felt its presence; but all I know is that it is what enables things to be simultaneously said and represented; that at the same time that the understanding grasps them, the soul is touched by them, the imagination sees them, and the ear hears them; so that the discourse is no longer a mere chain of energetic terms that explain a thought with energy and nobility, but instead a tissue of hieroglyphs piled on one another that paint it.]

He proceeds to show in a series of examples how the graphic, phonetic, and semantic elements interact to produce an effect that is greater than the sum of its parts. Terms such as "tissu," "entassé," and "emblème" (the last derived from the Greek for "thrown together") all bespeak non-linear connections.[38] "Entassé" of course echoes the etymological origin of *système*, allowing the hieroglyph to stand as an apt marker for Diderot's notion of systematicity, compelling and multifarious.[39]

While, like many of his contemporaries, Diderot was attracted to the notion of hieroglyphic writing as suggestive of both allusiveness and unreadability, his adoption of the term breaks with his contemporaries in significant ways. Various commentators have called attention to the 1744 translation by Léonard des Malpeines of part of William Warburton's *Divine Legation of Moses* as *Essai sur les hiéroglyphes des Egyptiens*, a work of considerable influence among the philosophes and the primary source for de Jaucourt's article "Hiéroglyphe" for the *Encyclopédie*.[40] Certainly for Diderot, as in Warburton, the hieroglyph bespeaks a peculiarly material concept of language, thought's embodiment rather than its vehicle.[41] Yet his poetic hieroglyph is both more and less than Warburton's. *The Divine Legation* is a refutation of Athanasius Kircher's account of hieroglyphic writing as divinely inspired and mystically revelatory; for Warburton, it is merely a system of writing.

Without endorsing Kircher's mystical mode, Diderot certainly sees the poetic hieroglyph as more than a "form of writing." It is complex, yet full, and in the intricacy of its operations something escapes analysis. And yet it remains resolutely material. When Diderot speaks of "un esprit qui ... meut et vivifie," what is at stake is not the insubstantial *esprit*, but rather movement, liveliness, and the conjoined resonance of the senses. Most importantly, however, the poetic hieroglyph is not "scrypture" in any sense; far from veiling meaning, it is productive of meaning, it performs meaning.[42] Several years after the *Lettre sur les sourds et les muets*, Diderot will elaborate his theory of dramatic *tableaux* for the theater, in which the physical disposition of the actors will strike the spectator through their expressive interrelationships: such will be one of the avatars of the hieroglyph in Diderot's thought.[43]

The meditation on language is also at the heart of "Encyclopédie." Having described the editorial structure and cultural aims of his project, but before elaborating his ideas on its internal organization, Diderot calls attention to an "oversight" on his part, the failure to assign an article on language (as opposed to grammar), which he proposes to rectify on the spot.[44] This "addition" quickly makes clear why the meditation on language is at the heart of the encyclopedic enterprise. A "common idiom" would change the world: "time and distance disappear; places touch; links form among all inhabited points of space and time, and all living and thinking beings converse" (189). Language is elastic, rhizomatic connectivity, *correspondance* in every sense and in every direction, both the measure of all that is known and the medium in which knowledge is transmitted. A medium and not a "vehicle" – knowledge and meaning are embodied in language and extend no further. The difficulty, however, is in transmission. For as language is in a perpetual state of change, the encyclopedists' desire to communicate is cast into danger. If the proper meanings of their words are lost, "We are halted in our project of transmitting knowledge" (194). The recurring question of the discussion becomes, how best to arrest language, *fixer la langue?*

Diderot offers a number of suggestions with a view to determining a reference point, *une base*, that will serve to locate meaning: proposing both an ordinary alphabet and an "alphabet raisonné" or general characteristic, the use of Greek and Latin roots and citations, and synonyms. At the same time, the excursus on language offers scenes and examples that cast doubt on the possibilities of any positive project. That the *Encyclopédie* should seek to spur its readers on to new creative experience of reflection and interpretation, as Anderson argues, is certainly one of its aims, and certainly constitutes "transmission" of an important kind, but this does not entirely resolve the problem of communication and *correspondance*. Part of the answer turns upon – in a typical Diderotian paradox – one's awareness of what language does not "transmit" – "an infinity of slight revolutions [*révolutions légères*], scarcely noticed events" (190). These events are not transmitted because they are not the object of any collective scrutiny; they fall outside the spotlight of linguistic designation. These non-events become events only to a later generation better able to see the "event" in what was earlier taken to be as natural as the air.

Language, or more precisely, a certain form of attentive reading, enables "communication" to take place even when the senders are unaware of their own "message."

... c'est en recueillant ainsi des mots échappés par hasard, & étrangers à la matière traitée spécialement dans un auteur où ils ne caractérisent que ses lumières, son exactitude & son indécision, qu'on parviendrait à éclaircir l'histoire des progrès de l'esprit humain dans les siècles passés. (191)

[... it is by thus collecting words let fall by chance, foreign to the specific matter at hand in an author in whom they characterize only his intelligence, his exactitude, and his indecision, that one might come to shed light on the history of the progress of the human mind in past centuries.]

Diderot admits that readers are capable of errors committed in ignorance of the context of certain expressions,

mais le bon esprit qui recueille ces expressions, qui saisit ici une métaphore, là un terme nouveau, ailleurs un mot relatif à un phénomène, à une observation, à une expérience, à un système, entrevoit l'état des opinions dominantes, le mouvement général que les esprits commençaient à en recevoir, & la teinte qu'elles portaient dans la langue commune. (191–2)

[... but the sound mind that collects these expressions, that seizes here upon a metaphor, there upon a new expression, elsewhere a word relative to a phenomenon, to an observation, to an experiment, to a system, glimpses the state of prevailing opinions, the general movement that minds were beginning to receive, and the tint that they brought into the common language.]

Diderot's ideal reader is rather different than the reader projected in Condillac's *Traité des systèmes*; not necessarily reading against the grain, but reading within the interstices, looking for the eloquent detail or turn of phrase; reading for "le mouvement général" and *with* the text, rather than from "une disposition d'esprit tout opposée"; in collaboration rather than in confrontation.

Language's capacity to transmit more than what it "says" is its great strength. In a passage harking back to the discussion of the hieroglyph in the *Lettre sur les sourds et les muets*, Diderot claims that the very imprecision of language renders it preferable to pictorial representation for his project. Visual representation fixes an image and thereby sets limitations on thought. Linguistic meaning depends on a "pact"; it requires and is part of social links, conversation and communication, so vital to Diderot. It possesses an "equivocal" character and "delicate nuances that remain forcibly indeterminate." Language occasions the social bond; it extends in every direction and provides material for generations of archaeologists of knowledge. It will not be "fixed" as such, or entirely. Certain procedures should be followed (giving definitions, etymologies, examples of use), but language and the *Encyclopédie* will reverberate and change through time.

It is helpful to follow Diderot's advice here and reflect on the resonance of his own "words let fall by chance." "Fixer" had a distinct meaning in the libertine discourse of Diderot's day, where it meant to make a lover faithful ("et puis, comment vous fixer?" Merteuil writes to Valmont in a moment of bittersweet remembrance). "Fixity" does not occur in Diderot's world, even between sincere lovers,[45] or in language where, he tells us, he is highly suspicious of "all general laws" (194). What is possible, however, is translation.

Translation is anything but fixity. The root meaning of translation, or *traduction*, is to carry over from one place to another, making the Latinate words etymological twins of the Greek-derived "metaphor."[46] For Diderot, translation figures less as practice than as trope, as a permanent feature of linguistic expression. Diderot began his career as a translator from English, producing a version of Shaftesbury's *Inquiry Concerning Virtue and Merit* in 1745. His comments on his own activity emphasize identification and mutual possession: "I read him and reread him: I filled myself with his mind; and I closed the book, so to speak, before taking up the pen" (DPV 1:300). There is a remarkable consistency in the images Diderot gives of himself in relation to a text, here and at the end of his life, in the *Essai sur les règnes de Claude et de Néron*, where he is again translating and immersed.[47] Translation becomes a particularly intensive version of Diderot's habit of constant interaction and commentary on other texts, a moment when marginal and interlinear glosses merge with the text being read.

But there are other moments when translation, whether explicit or implicit, begins to suggest a broader understanding of language. We have seen this occur in the *Lettres sur les aveugles*, when the series of encounters and examples leads to the realization that French could be a foreign language within French. Literal translation of the hieroglyphic examples in the *Lettre sur les sourds* is impossible; they exist in their materiality and do not refer to an ideal beyond language. Hence, Diderot concludes, he has demonstrated the "impossibility" of rendering a poet in another language (*Sourds* 190). Diderot constantly radicalizes all these notions in his rejection of synonymy. No words are indiscernibles, perfectly synonymous. The article "Encyclopédie" takes a more pragmatic route; but its instructions on how to treat terms "*as* synonyms" (207; emphasis added) only underscores their inability truly to coincide.[48]

In "Encyclopédie," Diderot proposes what may be seen as an odd method for acquiring a foreign language; he describes himself as having learned English by means of an English-Latin, rather than an English-French, dictionary (197). The passage comes in the middle of the excursus on language during the argument in favor of providing Greek and Latin translations of all root-words. The immediate reason given for this move is that while no language is entirely "fixed," dead languages are rather more stationary than others and afford some measure of certainty in establishing correspondence. A page later, Diderot offers a striking analogy to explain how one foreign language may be understood through another:

Il y a dans les idées, & par conséquent dans les signes (car l'un est à l'autre comme l'objet est à la glace qui le répète) une liaison si étroite, une telle correspondance; il part de chacun d'eux une lumière qu'ils se réfléchissent si vivement, que quand on possède la syntaxe, & que l'interprétation fidèle de tous les autres signes est donnée, ou qu'on a l'intelligence de toutes les idées qui composent une période, à l'exception d'une seule, il est impossible qu'on ne parvienne pas à déterminer l'idée exceptée ou le signe inconnu. (198)

[In ideas, and consequently in signs (for one is to another as an object to the mirror that repeats it) there is so close a link, such a correspondence; from each comes a light that they mutually reflect so brightly, that when one possesses the syntax, and the faithful interpretation of all the other signs is given, or when one understands all the ideas composing a period, with one exception, it is impossible not to succeed in determining the exception or the unknown sign.]

For all the talk of mirroring, "representation" is not at stake here. Instead, "ideas" and "signs" are held to be *corresponding* logical systems, the internal logic of each enabling one to ascribe sense to any unclear element. Each reflects the "light" of the other; language inflects thought as much as thought shapes language. Thinking between relational systems, languages, is clearly important to Diderot. Why, however, does he turn to a third language, Latin, in his attempt to coordinate French and English?

In the *Plan d'une université*, the discussion of learning languages through translation is, significantly, the text's most thoroughly "dialogued" passage. Here, Diderot's quick act of ventriloquism momentarily assumes Dumarsais's stance on pedagogical uses of translation, a position he immediately reverses when he offers his own views, in which both translation from a foreign language into one's own and translation from one's language into another ("composer," Diderot would say; "thème" in modern usage) are necessary for learning; indeed, "composition" in the foreign language, despite the potential for mistakes, is the more important of the two.

Et quel est le travail de l'esprit en composant? C'est de chercher, dans la langue étrangère qu'on apprend, des expressions correspondantes à celles de la langue qu'on parle, et qu'on sait.

Or il est évident que, dans cette dernière opération, ce n'est pas la langue qu'on sait, que l'on apprend; c'est donc celle qu'on ignore ... (474–5)

[What does the mind do in composition? It seeks, in the foreign language that one is learning, expressions that correspond to the language that one speaks and knows. Now, it is clear that in this last operation, it is not the language one already knows that one learns; it must therefore be the language one does not know...]

Diderot goes on to argue that by projecting oneself, linguistically and imaginatively, into the foreign structures, one acquires knowledge in a manner not possible as long as one remains within the familiar enclosure of one's native tongue.

Somewhat in the spirit of Foucault's "techniques of the self," we might speak of translation as Diderot's "technique of the other." Like metaphor, which engages substitution and connections throughout all sections of the linguistic field,[49] translation respects the differences between languages even as it connects them; as Walter Benjamin put it, translation makes us aware of the kinship of languages, but also functions as "a somewhat provisional way of coming to terms with the foreignness of languages."[50] Thus it is not surprising that, in speaking of translation in the *Plan d'une université*, Diderot should naturally shift into dialogue, his preferred mode, the theatrical instantiation within his text of other voices, connections, communication. Here as in the article "Encyclopédie," the form of mental "estrangement" produced by thinking in a foreign language, thinking "toward" a foreign other, becomes a space for creativity and invention, stabilized, but not arrested, by the detour through Latin. Like the hieroglyph in the *Lettre sur les sourds et les muets,* translation becomes a way for appreciating language in its ambiguity and complexity; it allows for the production and "transmission" of ideas while avoiding the trap of a linear, univocal notion of representation.

Some reflections and analogies by way of a conclusion. The language in which I originally learned to read and write, French, was not the language that I spoke with my parents at home, English, and for a period of a few months the systems remained compartmentalized, to the point that I could "read" and write words whose meaning I did not understand, while words written in the language I spoke the most fluently were still largely meaningless characters on the page. A moment would eventually come when, staring at English words on a page and hearing another child read them aloud, the invisible barriers would dissolve and the letters arrange themselves into familiar words. The memory conferred a continuing strangeness and seduction on both my "own" language and the "other" one, which I had possessed in such oddly separate ways; as Diderot says of the object reflected in the mirror, there was a correspondence between the two, yet a need to understand each on separate terms, and no one-to-one equivalence. So thence perhaps the profound resonance of the final words of Bergman's film *The Silence* – words that are read silently, never spoken – "Words in a foreign language." The list of unconnected terms and their supposed equivalents, given as a last letter to a small boy by his dying aunt, a translator, and read by him in a train speeding through an unfamiliar countryside – this list becomes a hieroglyph through which connect and throb the desire for communion, the strangeness and the kinship of languages, the messages left by the dying to posterity, *neveux.*

Another scene, one that Derrida calls attention to in his *Mémoires d'aveugle,* where he says of Diderot, "He knew how to write."[51] It is a letter written by Diderot to Sophie Volland, one of the earliest that we possess.

[Paris, le 10 juin 1759]

J'écris sans voir. Je suis venu. Je voulais vous baiser la main et m'en retourner. Je m'en retournerai sans cette récompense. Mais ne serai-je pas assez récompensé si je vous ai montré combien je vous aime? Il est neuf heures. Je vous écris que je vous aime, je veux du moins vous l'écrire; mais je ne scais si la plume se prête à mon désir. Ne viendrez-vous point pour que je vous le dise et que je m'enfuie? Adieu, ma Sophie, bonsoir. Votre coeur ne vous dit donc pas que je suis ici? Voilà la première fois que j'écris dans les ténèbres. Cette situation devroit m'inspirer des choses bien tendres. Je n'en éprouve qu'une, c'est que je ne scaurois sortir d'ici. L'espoir de vous voir un moment me retient, et je continue de vous parler, sans scavoir si je forme des caractères. Partout où il n'y aura rien, lisez que je vous aime.[52]

[I write without seeing. I came. I wanted to kiss your hand and leave. I shall leave without that reward. But shall I not sufficiently be rewarded if I have shown you how much I love you? It is nine o'clock. I write to you that I love you, at least I want to write it; but I don't know if the pen lends itself to my desire. Will you not come so that I may say it to you and flee? Farewell, my Sophie, good night. Your heart doesn't tell you that I'm here? This is the first time I am writing in the dark. This situation should inspire tender thoughts, but I am thinking only that I cannot leave. The hope of seeing you an instant retains me, and I continue talking to you, without knowing if I'm forming characters. Wherever there is nothing, read that I love you.]

"Not seeing" Sophie has a double meaning, and Diderot undertakes to dramatize his situation by writing without seeing, writing blind, "sans scavoir si je forme des caractères." Full of regret at not seeing his lover, Diderot writes in the dark, hoping to leave a written trace, hoping that at least his pen will "lend itself" to his desire since she is absent, hoping that she will see that he has been there. Powerful forms of fascination and desire are maintained in these circumstances. Writing-toward-another and becoming-blind overlap and interact in a moment of self projection and self erasure. Love letters written in the dark, like "words in a foreign language," bespeak moments shot through with subtle and complex intensities, multiple messages, time past, time future, time of now.

PLAGIARISM AND THE POETICS OF ADULTERY

Perhaps the eeriest moment in Julio Cortázar's novel *Hopscotch* occurs as the protagonist Horacio Oliveira, having become convinced that his best friend and alter ego Traveler intends him harm, barricades himself in his room with various strange objects – strings, basins of water, a stapler – and begins theorizing Traveler as "the territory." Division and territorialization mark the novel at this point, in the threads strung geometrically throughout the darkened room, in the misunderstanding between Horacio and his friend, in the manic classificatory system of an author that Traveler and his wife Talita have been reading; divisions which are traversed and territories which are undone, however, as the reader hops among the chapters following an almost random plan, and as Oliveira kisses Talita and thereby provokes (he thinks) the expected attack. Oliveira's momentary conflation of Talita and a former lover unsettles the novel's already shaky categories and precipitates closure.

In the last group of texts, we saw Diderot bringing into focus many familiar Enlightenment tensions and questions regarding order, logic, and meaning. His approach, as we have seen, is not to offer a simple solution, but rather to seek out creative ways of maintaining relations, translations, writing that enters into an ongoing process of becoming. Diderot's systematicity-without-closure requires rethinking the notion of "limit." In this section I have grouped several texts that foreground "limits," understood as boundaries, enclosures, and property rights, whether textual, affective, or social. As Foucault saw in the case of Kant, exploring limits entails experiencing trangression. So too in Diderot we find a tension between, on the one hand textual and social "territories" set off by recognized boundaries – boundaries that may be infringed upon – and, on the other, open spaces of communication and exchange in which the idea of boundaries seems irrelevant. Or, to put it differently, there are two ways of construing the way in which boundaries may be obviated: transgression and deterritorialization. As I use these terms, transgression recognizes and derives meaning from the notion of boundaries and connections; deterritorialization does not. Of course, analyses of the concept of transgression suggest that a culture's rejection of such phenomena is based on the fear of conflation, rather than on simple opposition, that is, the suspicion that what is excluded from one sphere may nevertheless be implicated in it or have claims on it.[53] Thus transgression and deterritorialization are neither opposites, nor complementary, but bear a sliding relationship to one another and even a tendency to merge.

Transgression and symbolic inversion have been seen as necessary outgrowths of Weberian rationalization and Foucaltian institutionalization that both constitute and destabilize the social order. In Diderot too, we see a staging of the Enlightenment gesture of self-preservation through self-regulation, demythologization through the eradication of value, purification and transcendence through rationalization and the domination of instinct – again, the "dialectic of Enlightenment." For Horkheimer and Adorno, however, rationalization is essentially irrational, based on exclusion and taboo in its heart of hearts. Transgression resists the rationalizing gesture by defining but ultimately endangering the rules and erupting from within. Unlike the "contained outsiders-who-make-the-insiders-insiders" studied by Stallybrass and White, however, I find Diderot less concerned with transgression as inversion and contamination, than with something I'll call "dissipation," a form of deterritorialization in which categories are neither reversed, nor denied, nor infringed upon, but simply allowed to fade, disintegrate, or remain partially and absurdly in place, irrelevant to the transaction at hand, even as other connections and configurations of meaning are hinted at and shadowed forth.

Of the numerous forms of transgression that fascinate the Enlightenment, I will concentrate on the disruptions of textual and sexual economies in plagiarism and adultery. These infractions are more closely related than may at first appear. Plagiarism already connects the domains of intellectual boundaries and bodies marked as off-limits. Etymologically, *plagiarius* referred to the kidnapping or wrongful appropriation of a person (either suborning a slave or selling a free person into slavery) before it came to refer to incursions on others' intellectual property. The Latin definition implies an interesting contradiction: on the one hand, plagiarism renders a *dependent* unfit for his or her status; on the other, it enslaves that which is rightfully *free*. Furthermore, the etymon *plaga* can refer either to a net or a trap, a device for distinguishing free from not-free, or to an undemarcated expanse of land (Fr. *plage*), free, deterritorialized space.

Freedom and constraint crisscross in the history of the word and in the practice it has come to represent. Plagiarism is threatening.[54] Plagiarism becomes a crime against identity – if by "crime" one understands the demystification of that which the culture prefers to maintain in its mystified state: the dissipation of identity into substitutability, mutability, and iterability. I take as emblematic in this regard an account of the 1560 condemnation of Arnaut du Tilh (better known by his usurped name, Martin Guerre) for "fausseté de nom, supposition de personne, adultère, rapt, sacrilège, larcin, plagiat."[55] An eighteenth-century source glosses *plagiat* as the crime "qu'on commet en retenant une personne qui est en puissance d'autrui."[56] Since "Martin Guerre" did not control serfs, the person in question is apparently Guerre's wife Bertrande de Rols. *Plagiat* thus slides into the same semantic space as *rapt*, kidnapping, and, of course *adultère*. The first two crimes furnish symmetrical descriptions of one act: "falsifying the name" can function as a gloss for "personal supposition" or "impersonation," but the expression is also a technical term in medieval logic (*suppositio personalis*) for using a general term to refer to a particular entity. The technical meaning enters into ironic dissonance with its context, since du Tilh has instead used a particular name promiscuously – rather it is his accusers who have particularized general terms in indicting him. The real Martin Guerre disappears, but, scandalously, a "representative" arrives who is not readily distinguishable from the original. Du Tilh "stands for" Martin Guerre. The promiscuous availability of what should be a particular name constitutes a scandal; the single act of impersonation – being appropriation of name, material goods, and the wife's body – must be named, renamed, then ceremoniously and redundantly condemned. It is a moot point whether the overarching concept in play here is *larcin*, theft, as several of the terms imply, or rather *sacrilège*, as the resonant disturbance of the order of things suggests.

Property is returned to its owner, propriety reestablished. But there is an aporia in any appropriation. In looking at the history of the concept of plagiarism, one discovers that textual boundary disputes, as noisy as they frequently become, are often accompanied by the acknowledgement that no text is perfectly autonomous. In eighteenth-century France, supposedly a moment when the originality and integrity of the author becomes a crucial cultural concept, both philosophers and traditionalists are at pains to decriminalize textual borrowings and recognize that imitation is as ineluctable as it is ubiquitous.[57] Diderot is a key figure in this regard. Accused of plagiarism on more than one occasion – generally in the context of the ideological debate between *philosophes* and *anti-philosophes* – what responses he gives generally underscore the necessity and even the desirability of textual overlap and interplay.

Utilitarian issues and ideologically-motivated attacks aside, however, Diderot's so-called "dialogism," his technique of writing through engagement with another voice, often as not another text, presents us with a world of border-crossings, infringements, and exchanges. In the *Essai sur les règnes de Claude et de Néron* written near the end of his life, he offers a comment on the ethics of appropriation: "I permit borrowing, but not theft, and certainly not insulting the person one has robbed."[58] The simple assertion is rendered more piquant by its immediate context. Diderot situates his remark on borrowing through a quotation from Montaigne, who thus functions as an authority and an example; his remark is accompanied, rather more problematically, by a long footnote by Diderot's editor Naigeon, attacking Rousseau for (among other things) plagiarism. In the main text, Diderot too complains of Rousseau, but his reproaches concern less literary property than the proprieties of friendship; throughout, the displacement of guilt onto the Other whom Diderot appears incapable of either dismissing or engaging hovers uneasily in the text. The footnote is not only not by Diderot himself, but its principal accusation bears more heavily on the *seduction* of Rousseau's prose and its capacity to "impose" on and sway unwary readers. "Seduction" and "plagiarism" are related terms: the Greek *plagios* means "oblique," suggesting deviation from a straight norm, as does *seducere*, and one of the meanings of the Latin *plagiarius* is suborning or seducing someone else's dependent. So perhaps Rousseau is guilty of plagiarism as much in the manner of Arnaut du Tilh as any other. Naigeon is particularly scornful of women's susceptibility to Jean-Jacques's textual prowess, and denounces them as "avides de jouissances." The note seems all the more out of place when one considers that it is in the *Essai*, as in few other works, that Diderot most consciously explores what it means to "lose oneself" in an author.[59] In explicating and justifying Seneca's life and works, Diderot dialogues with his subject, impersonates him, and responds to his own critics as much as to the Roman's.

ici, présentant au censeur le philosophe derrière lequel je me tiens caché; là, faisant le rôle contraire, et m'offrant à des flèches qui ne blesseront que Sénèque caché derrière moi. (229)

[here, presenting to the censor the philosopher behind whom I am hiding; there, taking the opposite role, offering myself to the arrows that will wound only Seneca hiding behind me.]

Rousseau figures in the text as a kind of anti-Seneca with whom no dialogue is possible. Diderot's attack on his former friend (120–30) describes the author of the *Confessions* as hypocritical and fundamentally *méchant*, closed to communication. Ironies crop up in such places as Naigeon's footnote, where Rousseau's crime and Diderot's writerly activity take on a similar structure, or in a passage later in the text, where Diderot makes an (unconscious?) allusion to *Julie* (278 n.543).

At first glance, Diderot's *Lettre sur la liberté de la presse* (also known as the *Lettre sur le commerce de la librairie*) offers a different perspective on textual property and propriety. Here Diderot insists on the consubstantial relation between the writer and his productions.[60] He invokes a Lockean notion of ownership through labor in order to underline the extent to which one's work is one's own. Although ultimately his view could be used to argue for copyright or *droit moral*, Diderot is concerned in this text to uphold the concept of publishers' *privilège*. Treating the writer's work as any piece of property enables Diderot to argue that the sale of such property is as irrevocable as any property transfer, and that *privilège* – a publisher's exclusively to publish a given work – is necessary to maintain the contracts by which both writers and publishers make their livelihood. The literary text is soul and substance of its author, insofar as it may be legally alienated, sold, in an agreement protected as any other binding contract. Of the "sources" of that production nothing is said – nothing to contradict Diderot's notion of a multiple authorial being of uncertain boundaries, from which the text is eventually produced. In his revised and reformed literary marketplace, the number of publishers is not impeded and the scope of what can be published greatly extended. "Tacit permission" – the enlightened censor's tool for allowing circulation of worthwhile, but officially inadmissible material, is to be "infinitely multiplied" (88). Thus, while recognizing an economic necessity in maintaining exclusive publication rights and avoiding piracy, Diderot also promotes a communication system in which voices multiply unrestrained. The aim is the proliferation of texts, not their duplication and repetition. As a single text is constituted through conversation, engagement, and exchange, so too is the republic of letters. Nevertheless, the *Lettre* also makes us aware of the potential for "dissipation": financial, moral, and cultural ruin, as properties are denatured and devalued, as commerce flees from the national publishers to foreign competitors, and as writers lose their ability to guarantee the contracts upon which their children's inheritance depends.

Both the *Essai* and the *Lettre* set up textual communications networks that function in quite similar ways, both on the level of the individual text and on that of its situation in the world. Both display certain quirks within an ongoing process of rationalization. In the *Lettre*, the process occurs in the transformation of a system of arbitrary royal mandate into a *système raisonné* of contract and exchange. In the *Essai*, the rational system is represented rather in the horizon of expectations set up through the various kinds of dialogues that constitute the text. Diderot proposes exchanges with Seneca, Seneca's critics, his own critics, Jean-Jacques Rousseau, and even himself. The interaction with Seneca, or rather with the Senecan text, is the freest and the most productive: we see Diderot at his most polymorphous and creative. The debate with the numerous named and unnamed critics falls into a recognizable set pattern of "accusation/reply." Only in the case of Rousseau, as we have seen, does the dialogue risk breaking down into an incoherent colloquy, with Naigeon's ill-considered insertion and the near-reversal of the figure of Jean-Jacques into that of Diderot. Thus something occurs to skew the otherwise smooth give and take of the textual conversation, whether between Diderot and Seneca or Diderot and the critics. Furthermore, insofar as one of the expectations created by the dialogue form is that the voices will remain separate, distinct identities, this expectation too is thwarted, or at least redirected, as the voice of Diderot becomes deliberately confused with the voice of Seneca and as Diderot appears inadvertently liable to some of the accusations made against the seductions of Rousseau's prose.

Diderot also stages a virtual dialogue with the addressee of the *Lettre*, the royal censor Sartine. This orderly conversation, even as it seeks to convince Sartine of the necessity of bringing the publishing business into a rational public sphere nevertheless beckons towards the disorderly and the unexpected in its call for the "infinite multiplication" of voices. That unimpeded conversation has its political impact is spelled out, not in the *Lettre* addressed to Sartine on behalf of the booksellers, but rather in the more personal ruminations of the *Essai*.

Il me semble que si jusqu'à ce jour l'on eût gardé le silence sur la religion, les peuples seraient encore plongés dans les superstitions les plus grossières et les plus dangereuses ... Il me semble que si jusqu'à ce jour l'on eût gardé le silence sur le gouvernement, nous gémirions encore sous les entraves du gouvernement féodal ... Il me semble enfin que si jusqu'à ce jour l'on eût gardé le silence sur les moeurs, nous en serions encore à savoir ce que c'est que la vertu, ce que c'est que le vice. Interdire toutes ces discussions, les seules qui soient dignes d'occuper un bon esprit, c'est éterniser le règne de l'ignorance et de la barbarie. (282)

[I believe that if until now we had maintained silence on the matter of religion, people would still be plunged in the most crude and dangerous superstitions ... I believe that if until now we had maintained silence on government, we would still be groaning in the shackles of feudalism ... Finally I believe that if until now we had maintained silence on morals, we would have yet to learn what is virtue, what is vice. To forbid these discussions, the only ones worthy of good minds, is to perpetuate the reign of ignorance and barbarism.]

Given the evident teleology invoked here, it is perhaps incorrect to speak of conversation as leading to "disorder." Diderot, in the *Lettre*, counts on a general public enlightenment and concomitant "laws of the marketplace" to maintain a minimum level of reason and harmony. Nevertheless, in the passage from the *Essai*, we are faced with real change, fundamental, ongoing change, which as it proceeds unhampered by either legislation or "silence" may yet take unforeseen turns. Diderot maintains his faith in progress, but cannot predict what form it will take. Both *Lettre* and *Essai* consider what happens when texts, freed from authorial or authoritarian control, are themselves authorized to circulate in the world, engage with other texts, and become part of the ongoing conversation among readers and critics. In whatever well-ordered, regulated context this occurs, no boundaries or definitions can forever remain as given. Although not explicitly confronted, contradicted, or infringed on, they cease to function, suspend relevant action.

Such a reevaluation of values occurs as well in Diderot's triptych of story-dialogues, "Ceci n'est pas un conte," "Madame de la Carlière," and the *Supplément au Voyage de Bougainville*. Although they were written for serial publication in the *Correspondance littéraire*, and despite various cross-references among them, these three texts are rarely treated as the triptych they represent, either by critics or by editors.[61] Although its greater importance, both in complexity and sheer length, doubtless warrants the greater critical attention paid the *Supplément*, reading all three in their original context deepens the resonances of each.

The three dialogued tales present the same pair of unnamed male interlocutors who together recount and consider the moral implications of stories concerning other people. Each dialogue sets up a rational discursive/affective economy of exchange, expectation, and the regulated circulation of objects (monetary and intellectual) and people. The friendly give-and-take of the dialogue form accentuates the mechanical aspects of the social network (society is twice referred to as a machine in the *Supplément*, 587, 640). The two interlocutors, to whom I will refer by their designations in the *Supplément*, "A" and "B," exchange stories, compare opinions, ask and answer, and eventually achieve agreement. Their conversation takes place against a double backdrop: on the one hand, insubstantial and unsatisfying society chit-chat, which acts as a foil to their more meaningful exchange; on the other, various beautiful and rational natural phenomena, a "superb vault of stars" and a perfectly functioning thermodynamic system of mist and clouds. A fair setting, one might say, for an "ideal speech situation."[62]

Despite these promising circumstances, the seeker of Habermassian harmony will be frustrated in her expectations, even as the various characters in the stories told by B and A find themselves puzzled and defeated by reality's resistance to normalization. Though set in a world of commercial transactions, reciprocal agreements, and promises, each dialogue recounts stories of faithlessness, unreimbursed expenditure, and absurdity – *inconséquence*. Only one of the stories literally concerns adultery as such, but all take up the issues of unforeseen or extra-contractual sexual relationships, and of gratuitous ruptures and unrealized expectations. These are not precisely accounts of "transgression," because the sense of "rules" is so unstable. Expectation replaces legislation; dissipation, infraction. In the *Supplément*, the juxtaposition of European expectations and Tahitian practice proves to be a useful critical device, if a two-edged one, but all of Diderot's libidinal economies are to some degree absurd, and even the presumably well-ordered exchange between A and B has its lapses and non sequiturs, rendering "judgment" or even consensus problematic. The wisest course appears in some ways that of the character Desroches, who renounces "la périleuse fonction de prononcer sur la vie des hommes" (552), but the texts continue to call on us to make judgments nonetheless. Their affective economies are constituted by the circulation of bodies, the investment of emotion, and the exchange of stories and opinions. Each text further concerns broader social issues of ownership, both through a recurring motif of tangible property and in terms of "publicity," and the extent to which one's story is appropriated by others.

"Ceci n'est pas un conte" begins by emphasizing the communicational context of its utterance:

Lorsqu'on fait un conte, c'est à quelqu'un qui l'écoute; et pour peu que le conte dure, il est rare que le conteur ne soit interrompu quelquefois par son auditeur. (521)

[When one tells a story, it is to someone who listens; and however long it lasts, it is rare for the teller not to be interrupted by the listener.]

In the conversation that follows, we learn that "communication" is expected to be "productive"; the listener character, A, expresses his annoyance that an anecdote recently recounted in society should have produced little or no effect. In A's view, it has been an evening of pointless expenditure and alienation; people speak only of what they don't know (522) and all participate in an ongoing cycle of displaced authority and unresolved issues.[63] Whereupon B promptly prolongs the games, by relating two stories of useless expenditures, emotional production that gets nowhere. The stories themselves are doubly "pointless." First because, as B admits, they illustrate the same moral as the anecdote already condemned by A, "something known for all eternity, that man and woman are two very wicked animals (521–2). As if to underline the redundancy, B will preface each story with the same moral.

The first tale is also "useless" inasmuch as it is more-or-less known to A already, who immediately recognizes the "belle Alsacienne" and in due course reveals himself to have been one of her recent lovers. Thus, what is given at the outset as a straightforward transfer of "knowledge" from B to A rapidly becomes a more complex affair as A and B both furnish information regarding events in which both are peripheral actors. The story itself is one of appetite, appropriation, and unrequited expenditure. Tanié takes on the most physical of manual tasks in order to support his mistress (he also begs in the streets, the only instance in which he receives without giving!). At last, disillusioned as to her character, Tanié attempts to fill the lack, exhausts himself, and dies. "Je savais tout cela," says A when B concludes the touching story, and admits that he was Tanié's successor not only as Reymer's lover, but also as one who over-extended himself financially for her (529).

Possibly in order to recoup his loss of narrative authority, B promptly launches a new story, a mirror image of the first. Again, the story is set in a context of give and take, closeness and reciprocity, first as B describes the vast collaborative project that provides the scholar Gardeil (and his lover and collaborator Mlle de la Chaux) with work, and then as he evokes his own intimate friendship with Gardeil. Like the story of Tanié and Reymer, this is an account of futile expenditure: Mlle de la Chaux gives up wealth and honor (532), all because of an overwhelming passion for the unprepossess-ing Gardeil – a passion which seems to have remained to some degree frustrated. B says that she "promised herself" sexual fulfill-ment, then suggests that, like other desires and expectations, this one too remained unrealized. A's astonishment that "Gardeil was un-grateful" hardly seems justified, but he has become a more receptive listener in this second story. His responses to B are those of a Greek chorus, intensifying the moment without derailing the production of the plot. His knowledge is not of the actors in the story, but rather of B himself – it is A who situates the story with regard to the events of B's life (531) and comments on his emotional involvement with the story. B, for his part, explains de la Chaux's motivations through reference to A's complicated love life ("your adventure with la Deschamps," 532).

Here, however, the reciprocity and equality ends in their relation-ship. This time, it is B who knows the story; A does not. Further-more, despite his having announced his subject in uncomplicated, dichotomized normative alternatives, B foils A's attempts to gener-alize from the events by offering counter-examples to whatever moral he attempts to draw (535, 546). His reflection that one should not be too hasty to pronounce judgment on someone's character based on a single action (546), although à propos of Gardeil's betrayal, could also apply to good actions. B continues to deplore Gardeil's moral vacuity, but the rejection has become more intuitive than rational. The point of the dialogue would seem to be the conversion of A, who allows himself to be guided, his ideas given depth and nuance, by B. But to what end? The answer remains ambiguous, as B retreats from his early position of clear-cut norma-tive designations and dramatic exemplifications.

Other forms of expenditure. Aesthetically – and emotionally – consider the scene in which de la Chaux seeks B's help to confront Gardeil: the moment corresponds to every aspect of Diderot's dramatic style, from the emphasis on physical presence and staging (535), to de la Chaux's superb paratactic lament ("Il ne m'aime plus, je le fatigue, je l'excède, je l'ennuie, il me hait, il m'abandonne, il me laisse, il me laisse"), and finally the inevitable "tears, cries, inarticulate words." The entire production evokes no response whatsoever from Gardeil. Similarly futile investments are Camus's passion for de la Chaux (who in return "offers herself" in a manner precisely calculated to guarantee a demurral) as well as de la Chaux's various efforts to express herself to a larger public. Two such efforts are squelched by B himself, who prevents her from accusing Gardeil in front of his patron (540), and advises her against publishing her novel. Offered financial help, de la Chaux demurs; B loses touch with her; she dies.

The interlocutors concur in seeing a bleak moral for the tales: A – "If there is a good and honest Tanié, Providence sends him to a Reymer. If there is a good and honest de la Chaux, she becomes the lot of a Gardeil, so that everything may be for the best" (546). Their fatalism stands in stark contrast to Gardeil's cold assessment of love's end. "All I know is that I began without knowing why, and I sense that it is impossible that this passion might return" (537), a sentiment oddly echoed by B (546). As he struggles with the question of whether or not he has been guilty of the same fault as Gardeil, B envisions "a question to be resolved only on Judgment Day" (547), but condemns him nonetheless. "Ceci n'est pas un conte," like its title, plays on foiling expectations from beginning to end, whether those of Mlle de la Chaux, Tanié, A, B, or the reader.[64] Words are produced in a vacuum, money is spent, texts are produced, to no clear effect. However strongly drawn or "exemplary" the characters, B has trouble drawing a moral from his tale, and he discourages A from doing so. The question of whether or not there is some kind of universal order, either a benign or vicious Providence, or whether events simply occur randomly and without motivation, is left hanging. This ambiguity does not obviate B's need to make a moral judgment, but it prevents him from giving a rational account of it.

These same issues permeate "Madame de la Carlière." Like the story preceding it, this second conversation between A and B involves a complex meditation on human affection and disaffection, on expectation and rupture, set within the framework of a gradual conversion of A, who becomes more critical of the whims of public opinion as he takes on more of B's ideas. The conversion is rendered problematic, however, insofar as the story of Desroches constantly destabilizes the category of "judgment." Whereas "Ceci n'est pas un conte" deals with expectation, emotional engagement, and failure in irregular if stable liaisons, "Madame de la Carlière" takes up the issue in the institutional context where such infraction is termed adultery. Legally speaking, adultery was a woman's crime in the ancien régime; wives could not prosecute their husbands. The distinction was not always so sharp in the social imagination, but the adulterous *wife* remained the figure in which the psycho-social tensions of bourgeois fiction most clearly emerge.[65] Nevertheless, Diderot's story involves a male transgressor. That society is more ambivalent, less categorically condemning, of male sexuality enables the story to make its point about normative vacillations; even so, having left the social network of public promises, expectation, and conventions, Desroches finds it difficult to return. A and B see him in a social gathering as a "dry, long, melancholy personage" left alone by the others (550).

Property and publicity are the key components of the social contract: the public recognition and affirmation of ownership and consensual boundary lines. Mme de la Carlière embodies both principles. In terms of publicity, the major events of her life are highly public, dramatically staged and presented to a select society of family and friends. She is even more closely identified with property and possessiveness. Desroches meets her on her territory, *à sa terre*; he wins her affection by helping her win a lawsuit. Carlière describes emotional commitment in revealing terms, speaking of "belonging" [*appartenir*] and of personal "price" [*prix*]: "je prétends vous acquérir sans réserve" ["I expect to acquire you unreservedly"].[66] Even that which Desroches gives *to* his wife, his name, is reinscribed among her prerogatives. She chooses to be called Madame Desroches beginning at the pre-nuptial ceremony – *suppositio personalis*? – just as she later announces her return to "Carlière" at her public disavowal of the marriage.

The object of her acquisitive affection seems singularly ill-chosen from the outset; as she is driven to fixation, he is the emblem of "dissipation" and diversity, having earlier circulated avidly throughout society, passing not only from woman to woman, but also from profession to profession. Desroches's career as a magistrate receives the most attention. He resigns his function upon learning that a man he had condemned was convicted on badly construed evidence. It is at this moment that he renounces "the perilous function" of judging others. Now it is the case that the judgment was "correct" inasmuch as the condemned man had actually committed the crime imputed to him. The incident which closes Desroches's juridical career thus stands as a sign of incoherence, illogic, and *inconséquence*: the facts do not add up to the truth. There is neither rhyme nor reason to Desroches's changes of status; but despite his "penchant for inconstancy," both his attachment to Carlière and the liaison that brings about his downfall are given plausible explanations. It is instead Carlière, the figure of possessive identity and one-to-one correspondences, who will be described by A as "bizarre to the end" (571). Her *bizarrerie* is of course enhanced by her transgression of gender categories and assumption of a traditionally male role in the prosecution of adultery.

Any characterization of either Desroches or his estranged wife implies the dubious source from which all such characterizations are generated: *le jugement public*. No enlightened marketplace of freely circulating public opinion, "judgment" is univocal, categorical, and capricious. Like Desroches the judge, the public inspects some events, remains blind to others, and indulges itself in various interpretative games, hermeneutic epicycles leading to neither closure nor verifiability, but only to partisanship and further speculation. In spite of its irrationality, B still seems to entertain the notion that the public might yet be as predictable as the meteorological phenomena he interprets in the opening sequence. So too, he predicts a slow rise in Desroches's stock as his story becomes better known and understood; he also suggests that Mme de la Carlière will eventually be remembered as "a haughty inflexible prude [*bégueule*]" (574). There is, of course, no more reason to accept this account as definitive, than Desroches had to believe in the validity of a judicial decision rendered on the basis of complete, but incorrectly construed, evidence. B himself classes both Carlière and Desroches along with Tanié, Mlle de la Chaux as "des infortunés à propos de rien" ["wretches for nothing"] at the end of the *Supplément* (643).

The problem of nothingness and *inconséquence* haunts both plot and commentary. Despite B's reasoned prediction of a "change of season" for Desroches's public image, not only the sways in *jugement* but also the events of the individual life are, as in "Ceci n'est pas un conte," perceived as aleatory or ascribed to fate or *le hasard* (501). Desroches has an unlucky roll when his wife finds the letters from his mistress (574). This fundamental obscurity belies the serene weather predictions B makes to A at the beginning of their conversation. Those weather predictions and the promise of a story are however the only kept promises in the story. As such, they provide a misleading frame. Also as before, this frame – the storytelling pact – is rendered problematic through the specifics of its occurrence. Again, A already knows much of the story, although his initial failure to recognize Desroches is in many ways emblematic of his relation to the rest of the plot. B, on the other hand, proves to have been among the select group privy to the domestic marriage and annulment scenes. Predictably, part of the overall strategy of the dialogue involves A's conversion from unreflective society gossip to more distanced observer.

Like "Ceci n'est pas un conte," "Madame de la Carlière" puts into play a number of situations reflecting lapsed or broken contracts and thwarted expectations. The leitmotivic expenditures of the first story are replaced by Carlière's relentless, if fruitless, efforts to acquire and possess her husband, and her subsequent renunciation of all: she leaves her tangible property to him and then loses health, child, and life. The exchange between A and B again fails to reflect a straightforward transmission of information as governing model, appearances to the contrary notwithstanding. Communication between A and B is to be seen within the set of issues raised by the story regarding the construction of knowledge and the production of opinion and judgment, neither of which apparently happens without the destabilizing effects of desire and pure chance. And yet, like the previous story, "Madame de la Carlière" impels us to judge even as it questions the possibility of judgment. B, in contrast to his earlier rejection of Gardeil, says he could imagine marrying his daughter to Desroches "without hesitation" (574). Desroches's adultery – the word never actually appears in the text – thus loses what little "transgressive" status it may have had amidst the vagaries of public opinion. The tendency is to forget the physical act altogether, and to see the real crime as the breach of promise. As desacralized as marriage has become in the world of the story, the vow of sexual fidelity is seen by Carlière as the cornerstone of the institution. When the public later blames her for "going too far," it is almost as though the crime were hers – a crime one could almost call plagiarism, the wrongful possession of a free human being.

What does it all mean? one asks of the conflicting signals and incomplete structures. At the end of "Madame de la Carlière," B ventures some reflections on the social implications of the story just told, and prepares us for the last part of the triptych:

Et puis j'ai mes idées, peut-être justes, à coup sur bizarres, sur certaines actions que je regarde moins comme des vices de l'homme que comme des conséquences de nos législations absurdes, source de mœurs aussi absurdes qu'elles et d'une dépravation que j'appellerais volontiers artificielle. (575)

[And so I have my own ideas, perhaps correct, undoubtedly bizarre, about certain actions that I regard less as our vices than as the consequences of our absurd legislation, source of morals that are as absurd as it is and of a deprivation that I would gladly call artificial.]

It is not simply that *la loi appelle la transgression*, but rather that both concepts dissipate in the denial of the categories. This is the subject of the *Supplément au Voyage de Bougainville*.

The *Supplément* goes far beyond either of the two previous stories in both length and complexity as it alternates between Europe and Tahiti and gives voice to other interlocutors, other texts. The *Supplément* has always been taken as a stinging criticism of European mores and institutions, and so it is. Like Montesquieu's Persians, the Tahitian patriarch and Orou see the Europeans with other eyes; they denounce the apparently natural and God-given as artificial and unnecessarily restrictive. The criticism invokes two themes from the earlier stories. On the one hand, European life is shown as rife with *inconséquence*, as shown by the absurdities that arise when people are compelled to live according to the contradictory dictates of nature, civil and religious law, "forced to transgress one after another these three codes that have never been in agreement" (629). On the other hand, there is the perversity of possession, particularly of people (590, 633, 636). As various critics have pointed out, however, Diderot is not content to hold up Tahiti as a perfect model, unsullied and untrammelled "nature" as opposed to corrupt European "culture"; instead, the interplay of various sections of the text alerts the reader to the extent to which the Tahitian sexual economy is hierarchizing, dominating, blind to itself, incapable of adaptation and therefore doomed.[67] However, without denying the *Supplément*'s critical function or its engagement with various other texts in travel literature and natural rights theory, I shall concentrate on the daring way in which it apparently unsettles its own critical impetus through a renunciation of discursive authority. Who speaks in the *Supplément?* How can the text refuse to constitute a "message" and nevertheless remain viable in its opposition to accepted practices? In dealing with these issues, Diderot radicalizes the previous stories' reflections on intellectual and affective investments, unrealized expectations, appropriation, and communication.

The problem of authorship is neatly posed at the end of Part 3, close to the center of the work, when B relates the anecdote of Polly Baker, the young woman in the American colonies who contested the accusations of immorality made against her on account of her illegitimate children. He attributes the story to the abbé Raynal's *Histoire des deux Indes.* The reference to Raynal leads to a brief exchange on the difficult relation of author to public – and utterly elides the fact that Diderot himself had a hand in the work, a project that made him very much aware of the problem of "voice" and self-assertion in social and political criticism (617). This passage, with its deferrals and dissimulations, constitutes an anti-signature, a de-authoring gesture in which we perceive Diderot by his shadow or by *via negativa.*[68]

The *Supplément* further de-authors itself through its complex staging and filtering of the entire Tahitian sequence. We see this initially in the overt skewing of regular narrative chronology in the references to Bougainville's presence on Tahiti. "Go straight to the farewell," advises B as he hands the manuscript to A. Part 2, "Les Adieux," barely mentions the Europeans' arrival (during which the patriarch maintained an obdurate silence) and passes directly to their departure and his eloquent harangue. The later parts of the dialogue occur earlier and are furthermore intercut with scenes returning us to A and B. Part 5 begins with B's paraphrase of the almoner's regrets upon leaving the island, his fantasy of returning, and his anticipatory nostalgia (628).

In addition to denaturalizing the sequence of events, the text emphasizes its precarious transmission through an accumulation of details regarding its translation and its incomplete realization in the dialogue. A's first reaction upon learning the topic of the first segment draws our attention to the problem of language – "How did Bougainville understand this farewell given in a language he didn't know? (588). B's answer, deferred until after the speech itself, involving an intermediate translation into Spanish, is somehow less than compelling (596). The transformation of the confrontation into a delivery of prepared remarks considerably attenuates the scene's drama; furthermore, as Diderot's editors have pointed out, Diderot seems to have "confused" Spanish and Portuguese, the language spoken by the first Europeans on Tahiti. Translation between Tahitian and French has already been declared all but impossible in B's account of the Tahitian Aotourou's visit to Paris (586). When A imagines what Aotourou might say of Europe to other Tahitians, B dampens his enthusiasm: "Not much and they won't believe it. A: Why not much? B: Because he conceived little, and because he cannot find in his own language terms corresponding to the few ideas he has formed" (587).

Despite linguistic incompatibility, Orou and the almoner do converse, although such European categories and terms as religion, sin, God, adultery, incest, etc. pose difficulties for Orou (who nevertheless understands them well enough to criticize them like any *philosophe*). Revealingly, both the patriarch's speech and the dialogue are thought by A to be "slightly Europeanized" (627; see also 596). Thus the meticulous concern with translation and transmission, instead of serving its usual function in eighteenth-century fiction of enhancing verisimilitude, produces the opposite effect, by distancing the text and casting doubts on its authenticity.

Finally, the impact of the "supplement" within the *Supplément* is lessened by the incomplete disclosure of the manuscript being discussed. B initially declines to give it to A, suggesting only that they look it over together. If his remark that the dialogue will be less interesting to A than the harangue can be seen as disingenuous, given the dialogue's libertine appeal, as much cannot be said of his elision of the manuscript's "meaningless" preamble (588) and of a third section that he has skipped (633), since they are not reported. Various parts of the almoner's narrative are simply taken over or abridged by B, and on one occasion, the almoner himself censors the dialogue (613). Once again, we are led to expect a form of regularization or normalization, whether in the social rules invoked, the promises exchanged, or the communicational logic established in the dialogue itself. In each case the system is rendered inoperative, or at least revealed as behaving in unforeseen ways. The irregularities in each system are invariably intensified, as we have seen, whenever there is a question of property or ownership, whether intellectual, sexual, or textual. Infraction and transgression are recognized phenomena, even in Tahiti (or all the more so in Tahiti): "wherever there is interdiction, it is inevitable that one is tempted to do the forbidden thing and that one does it" (621). But there is nothing "natural" about Tahiti and its regulations; and transgression dissipates in the critical glare of *inconséquence*. What then?

At least part of the answer lies in the communicative model, the indefatigable dialogue between A and B, although, as we have seen, the logic of their exchange defies most conventional scenarios such as the transmission of information or the conversion from one viewpoint to another. If there has been some element of the latter in "Ceci n'est pas un conte" and "Madame de la Carlière," little remains in the *Supplément*. While the conversation between Orou and the almoner leads to the priest's seduction, the seduction is not conversion, since the priest eventually leaves the island. "Let us imitate the good almoner," proposes B, "monk in France, savage in Tahiti" (643). As for the dialogue between A and B, the faint differences in their attitudes remain constant, and A continues to be rather more attuned to the titillating aspects of the text than to its didactic side. His final proposal, to read the dialogue to their women friends seems almost to return us to the world of society conversation at the beginning of "Ceci n'est pas un conte," where no one is entirely invested in what she or he says.

B. A votre avis, qu'en diraient-elles?
A. Je n'en sais rien.
B. Et qu'en penseraient-elles?
A. Peut-être le contraire de ce qu'elles en diraient. (644)

[B: What do you think the ladies would say? A: I have no idea. B: And what would they think? A: Perhaps the opposite of what they would say.]

Among other things, then, the *Supplément* constitutes a refusal of any simple or positivist notion of "critique," inasmuch as criticism implies a critic, an authorizing figure in possession of her or his language. Through its various de-author(iz)ing and distancing gestures, the *Supplément* presents communication as collaboration, complicity, and role-playing. It is not clear what precisely is "communicated" here: rather various relations are enacted. Who speaks? In whose name? These questions have been suspended.

Other questions continue to press, however. Just as the previous stories ended with various calls to judgment ("Would you marry your daughter to Desroches?"), so too the *Supplément* repeatedly asks us to choose sides between "civilization" and "instinct," more and more insistently as we near the end (638, 640, 641). "What shall we do? Return to nature? Or submit to the laws" (643). In response to this last, B says, "We shall speak up against senseless laws until they are reformed, and submit to them in the meanwhile. He who on his private authority breaks a bad law, authorizes others to break good ones" (643). Has Diderot questioned the social structure so persistently, only to arrive at an injunction to wait and "submit"? How is the "system" to be changed?

The answer lies in a new understanding of the terms of both question and answer. Recalling the passage we earlier examined from the *Essai* ("If we had maintained silence on government ...") makes clear the emphatic ring of *Nous parlerons*. "Speaking" calls up the limitless exploratory, creative, and transformative potential of human communication.[69] At the same time, the subjects who speak are heteronomous; their language is borrowed, transcribed, misappropriated. "Communication," in order that it not be bound to replicating structures it seeks to criticize, takes on a different form. B's warning sums up much of the thrust of the *Supplément* by signalling the danger of *autorité privée* that attempts to legislate on its own, without any consideration of the social network. Such apparent freedom is a form of tyranny, and an avoidance of reform.

Diderot's texts may be described as what William Paulson calls "autonomous systems" that "do not intrinsically communicate, but ... may, through a history of mutual interactions, come to behave in ways that can be described as communicative or instructive."[70] "Instructive" is particularly pertinent here. Diderot's texts are "dissipative structures" whose insistence on *inconséquence* does not preclude them from offering an emancipatory pedagogy. To the extent that communication equals transmission and conforms to pre-determined systems, it implies unequal power relations and limited possibilities for change. To the extent that desire is rigidly channelled and defined in systems of possession, it creates tension and incoherence. A and B speak of society as a machine, a homeostatic system which remains unpredictable at the level of the individual. "Méfiez-vous de celui qui veut mettre de l'ordre; ordonner, c'est toujours se rendre le maître des autres en les gênant" ["Don't trust someone who wants to put things in order; setting in order is a way of becoming master of others by restraining them"]

(639), notes B. Desire, *inconséquence*, and the limitless interactions of texts with other texts, present and future, resist the imposition of constrictive order and maintain the possibility of change.

POSTSCRIPT – AFFECT AND RATIONALIZATION

In the view of sociological systems theorist Niklas Luhmann, the transition of the vertically stratified society of "simple" identities to a "functionally differentiated" one in which members might belong to more than one subsystem necessitates new kinds of subject-object relations; i.e., the need for the ability to distance, distinguish, and analyze. In his study of affective "codes" from the seventeenth to the nineteenth centuries, Luhmann sees semantic realignment of the concepts of love, friendship, and duty, which points toward a simultaneous strengthening of internal self-discipline and a compensatory valuing of sympathy and emotional reciprocity. This process leads in turn to the eventual replacement of "fusion" with "interpenetration" between distinct selves.[71] Luhmann sees this evolution as a drive toward harmony and enlarged personal experience, but there is in his scheme a paradoxical echo of Horkheimer and Adorno's reading of the Sirens episode in the Odyssey. So that he may fully give himself up to the enchantment of the sirens' song, Odysseus has himself physically restrained and his men's ears blocked, thus exemplifying how an appropriately bracketed sensuous enjoyment may be obtained at the price of the domination of self and others.

If one leaves Homer for Book IV of the *Aeneid*, one comes upon another, gendered version of the dialectic, one that I call the Dido variant. It will be recalled that, following a period of amorous fusion in Carthage, Aeneas is warned by the gods that he still has a mission to accomplish. Dido's pain notwithstanding, he sets sail. There is no denying that Aeneas suffers a loss (even in the Underworld, she denies him either understanding or forgiveness), but he is allowed the compensatory satisfaction of the divine mandate: it is she who suffers the ultimate self-denial through violent death at her own hands.

The Dido variant is played out in any number of fictions in which the social order is preserved through the sacrifice of the heroine: *La Princesse de Clèves, Manon Lescaut, Julie,* the "Caliste" sequence in *Lettres de Lausanne, Adolphe, Corinne.* Diderot's triptych also conforms in certain respects to the pattern. Each segment stages an elaborate form of female sacrifice, whether in the martyrdom of Mlle de la

Chaux, the mortal chagrin of Mme de la Carlière, or the wholesale incorporation of the Tahitian women into their island's Gross National Product. Clearly, however, the rationalizing process is undercut in these same texts, as both its ideological slant and its ultimate impossibility are amply demonstrated. The sacrifice of the woman should thus be seen, not as a regrettable necessity to an unavoidable end, but rather as that which most consistently gives the lie to the supposed "neutrality" of the normalizing process. It is no longer possible to point to a social good or to the maintenance of order as the outcome of these deaths. Chaux and Carlière in particular continue to evoke pain even though the possibility of their absorption into some grand plan has dissolved. Like the Dido of the hieroglyph, they are meaningful in themselves, yet untranslatable, never to be recuperated as negative "exemplars" for feminity.[72]

In this chapter, I have not sought to prove that Diderot alone of all his age manages to "solve" the problems besetting *l'esprit systématique*: certainly we have seen insightful approaches in the other writers of this study. Diderot, however, does give us a body of work in which the reflection on systematicity is pursued with exceptional variety and depth. He "changes the system" by leaving it open, accepting it as *complex*, and seeing what can be accomplished thereby.

Having begun this discussion amidst the feverish divisions and territorializations of Cortázar's novel, let us close with an opposite image. At the end of *Qui se souvient de la mer*, Mohammed Dib's hallucinatory rendering of the Algerian revolution, the protagonist escapes the terrors of his city and finds himself in a parallel underground city, like the one he has left but infinitely proliferating, labyrinthine. The physical and conceptual constraints of the former city dissipate: first, in the new complexity, where systems interact with other systems, replicating but extending the original structure, and, second, in the original city's dramatic overwhelming by the vast, structureless sea.

"Explosant l'une après l'autre, les nouvelles constructions sautèrent jusqu'à la dernière, et aussitôt après les murs se disloquèrent, tombèrent: la ville était morte, les habitants restant dressés au milieu des ruines tels des arbres desséchés, dans l'attitude où le cataclysme les avait surpris, jusqu'à l'arrivée de la mer dont le tumulte s'entendait depuis longtemps, qui les couvrit rapidement du bercement inépuisable de ses vagues."

Quelquefois me parvient encore un brisement, un chant sourd, et je songe, je me souviens de la mer.[73]

Conclusion – labyrinths of Enlightenment

Consider an episode from the history of landscape architecture. There once was a labyrinth in the gardens at Versailles. Located to the east of the Bassin d'Apollon and part of Le Nôtre's original plans for the garden, the Labyrinth achieved its final form in 1672.[1] Among the many *salles d'eau* and *bosquets*, the Labyrinth was the most elaborate. Charles Perrault recommends it "for the novelty of its design and the number and diversity of its fountains."

Il est nommé Labyrinte, parce qu'il s'y trouve une infinité de petites allées tellement mélées les unes dans les autres, qu'il est presque impossible de ne s'y pas égarer: mais aussi afin que ceux qui s'y perdent, puissent se perdre agréablement, il n'y a point de détour qui ne présente plusieurs Fontaines en mesme temps à la veûë, en sorte qu'à chaque pas on est surpris par quelque nouvel objet. (3–4)

[It is named Labyrinth because there are an infinity of little paths so mixed together that it is nearly impossible not to become lost; but in order that those who become lost, do so pleasantly, there is not a single turn that does not present several fountains to one's view, so that with each step one is surprised by a new object.]

The forty fountains, as Perrault's book with full-page engravings by Sébastien Le Clerc amply testifies, were themselves small marvels, each incorporating *rocailles* and lifelike painted lead sculpture to illustrate one of Aesop's fables. A quatrain by Isaac Benserade recounting each fable was engraved on a plaque by each fountain.

As can be seen from a contemporary engraving (see Fig. 1), the overall design of the maze is a pleasing asymmetrical grouping of familiar design elements – semi-circles, variously bisected squares and rectangles, serpentine curves – that are reminiscent of other classical garden features. Here, however, thanks to the high, thickly-planted trellises lining the walks, their irregular disposition would certainly have been disconcerting to the walkers within.

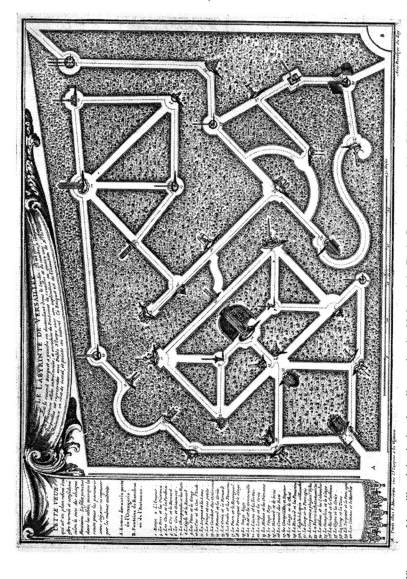

Figure 1 Versailles, labyrinth, plan. Engraving by N. Langlois, Paris. By courtesy of the Bibliothèque Nationale, Paris.

Perrault's 1677 guide (actually more of an elegant in-quarto "coffee-table" book) takes us through the maze; the order of the plates and descriptions is the order of the walk, which is traced on the plan with a dotted line. Successful completion of the maze involves viewing each fountain once and once only (excepting #30, passed a second time as one returns from a cul-de-sac), thus preventing a full exploration of all the paths. In his introduction to Le Clerc's plates, Perrault renders the labyrinth singularly linear, even abstract. There is no attempt to describe the spatial experience of the garden, no account of turns, directions, or perspectives, only the sequence of fountains as keyed to the map. This approach is not unique to Perrault. Other official guides and accounts offer similar strategies for apprehending the gardens as a sequence of stops and events. Thus the peremptory future tense of Louis XIV's "Manière de montrer les jardins de Versailles":

On entrera dans le Labirinte, et après avoir descendu jusques aux canes et au chien, on remontera pour en sortir du costé de Bachus.[2]

[Enter the Labyrinth, and having gone far as the ducks and the dog, come out beside the Bacchus.]

The select group of courtiers in Madeleine de Scudéry's 1669 *Promenade de Versailles* must indeed forego the experience of the Labyrinth in order to take in the entire garden properly in a limited amount of time: "If we had the time [says Telamon], I would take you in a labyrinth filled with rustic bowers and statues, where you would find an untamed solitude [*solitude sauvage*] that would not displease you."[3] A significant function of accounts such as Scudéry's is to condition the reader/spectator to accept that Versailles, and by extension Louis XIV, has so surpassed ordinary human achievement as to be unrepresentable, and furthermore, to believe that, however narrowly the promenade may be articulated, there is only one inevitable way to experience the garden, thus legitimating and naturalizing the exercise of power.[4] Certainly in Scudéry's text, the unseen marvels of the labyrinth function both as a form of the unrepresentable and as a lure, a tempting distraction that must be renounced in order to see the garden "correctly."

It would be fair to say that, while greatly admired for its design and the execution of its fountains, the maze was somewhat at odds with the spirit of Le Nôtre's overall plan. *Solitude sauvage* is not what Versailles was about. The disposition of space, the manipulation of perspective, and the use of sun-myth imagery contribute to an overwhelming representation of kingly power, "the symbolic pro-duction of the exemplary royal portrait."[5] The labyrinth, offering an art of detour and surprise, is the opposite of the grand central perspective. Perrault, in his account, is concerned with suppressing the ambiguities, underplaying the detours, and "geometricizing" the maze in the spirit of the main garden. Even so, the limits to the geometrical approach can be seen in the engraved plan's impossible multiple perspective that requires the viewer to "turn the map according to the direction of each fountain." Even when mapped and mastered, the labyrinth is not available to a single dominant point of view.

The labyrinth proved difficult and expensive to maintain. After several restorations, it received little attention after 1705 and fell into disrepair. It also acquired a dubious reputation, especially once the gardens were again open to the public in the eighteenth century, and was finally destroyed in 1774. Replanted as the "Bosquet de l'ancien labyrinthe" or "Bosquet de Vénus," it was later dubbed the "Bosquet de la Reine," as a lingering memory of an evening in 1784, when the Cardinal de Rohan came to the spot to offer a celebrated diamond necklace to a woman he believed to be Marie-Antoinette, thus setting off a political labyrinth of in-calculable dimensions ...

What is a labyrinth? The Le Nôtre design, with its fragmentary, asymmetrical forms and its multiple paths, is a far remove from most classical and medieval models of the figure, which are most often "unicursal," with one entrance, one exit, and one winding and folded path to and from the center. The multicursal maze, while described in numerous literary sources, is rarely given graphic representation or constructed before the sixteenth century. Despite what appear to be striking differences between these two models, in the place each gives to individual choice and in the possibility of getting lost, their co-presence in classical and medieval culture points to the greater importance of common features: emblems of artistry and confusion, divine simultaneity and human temporality.[6] Labyrinths could be either positive or negative: imprinted or inlaid in cathedral floors either as injunctions to patience in the progress toward an ultimate goal, or reminders of the confusions of a fallen world. For Petrarch, the labyrinth bespeaks passion:

Nel laberinto intrai, né veggio ond'esca

(Sonnet 211)

For Calvin, it represents the deadly tangle of pernicious worldly institutions, counter-balanced by another anxiety, the "abyss" or void, the sense of being adrift in the cosmos.[7] In the philosophical tradition, certainly the labyrinth looms as that which must be avoided or resolved: "The affective base of the labyrinth analogy is ... fear," writes one commentator of Bacon and Descartes.[8] And yet, from the Middle Ages on, there is also a courtly tradition of labyrinths built "for the pleasure of getting lost," as Emilie Du Châtelet put it, alluding simultaneously to philosophy and castle gardens. Order and disorder, vision and confusion, simultaneity and linearity, passion and method, all find themselves in this image.

The presence of the labyrinth at Versailles is an apt emblem for that hidden problematic, that potential for disorder, that beset the grand designs of classicism and *l'esprit systématique*. The political aesthetics of the absolute gaze, the angelic eye, the purifying of reason are rendered not only in gardens, but also in signifying spaces such as those of classical theater architecture. According to a certain kind of narrative, new formations, the valorization of sentiment or individualism for example, gradually displaced the single absolute point of view. In the theaters, three-dimensional sets offering depth when seen from either side, as opposed to the multiple flats whose illusion functioned only from one perspective, could be said to have made possible full audience participation in the spectacle. Such accounts, however, overlook the complexities of spectatorship, the forms of knowledge and pleasure available in the oblique gaze, which sees the dramatic illusion for what it is – unlike the central royal box.[9] Similarly, while at Versailles the progressive decentering of Le Nôtre's plan towards the Trianons and the Hameau offers room for speculation on the blurring of the definition of monarchy, it is important to remember that the main garden was never an entirely simple, unified space.

What is a labyrinth in the French Enlightenment? For many, as we have seen, it is an image of moral and philosophical confusion. For d'Alembert, Bailly, Condillac and others, the application shifts. Sometimes it is the phenomenal world that is the labyrinth, sometimes the constructions that we attempt to put on that world –

The general system of the Sciences and Arts is a sort of labyrinth, a twisted path where the mind sets out without really knowing the way to go. (D'Alembert, *Discours préliminaire*, XIV)

For some, the labyrinth represents a problem in need of a solution, or a high place from which the wandering paths will make sense, or an Ariadne's thread in the form of a sound demonstration. As we have seen, d'Alembert's attempts to dispel the labyrinth in favor of the encyclopedic Tree are not entirely successful.[10] For others, awareness of complexity is not so much a problem to be solved as simply the basis for existence. We see this in Diderot, as well as in Du Châtelet:

Tout est lié dans le monde; chaque Etre a un rapport à tous les Etres qui coexistent avec lui, & à tous ceux qui l'ont précédé, & qui doivent le suivre: nous sentons nous-mêmes à tout moment que nous dépendons des Corps qui nous environnent; qu'on nous ôte la nourriture, l'air, un certain degré de chaleur, nous périssons, nous ne pouvons plus vivre; la Terre dépend de l'influence du Soleil, & elle ne sauroit se conserver, ni végéter sans son secours. Il en est de même de tous les autres Corps; car quoique nous ne voyions pas toujours distinctement leur liaison mutuelle, nous ne pouvons cependant par le principe de la raison suffisante & par l'analogie, douter qu'il n'y en ait une, & que cet Univers ne fasse un tout, un entier & une seule machine dont toutes les parties se rapportent les unes aux autres, & sont tellement liées les unes aux autres, qu'elles conspirent toutes à une même fin. (Du Châtelet, *Institutions*, 147–8)

[Everything is linked in the world; each being is related to all other coexisting beings, to all that have preceded it and to all that must follow: at every instant we feel within ourselves that we depend on the bodies that surround us; if food, air, a specific degree of warmth are taken from us, we perish, we can no longer live. The earth depends on the influence of the sun and could neither maintain itself nor flourish without its help. So it is with all other bodies; for although we do not always distinctly see their mutual connection, the principle of sufficient reason and analogy do not allow us to doubt that the universe is a whole, a single entire machine whose parts relate to one another, and are so connected that they conspire to the same end.]

From one contemporary perspective, Du Châtelet's single "end" may appear as the regimenting unifying factor representing closure and control – but surely the weight of this passage points in another direction, towards time, materiality, human possibility and ecology. The interdependence of phenomena is creative, not coercive.

Whether they seek to solve the labyrinth or to embrace it, these writers, philosophers and epistolary strategists alike, share an awareness of the complexity and interconnectedness of knowledge, the uncertainties attendant on its construction and transmission, that is far more critical, self-aware, and wide-ranging, than has often been thought. There is less distance between the notion of "the general system" as thought by d'Alembert and as thought by Derrida than many of Enlightenment's critics and defenders have been willing to recognize. This kinship also reminds us of the progressive, emancipatory potential in the discourse of complexity and critical self-reflection.[11] What Katherine Hayles says of the "politics of chaos" is also true of the Enlightenment's language of systems: both yield multiple strata and possibilities for articulating stability and movement, totalizing patterns and random events, local and global.[12] It is not necessary to locate in the eighteenth century technical prefigurations of contemporary work in complexity theory or non-linear dynamics, in order to understand both, transhistorically, as investigations into the multiple patterns of the real, and, historically and contextually, as analogous cultural moments of coming to terms with the foreignness of the everyday.

L'esprit systématique, or systematic reason as I have been calling it, is a powerful critical and analytic tool, capable of representing the world, organizing knowledge, and interpreting phenomena. As such it has been both admired and attacked. Yet the call to understand the system of nature becomes for many an invitation to reflect on the nature of systematicity as such, to interrogate the foundations of knowledge and representation, and to see boundaries and limits of all sorts as constructed, rather than natural, and therefore open to question. In this way, systematic reason contains its own critique. Diderot and his contemporaries explored the ambiguity and the potential of their systems, categories, and forms of order. We continue to carry out the Enlightenment project.

There is a labyrinth in the garden. Or rather, the classical garden is more labyrinthine than was previously thought. Figures of the labyrinth abound in modernity, from Joyce to Benjamin to Borges, to name only the most obvious. Few have so carefully grafted it onto classicism, however, as Alain Robbe-Grillet in the conclusion to the film *L'Année dernière à Marienbad*. A man has pursued a woman through a geometrically disposed garden and through a maze-like baroque hotel, recounting multiple and often contradictory narratives of a past that they may or may not have shared. In the end, she agrees to leave with him, and they descend the steps from the hotel into the garden.

Le parc de cet hôtel était une sorte de jardin à la française, sans arbre, sans fleur, sans végétation aucune … Le gravier, la pierre, le marbre y marquaient des espaces rigides, des espaces sans mystère. Il semblait au premier abord impossible de s'y perdre … au premier abord … Le long des allées rectilignes, entre les statues aux gestes figés et les dalles de granite où vous étiez maintenant déjà en train de vous perdre, pour toujours, dans la nuit tranquille, seule avec moi.[13]

What is Enlightenment? This: the recognition that a labyrinth is perpetually available within the most carefully conceived geometric space, within every system and every language; that within the general system, fiction and seduction are ineluctably bound to knowledge of self and of the world.

Notes

1 Myles na Gopaleen, pseud. (Brian O'Nolan), *The Poor Mouth*, trans. Patrick Power (London: Hart-Davis, MacGibbon, 1973), 30–4.
2 Gilles Deleuze and Félix Guattari, *Capitalisme et schizophrénie: L'Anti-Œdipe* (Paris: Minuit, 1972), 54; *Anti-Œdipus: Capitalism and Schizophrenia*, trans. Robert Hurley, Mark Seem, and Helen R. Lane (Minneapolis: University of Minnesota Press, 1983), 45.

1 Jean-François Lyotard, *The Postmodern Condition: A Report on Knowledge*, trans. G. Bennington and B. Massumi (Minneapolis: University of Minnesota Press, 1984).
2 Jürgen Habermas, *The Philosophical Discourse of Modernity: Twelve Lectures*, trans. Frederick Lawrence (Cambridge: MIT Press, 1987), 253.
3 Michel Foucault, "What is Enlightenment?" trans. Catherine Porter, in *The Foucault Reader*, ed. Paul Rabinow (New York: Pantheon, 1984), 35. (Long known only in the English version, Foucault's original French text has recently been published: "Qu'est-ce que les Lumières?" in Foucault, *Dits et écrits 1954–1988*, ed. Daniel Defert and François Ewald, 4 vols. [Paris: Gallimard, 1994] 4:562–78). On the vexed question of whether or not Enlightenment should be "defined" at all, see Lester Crocker, "The Enlightenment: What and Who?" *Studies in Eighteenth-Century Culture* 17 (1987): 335–47. Although its publication came too late for me to take full account of it here, James Schmidt's recent volume speaks very much to these issues: *What is Enlightenment? Eighteenth-Century Answers and Twentieth-Century Questions* (Berkeley: University of California Press, 1996).
4 Benedict Anderson, *Imagined Communities: Reflections on the Origin and Spread of Nationalism*, revised edn. (1983; London: Verso, 1991), 6.
5 Karlis Racevskis, *Postmodernism and the Search for Enlightenment* (Charlottesville: University of Virginia Press, 1993).

6 Daniel Brewer, *The Discourse of Enlightenment in Eighteenth-Century France: Diderot and the Art of Philosophizing* (Cambridge University Press, 1993), 6.

7 Immanuel Kant, First Preface to *The Critique of Pure Reason*, trans. Norman Kemp Smith (London: MacMillan and Co., 1963), 9n.

8 On the resemblance, see among others, Michael Ryan, *Marxism and Deconstruction: A Critical Articulation* (Baltimore: Johns Hopkins University Press, 1982), 65–81.

9 Theodor Adorno, *Negative Dialectics*, trans. E.B. Ashton (New York: Seabury Press, 1973), 146.

10 Max Horkheimer and Theodor Adorno, *Dialectic of Enlightenment*, trans. John Cummings (1972; reprint, New York: Continuum, 1987), 3.

11 Michel Foucault, *Les Mots et les choses* (Paris: Gallimard, 1966) and *Surveiller et punir* (Paris: Gallimard, 1975); See also Timothy Reiss's discussion of the epistemic replacement of "patterning" with "analytico-referentiality," and Evelyn Fox Keller's and Susan Bordo's critiques of the suppression of alchemical (and feminized) engagement with nature by "objective" (and masculinized) science. Timothy Reiss, *The Discourse of Modernism* (Ithaca: Cornell University Press, 1982); Evelyn Fox Keller, *Reflections on Gender and Science* (New Haven: Yale University Press, 1985); Susan Bordo, *The Flight to Objectivity: Essays on Cartesianism and Culture* (Albany: SUNY Press, 1987). On the relation of Foucault to the Frankfurt School, see Charles C. Lemert and Garth Gillam, *Michel Foucault: Social Theory and Transgression* (New York: Columbia University Press, 1982), 106–7.

12 Andreas Huyssen, Foreword to Peter Sloterdijk, *The Critique of Cynical Reason*, trans. Michael Eldred (Minneapolis: University of Minnesota Press, 1987), xv.

13 Sloterdijk, *Critique*, 74.

14 Seyla Benhabib, *Critique, Norm and Utopia: A Study of the Foundations of Critical Theory* (New York: Columbia University Press, 1986), 163–82. Jürgen Habermas, *Philosophical Discourse*, esp. 106–60. For a similar argument that Enlightenment ideals are best carried out by "liberal," anti-foundational debate, see Richard Rorty, *Contingency, Irony, and Solidarity* (Cambridge University Press, 1989), 56–7.

15 Larry Langford defines Enlightenment as "oppositional critique ... or nothing at all," in "Postmodernism and Enlightenment, Or, Why Not a Fascist Aesthetics," *Sub-Stance* 67 (1992): 24–43. Richard Bernstein links up Habermas and Rorty, as well as Derrida, Foucault, and Lyotard: " ... when we try to make sense of their own moral passion, we are led back to the fragile, but persistent 'ideal' of dialogical, communicative rationality ... " "The Rage Against Reason" in *Construction and Constraint: The Shaping of Scientific Reason*, ed. Ernan McMullin (University of Notre Dame Press, 1988), 216. While it may be helpful to appreciate certain common aims among these thinkers, it would be unwise to pursue too rapid a conflation of their positions.

16 Morris Berman, *The Reenchantment of the World* (Ithaca: Cornell University Press, 1981); Anthony Wilden, *System and Structure: Essays in Communication and Exchange*, 2nd edn. (New York: Tavistock, 1980).

17 Charles Taylor, *The Sources of the Self: The Making of Modern Identity* (Cambridge: Harvard University Press, 1989), 171–2.

18 Michel Foucault, "Sexuality and Solitude," a 1980 lecture given jointly with Richard Sennett. *Humanities in Review* 1 (1982): 10.

19 Jürgen Habermas, "Taking Aim at the Heart of the Present," in *Foucault: A Critical Reader*, ed. David Couzens Hoy (Oxford: Blackwell, 1986), 106.

20 I have amended Catherine Porter's translation of Foucault's last phrase, "critique permanente de notre *être* historique" (my emphasis). As he makes quite clear in this passage, he is talking not about purely chronological "eras," but of our human being-in-time. Michel Foucault, "Qu'est-ce que les Lumières?" *Dits et écrits* 4:571.

21 Habermas emphasizes the resemblances of Foucault's and Kant's critiques by summing up their common paradox: "the cognitive subject, having become self-referential, rises out of the ruins of metaphysics in order to take on, in full awareness of its finite powers, a project that would demand unlimited power" ("Taking Aim," 106).

22 Thomas P. Bonfiglio, "The Patrilineal Discourse of Enlightenment: Reading Foucault Reading Kant," *Bulletin de la société américaine de philosophie française* 6 (1994): 111.

23 Richard J. Bernstein, "Foucault: Critique as a Philosophical Ethos," in *Philosophical Interventions in the Unfinished Project of Enlightenment*, ed. Axel Honneth *et al.* (Cambridge: MIT Press, 1992), 303. See also Christopher Norris, *The Truth About Postmodernism* (Oxford: Blackwell, 1993), 34–5. David Hiley defends Foucault against such critics in *Philosophy in Question: Essays on a Pyrrhonian Theme* (University of Chicago Press, 1988), 91.

24 In an illuminating essay that touches on Foucault and Kant, Geoffrey Galt Harpham argues that the "form of paradox is stamped on everything in the Enlightenment." "So ... What *Is* Enlightenment? An Inquisition into Modernity," *Critical Inquiry* 20 (1994): 531. Harpham's essay outlines a provocative connection between the Enlightenment and its ostensible other, the Inquisition, and proposes a theoretical construct of "transgressable distinctions" similar to the forms of "dissipation" to be explored in the chapter on Diderot, 163–64.

25 See Bonfiglio, "The Patrilineal Discourse," 108–115. For a detailed feminist reading of the Kant essay, see Jane Flax, "Is Enlightenment Emancipatory?" in *Disputed Subjects: Essays on Psychoanalysis, Politics, and Philosophy* (New York: Routledge, 1993), 75–91.

26 "Jagged and complex," says Harpham of Foucault. The problem appears to transmit itself to each successive commentator; Christopher Norris refers to his own reading of Foucault's essay as "a tortuous commentary" (*Postmodernism*, 75).

27 One is reminded of various unsuccessful eighteenth-century attempts to discipline texts through numeric sequencing: Rousseau's sporadically numbered series in Books I and VII of the *Confessions*, or Sade's accounting errors when he tallies up the damages at the end of the ultra-numeric *Cent-vingt journées de Sodome*.

28 Jean-Jacques Rousseau, *Œuvres complètes*, ed. Bernard Gagnebin and Marcel Raymond, 5 vols. (Paris: Gallimard, 1964–1995) 3:601–616.

29 On the connection between hostility to "systems" and attacks on Hobbes, see J.W.N. Watkins, *Hobbes's System of Ideas: A Study in the Political Significance of Philosophical Theories* (New York: Barnes and Noble, 1968), 169; Richard W.F. Kroll, *The Material Word: Literate Culture in the Restoration and Early Eighteenth Century* (Baltimore: Johns Hopkins University Press, 1991), 75; and, more broadly, Steven Shapin and Simon Shaffer, *Leviathan and the Air-Pump: Hobbes, Boyle, and the Experimental Life* (Princeton University Press, 1985). However, as Samuel I. Mintz points out, Hobbes's rationalism infiltrates his opponents' reasoning. See *The Hunting of Leviathan: Seventeenth-Century Reactions to the Materialism and Moral Philosophy of Thomas Hobbes* (Cambridge University Press, 1969), 149–51.

30 Robert Derathé, *Jean-Jacques Rousseau et la science politique de son temps*, 2nd edn. (Paris: Vrin, 1974), 100–12, 338–39, etc.

31 Thomas Hobbes, *Leviathan*, ed. C.B. MacPherson (1968; London: Penguin, 1985), 160–61. [Book I, Chapter II].

32 Thomas A. Spragens, Jr., *The Politics of Motion: The World of Thomas Hobbes* (Lexington: University Press of Kentucky, 1973), 188–89.

33 See Paul de Man on the "political thermodynamics" in "L'Etat de guerre" and *Le Contrat social*. *Allegories of Reading* (New Haven: Yale University Press, 1979), 272.

34 For readings emphasizing this originary violence in the *Discours sur l'inégalité*, see Thomas Kavanagh, *Writing the Truth: Authority and Desire in Rousseau* (Berkeley: University of California Press, 1987), esp. 140–45; and Pierre Saint-Amand, *Les Lois de l'Hostilité: La Politique à l'Âge des Lumières* (Paris: Seuil, 1992), 101–41.

35 De Man, *Allegories*, 135–59.

36 Friedrich Nietzsche, *On the Genealogy of Morals*, trans. Walter Kaufmann and R.J. Hollingdale (1967; New York: Vintage-Random House, 1989), 17.

37 Marcel Détienne and Jean-Pierre Vernant, *Cunning Intelligence in Greek Culture and Society*, trans. Janet Lloyd (Atlantic Highlands, NJ: Humanities Press, 1978), 3–4.

38 The model of "counter-discourse" proposed here is less distinctly oppositional or agonistic than that of Richard Terdiman in *Discourse/Counter-Discourse: The Theory and Practice of Symbolic Resistance in Nineteenth-Century France* (Ithaca: Cornell University Press, 1985). Terdiman rightly points out that we "must not be taken in by the rhetorical abbreviation in the phrase 'dominant discourse' ... dominant discourse is not a 'thing'

but a complex and shifting formation" (57). See Raymond Williams's discussion of tensions between "residual" and "emergent" cultural formations. "Base and Superstructure in Marxist Cultural Theory," in *Problems in Materialism and Culture* (London: Verso, 1980), 31–49.

I "SYSTÈME" – ORIGINS AND ITINERARIES

1 Pontus de Tyard, *Solitaire second ou discours sur la musique*, ed. Cathy Yandell (Genève: Droz, 1980), 71–2.

2 "Between these two aspects of the notion of system lies no less than the gulf between thought and reality, the same gap that philosophy strives to bridge." Daniel Parrochia, *La Raison systematique* (Paris: Vrin, 1993), 12. Parrochia's study offers a formal analysis of the systems of Plato, Spinoza, Kant, and Hegel.

3 [Marin Cureau de la Chambre], *Le Systeme de l'âme* (Paris: Chez Jacques d'Allin, 1664).

4 Walter J. Ong, "System, Space, and Intellect in Renaissance Symbolism," *Bibliothèque d'humanisme et Renaissance* 18 (1956): 232. See also his *Ramus, Method, and the Decay of Dialogue* (2nd edn. [1958; Cambridge: Harvard University Press, 1983]), esp. the discussion of medieval place-logic and the notion of linguistic and mental "structures" (*Ramus*, 104–30), and the relation of these developments to printing (*Ramus*, 306–14).

5 [P. Dominique Bouhours], *Remarques nouvelles sur la langue françoise* (Paris: Chez Sébastien Marbre-Cramoisy, 1675), 57–8.

6 [Marie Huber], *Le Sisteme des anciens et des modernes, concilié par l'Exposition des Sentimens de quelques Theologiens, sur l'état des âmes séparées des corps. En quatorze lettres*, 2nd edn. (1731; Amsterdam: Wetsteins & Smith, 1733). The pamphlet has nothing to do with the Quarrel of Ancients and Moderns, and is concerned with biblical exegesis.

7 *Le Systême du melange dans l'oeuvre des convulsions, Confondu par ses ressemblances avec le Systême des Augustinistes, & par les erreurs, & les défauts qu'il renferme* (n.p., 1735), 7.

8 Voltaire, *Œuvres*, ed. Beuchot. 72 vols. (Paris: Lefèvre, 1829–40), 14:251.

9 On Law's system as "a new semiology of value," see Thomas Kavanagh, *Enlightenment and the Shadows of Chance: The Novel and the Culture of Gambling in Eighteenth-Century France* (Baltimore: Johns Hopkins University Press, 1993), 67–104. In a suggestive passage, Naomi Segal discusses "Law's shares [as] the extreme case of the fluctuating sign, expanding and contracting according to the wild dynamics of public desire." *The Unintended Reader: Feminism and Manon Lescaut* (Cambridge University Press, 1986), 123.

10 "Monsieur de Clarigny" [E.S. de Gamaches], *Système du coeur, ou conjectures sur la manière dont naissent les différentes affections de l'ame, principalement par rapport aux objects sensibles* (Paris: Denys Dupuis, 1704).

11 René Descartes, *Les Passions de l'âme* in *Œuvres*, ed. Adam-Tannery, 13 vols. (Paris: Vrin, 1964–69) 11:485.

12 Fontenelle, "Sur l'utilité des Mathématiques et de la Physique," *Histoire du renouvellement de l'Académie royale des sciences en MDCXCIX* (Amsterdam: Chez Pierre de Coup, 1709).

13 James L. Larson, *Reason and Experience: The Representation of Natural Order in the Work of Carl von Linné* (Berkeley: University of California Press, 1971).

14 See Philip R. Sloan, "The Buffon-Linnaeus Controversy," *Isis* 67 (1976): 356–75; Gunnar Broberg, "The Broken Circle," *The Quantifying Spirit in the Eighteenth Century*, ed. Tore Frängsmyr, J.L. Heilbron, and Robin E. Rider (Berkeley: University of California Press, 1987), 61; David Goodman, "Buffon's *Histoire naturel* as a Work of the Enlightenment," *The Light of Nature*, ed. J.D. North and J.J. Roche (Dordrecht: Nijhoff, 1985), 57–65. For context and biographical treatment, see Jacques Roger, *Buffon: Un philosophe au Jardin du Roi* (Paris: Fayard, 1989).

15 See Nancy Fraser, "Foucault on Modern Power: Empirical Insights and Normative Confusions," *Praxis International* 1 (1981, October): 272–88; Habermas, *Philosophical Discourse*, 266–93.

16 For a broad overview, see David Knight, *Ordering the World: A History of Classifying Man* (London: Burnett Books, 1981). M.M. Slaughter (*Universal Languages and Scientific Taxonomy in the Seventeenth Century* [Cambridge University Press, 1982]) concentrates on the rise and fall of the "taxonomic episteme" as well as Aristotelian taxonomy.

17 On taxonomy as "cultural need," see Vernon Pratt, "System-Building in the Eighteenth Century," (North and Roche, *Light of Nature*, 421–31). Patrick Coleman argues that "anxiety" produced by classifying enterprise spurred developments in political theory, anthropology, and aesthetics ("Character in an Eighteenth-Century Context," *The Eighteenth Century: Theory and Interpretation* 24 [1983]:51–63). A crucial reference continues to be Arthur Lovejoy, *The Great Chain of Being: A Study in the History of an Idea* (Cambridge: Harvard University Press, 1936), esp. 227–41.

18 Georges-Louis Leclerc, comte de Buffon, "Histoire naturelle: Premier discours," *Œuvres philosophiques*, ed. Jean Piveteau (Paris: PUF, 1954), 9a.

19 Emile Callot, "Système et méthode dans l'histoire de la botanique," *Revue d'histoire des sciences* 18 (1965): 45–53.

20 For an overview of the state of natural history, see Jacques Roger, "The Living World," *The Ferment of Knowledge*, ed. G.S. Rousseau and Roy Porter (Cambridge University Press, 1980), 255–83; and Thomas L. Hankins, *Science and the Enlightenment* (Cambridge University Press, 1985), 147–53.

21 See his essay on "certitude morale" *Œuvres*, 456–88.

22 For a similar account emphasizing complex bifurcations and unravelling within "method," see Derrida's discussion of Descartes, "La

Langue et le discours de la méthode," *Cahiers du groupe de recherches sur la philosophie et le langage* 3 (1983): 35–51.

23 Walter Moser, "D'Alembert: L'Ordre philosophique de ce discours," *MLN* 91 (1976): 722–33, and "Le Discours dans le *Discours préliminaire,*" *Romanic Review* 67 (1976): 102–16.

24 Jean le Rond d'Alembert, *Discours préliminaire,* in *Encyclopédie ou dictionnaire raisonné des sciences, des arts & des métiers* (1751–61; New York: Readex Microprint Corporation, 1969) 1:i. All further references to this facsimile edition will use the original pagination and volume numbers.

25 Diderot, "Prospectus," DPV 5:91.

26 Diderot's image is more radical than d'Alembert's (which continues to presuppose real links – "la liaison ... cachée" – among things); the difference is particularly evident in the version given in "Encyclopédie," which carries the notion of arbitrariness further and deletes the reference to the "vraies institutions de la philosophie."

27 Ernst Cassirer, *The Philosophy of the Enlightenment,* trans. F.C.A. Koelln and J.P. Pettegrove (Princeton University Press, 1951), VII.

28 See Kavanagh, *Enlightenment and the Shadows of Chance,* 9–28 (see 2–5 for a discussion of the semantics of *hasard*); Lorraine Daston, *Classical Probability in the Enlightenment* (Princeton University Press, 1988), especially her discussion of probabilism and "reasonableness," 49–111.

29 Gilles Deleuze and Félix Guattari, *A Thousand Plateaus: Capitalism and Schizophrenia,* (trans.) Brian Massumi (Minneapolis: University of Minnesota Press, 1987), 21.

30 Cf. Sylvain Auroux, *La Sémiotique des encyclopédistes* (Paris: Payot, 1979), 313–25. For a discussion of alphabetical order as a consequence of the epistemological exigencies of the period, see Charles Porset, "Figures de l'encyclopédie," in *Le Siècle de Voltaire,* ed. Christiane Mervaud and Sylvain Menant, 2 vols. (Oxford: Voltaire Foundation, 1982) 2:719–33. A more traditional approach to alphabetical order as merely expedient is taken in Hugh M. Davidson's "The Problem of Scientific Order versus Alphabetical Order in the *Encyclopédie,*" *Studies in Eighteenth-Century Culture* 2 (1972): 33–49.

31 Charles Palissot, *Mémoires pour servir à l'histoire de notre littérature* (1771), cited in John Lough, "Contemporary Books and Pamphlets on the *Encyclopédie,*" in *Essays on the Encyclopédie of Diderot and d'Alembert* (London: Oxford University Press, 1968), 329. Although rich in detail on the debate surrounding the *Encyclopédie,* this article and the one accompanying it on periodical literature make only passing mention of the controversy over alphabetical order and the *renvois,* claiming that such "technical" questions "throw no light whatsoever ... on the ideological conflict of the 1750s and 1760s" (397 n.3).

32 Georges Benrekassa, *Le Langage des Lumières: Concepts et savoir de la langue* (Paris: PUF, 1995), 235.

33 The expression is from Pierre Saint-Amand, *Diderot: Le Labyrinthe de la relation* (Paris: Vrin, 1984), 71. As his title implies, Saint-Amand sees Diderot's practice in general as a wilful assumption of the labyrinthine, as opposed to its rejection by a Descartes or a d'Alembert.

34 Wilda Anderson, *Diderot's Dream* (Baltimore: Johns Hopkins University Press, 1990), 78–91.

35 See their discussion of "linear systems" vs "punctual systems," *A Thousand Plateaus*, 294–8.

36 Jean le Rond d'Alembert, *Recherches sur differents points importans du système du monde*, 3 vols. (Paris: David l'aîné, 1754), 1:v–vi.

37 On the relation of Newtonianism to evolving notions of *systèmes*, and on Buffon's relation to the debate, see Jeff Loveland, "Buffon's *Histoire et théorie de la terre* in the Quarrel over Systems," *Studies in Voltaire and the Eighteenth Century* (forthcoming).

38 [Jean-Sylvain Bailly], *Eloge de Leibnitz* (n.p.: n.d.), 154, 164. (Pages numbered 129– 218 in the copy at the Bibliothèque Nationale.)

39 [Jean-Sylvain] Bailly, *Histoire de l'astronomie moderne*, 3 vols. (Paris: Chez les Frères de Bure, 1779–82).

40 Paul Henri Thiry, baron d'Holbach, *Système de la nature, ou des loix du monde physique & du monde moral*, 2 vols. (London, 1770; Genève: Slatkine, 1973) 1:5.

41 On Senebier in his intellectual context, see Jacques Marx, "L'Art d'observer au XVIIIe siècle: Jean Senebier et Charles Bonnet," *Janus* 61 (1974): 201–20; Hankins, *Science*, 122.

42 Jean Senebier, *Essai sur l'art d'observer*, 2nd edn., 3 vols. (1775; Genève: J.J. Paschoud, 1802) 2:48.

43 *Le Système des colonies* (n.p.: n.d.).

44 *Lucie, ou le système d'amour* (Lyons: n.p., 1791).

2 THE EPISTOLARY MACHINE

1 See Dena Goodman, *The Republic of Letters: A Cultural History of the French Enlightenment* (Ithaca: Cornell University Press, 1994) and her related article, "Enlightenment Salons: The Convergence of Female and Philosophic Ambitions," *Eighteenth-Century Studies* 22 (1989): 329–50. Jerome Christensen offers insightful comments on the range of meanings of "correspondence" in Enlightenment culture, in *Practicing Enlightenment: Hume and the Formation of a Literary Career* (Madison: University of Wisconsin Press, 1987), 203–10 and 226–42 (a reading of Hume's correspondence with the comtesse de Boufflers). For the seventeenth-century background, see Elizabeth MacArthur, *Extravagant Narratives: Closure and Dynamic Form in the Epistolary Form* (Princeton University Press, 1990) 36–61; and Elizabeth Goldsmith, *Exclusive Conversations: The Art of Interaction in Seventeenth-Century France* (Philadelphia: University of Pennsylvania Press, 1988), especially 17–40.

2 Terry Eagleton, *The Rape of Clarissa* (Minneapolis: University of Minnesota Press, 1982), 52.

3 As English Showalter puts it, "*After* 1735 [the date of publication of Sévigné's letters] every literate French man or woman writing a private letter would have been aware of the possibility of publication, intended or not." "Authorial Consciousness and the Familiar Letter: The Case of Madame de Graffigny," *Yale French Studies* 71 (1986): 115.

4 [Pons-Augustin Alletz], *Manuel de l'homme du monde, ou Connoissance générale des principaux états de la Société, & de toutes les matieres qui sont le sujet des conversations ordinaires* (Paris: chez Guillyn, 1761), 315–16.

5 Vaugelas is unambiguous on this point. "Car enfin la parole qui se prononce, est la premiere en ordre & en dignité, puis que celle qui est escrite n'est que son image" [iii]. "Il faut estre assidu dans la Cour & dans la fréquentation de ces sortes de personnes ... , & il ne faut pas insensiblement se laisser corrompre par la contagion des Provinces en y faisant un trop long séjour." Claude Favre de Vaugelas, *Remarques sur la langue françoise* (1747; rpt. Paris: Droz, 1934), [v].

6 Goodman, "Enlightenment Salons," 350.

7 As Jerome Christensen notes, "The free correspondence of the social and intellectual coteries of the Enlightenment was penetrated, fissured, and diverted by secret correspondences and hidden affiliations elsewhere." (*Practicing Enlightenment*, 203).

8 These issues are treated in a number of the essays in several collections to which I will refer by their editors: *Yale French Studies* 71 (1986), *Men/Women of Letters*, ed. Charles Porter; a special number of *Textuel* 24 (1992), *La Lettre d'amour*, ed. J-L Diaz, and the anthology *Writing the Female Voice*, ed. Elizabeth Goldsmith (Boston: Northeastern University Press, 1989).

9 Although he offers an epistolary poetics rather different from the one sketched here, Benoit Melançon's analysis in *Diderot épistolier* ([Saint-Laurent, Québec]: Fides, 1996) overlaps mine in several areas: on the potential for "euphoria" in absence (73–6); the complexity of epistolary "pacts" (134–62) and other forms of exchange or "commerce"; the interrelation of private and public, reading and publishing (217–47).

10 See Charles Porter on the levels of complexity inherent in even so simple a scheme. "Introduction," in Porter, *Men/Women*, 7–8.

11 Christie V. McDonald, *The Dialogue of Writing* (Waterloo, Ontario: Wilfrid Laurier Press, 1984), 12.

12 Janet Altman, *Epistolarity: Approaches to a Form* (Columbus: Ohio State University Press, 1982), 140.

13 As Richardson writes to Sophia Westcomb: "The pen makes distance, presence; and brings back to sweet remembrance all the delights of presence; which makes even presence, mere body, while absence becomes the soul ..." Cited by Bruce Redford, *The Converse of the Pen: Acts of Intimacy in the Eighteenth-Century Familiar Letter* (University of

Chicago Press, 1986), 1. On the active production of "distance" in the letters of writers from Baudelaire to Artaud, see Vincent Kaufmann, *L'Equivoque épistolaire* (Paris: Minuit, 1990).

14 On the Sade correspondence, see my "Sophistry and Displacement: The Poetics of Sade's Ciphers," *Studies on Voltaire and the Eighteenth Century* 242 (1986): 335–43. Marc Buffat underscores the importance of Sophie Volland's presence in Diderot's letters in "Les Lettres à Sophie Volland: Relation amoureuse et relation épistolaire," In Diaz, *Lettre d'amour*, 33–45.

15 On the remarkably successful "fusion" in the Diderot-Sophie Volland correspondence, at least from the only perspective we have access to, his, see Buffat, "Relation amoureuse," as well as "Conversation par écrit," *Recherches sur Diderot et l'Encyclopédie* 9 (1990): 55–69.

16 Roland Barthes distinguishes between "tactical" epistolary writing, such as that of *Liaisons dangereuses*, where the writer consciously seeks to touch and seize upon the other; and the lover's correspondence, bereft of tactics and indeed empty of meaning per se, rather "expressive." *Fragments d'un discours amoureux* (Paris: Seuil, 1977), 187–88. It is a rare idyllic moment, however, in which the lovers' correspondence is touched with none of the incertitude of interpretation, and on the whole, I would argue, these two "types" are better situated as points along an extremely mobile continuum.

17 On the resistance of the epistolary to closure or finality in meaning, see Elizabeth MacArthur, *Extravagant Narratives*, 25–28.

18 Julie de Lespinasse, *Lettres* (1893; rpt. Paris: Editions d'aujourd'hui, 1978), 235. [Lettre CII, 1775].

19 Camillo Baldi, *Trattato come da una lettera missiva si conoscano la natura e le qualità dello scrittore*, translated into French as *La Lettre déchiffrée*, trans. Anne-Marie Debet and Alessandro Fontana (Paris: Les Belles Lettres, 1993).

20 Janet Altman, "The Letter Book as a Literary Institution 1539–1789: Toward a Cultural History of Published Correspondences in France," in Porter, *Men/Women*, 33.

21 For a useful account of the debate, see Louise Horowitz, "The Correspondence of Madame de Sévigné: Letters or Belles-Lettres?" *French Forum* 6 (1981): 13–27.

22 Redford, *Converse of the Pen*, 9.

23 Hence the importance of projects such as Altman's on letter books, or Marie-Claire Grassi's archival findings, in "Friends and Lovers (or the Codification of Intimacy)"(In Porter, *Men/Women*, 77–92) and her "Lettres d'amour en archives" (In Diaz, *Lettre d'amour*, 47–55).

24 Part of the drama in the letters of Heloise and Abelard is in the pair's difficulty in discerning one another and themselves as writing subjects in relation to each other. Their struggle to find a common language in which to preserve the personal, affective dimension in their relationship

is apparent in their forms of address, prayers, and readings of scripture. *The Letters of Heloise and Abelard*, ed. Betty Radice (Middlesex: Penguin, 1973). Peggy Kamuf sees the couple as willfully misreading each other in their first four letters (*Fictions of Feminine Desire: Disclosures of Heloise* [Lincoln: University of Nebraska Press, 1982] 9–41); I would however argue that they ultimately achieve their aim of mutual reassurance through a "common language," in the final letters of the series.

25 Tourvel defends Valmont to Volanges in Letter 22 ("Monsieur de Valmont is perhaps simply another example of the danger of liaisons"); Merteuil twists the truth for Volanges by referring to Cécile's relation to Danceny as "une liaison dangereuse" in Letter 63; and Volanges, still ignorant of her own daughter's story, offers the reductive conclusion to the novel ("Who would not shudder in reflecting on the unhappiness caused by a single dangerous liaison?") in Letter 175.

26 Lespinasse, *Lettres*, 66. In his introduction to this reprint edition, Jean-Noël Pascal explicitly (and exclusively) describes Lespinasse in comparison with the Portuguese Nun.

27 Lespinasse, *Lettres à Condorcet*, ed. Jean-Noël Pascal (Paris: Desjonquières, 1990).

28 Mireille Bossis, "Methodological Journeys Through Correspondences," in Porter, *Men/Women*, 69.

29 I have loosely based my English terminology on that of the translation by Robert Hurley, Mark Seem, and Helen R. Lane. *Anti-Œdipus* (Minneapolis: University of Minnesota Press, 1983).

30 Jean-François Lyotard, *The Differend: Phrases in Dispute*, trans. Georges Van Den Abbeele (Minneapolis: University of Minnesota Press, 1988). Lyotard writes of the ongoing conversation or "deliberation": "The deliberative is more 'fragile' than the narrative . . . , it lets the abysses be perceived that separate genres of discourse from one another and even phrase regimens from one another, the abysses that threaten 'the social bond'" (150). Yet the refusal to inaugurate a decisive metalanguage, a narrative, allows the diversity of genres to flourish and provides the most sure resistance to the totalitarian.

31 Ernesto Laclau and Chantal Mouffe, *Hegemony and Socialist Strategy: Toward a Radical Democratic Politics*, trans. Winston Moore and Paul Cammack (London: Verso, 1985).

32 Terry Castle, "The Female Thermometer," *Representations* 17 (1987): 20.

33 See Derrida on the "encounter" between paradox, sinuosity, and chance, on the one hand, and a "methodology of the straight path" (*méthodologie du droit*). "La Langue et le discours de la méthode," *Cahiers du groupe de recherche sur la philosophie et la langue* 3 (1983): 50. More recently, Claudia Brodsky Latour has examined the figural "architectonic" qualities of "the line" in Descartes (*Lines of Thought: Discourse, Architectonics, and the Origin of Modern Philosophy* [Durham: Duke University Press, 1996]).

34 On the political context and its relation to Descartes's thought, see Timothy Reiss, "Descartes, the Palatinate, and the Thirty Years War: Political Theory and Political Practice." *Yale French Studies* 80 (1991): 108–45.

35 Elizabeth to Descartes, September 30, 1645. In Descartes, *Lettres sur la morale: Correspondance avec la princesse Elisabeth, Chanut et la reine Christine*, ed. Jacques Chevalier (Paris: Boivin, 1953), 96. All subsequent references to the letters will be from this edition.

36 *Descartes, la princesse Elisabeth et la reine Christine, d'après des lettres inédites*, ed. Louis-Antoine Foucher de Careil (Paris and Amsterdam: Germer-Baillière and Mulier, 1879). The Foucher de Careil edition served as the basis for Elizabeth's letters in the Adam-Tannery edition; several emendations were made for the Chevalier edition.

37 See Erica Harth's excellent discussion in *Cartesian Women: Versions and Subversions of Rational Discourse in the Old Regime* (Ithaca: Cornell University Press, 1992), 67–78.

38 See also her letter of December 27, 1645, in which she expresses concern lest an earlier letter fall into the hands of "critics" (123).

39 See Joan DeJean, *Tender Geographies: Women and the Origins of the Novel in France* (New York: Columbia University Press, 1991), 130–34, on Desjardins's reputation as a "public woman" owing to her independence as a writer. For the biographical details I rely on Micheline Cuénin's introduction to Desjardins, *Lettres et billets galants*, ed. M. Cuénin (Paris: Publications de la société d'étude du XVIIe siècle, 1975), 7–32.

40 See, among others, Elizabeth Goldsmith, "Publishing Passion: Madame de Villedieu's *Lettres et billets galants*," *Papers on Seventeenth-Century French Literature* 37 (1987): 439–50; and the chapters on Desjardins/Villedieu in MacArthur, *Extravagant Narratives*, 44–61, and Katherine Ann Jensen, *Writing Love: Letters, Women, and the Novel in France 1605–1776* (Carbondale: Southern Illinois University Press, 1995), 36–72.

41 Linda S. Kauffman offers a very different reading of the "classic" situation in her account of the *Lettres portugaises*, where "Writing is … a strategy of recuperation, in the senses both of healing and of reparation." *Discourses of Desire: Gender, Genre, and Epistolary Fictions* (Ithaca: Cornell University Press, 1986), 116.

42 Jensen is disarmingly frank about her own scholarly investments: "As part of my own wish fulfillment, I would have liked to outline an unequivocal evolution from women's rehearsals of seduction and betrayal in the seventeenth-century love letter to their *absolute undoing* of Epistolary Woman in eighteenth-century letter novels, depicting *female bonding* and *collective social change* in class and gender arrangements" (159; original emphasis). This is a powerful reading in many respects, but I do question the extent to which the avowed goals of *Writing Love* have not inflected the reading by indicating some choices and closing off others.

43 See the introduction, *Correspondance de Madame de Graffigny*, ed. J.A. Dainard *et al.* (Oxford: Voltaire Foundation, 1985–) 1:x–xviii, for an account of the history of the Graffigny correspondence, its compilation and previous partial publication. As English Showalter has recently shown, the "Graffigny" of the 1820 edition of the Cirey letters was to a large extent an editorial creation. See "Graffigny at Cirey: A Fraud Exposed," *French Forum* 21 (1996): 29–44.

44 This is precisely Sainte-Beuve's purpose in his *causerie* of June 17, 1850, in which he promises not to talk about *Cénie* or *Les Lettres péruviennes*, which are "passés," but rather about the thirty-one letters from Cirey, claiming that the "secondary genres (diaries, correspondances, memoirs)" enable one to infiltrate "life itself." Charles-Augustin Sainte-Beuve, *Causeries de lundi*, 9th edn. (Paris: Garnier, n.d.) 2:208.

45 Patricia Meyer Spacks offers a similar account of the role of "trivia" and "idle talk" in social life and the creation of intimacy, in *Gossip* (New York: Knopf, 1985). In my reading of Graffigny's correspondence, however, I would give less weight than she to the urge to "plot."

46 Derrida, *The Post Card*, trans. Alan Bass (University of Chicago Press, 1987), 79.

47 Frank Kermode and Anita Kermode, introduction to *The Oxford Book of Letters* (Oxford University Press, 1995), xxiii.

3 PHYSICS AND FIGURATION IN DU CHÂTELET'S 'INSTITUTIONS DE PHYSIQUE'

1 Margaret C. Jacobs, *The Radical Enlightenment: Pantheists, Freemasons, and Republicans* (London: George Allen and Unwin, 1981), 94. See also Steven Shapin, "Social Uses of Science," in G.S. Rousseau and R. Porter, eds., *The Ferment of Knowledge: Studies in the Historiography of Eighteenth-Century Science* (Cambridge University Press, 1980), 93–109, and "Of Gods and Kings: Natural Philosophy and Politics in the Leibniz-Clarke Disputes," *Isis* 72 (1981): 187–215. Steven Shapin and Simon Schaffer offer an exemplary case study of the intersection of sociopolitical regulation and the development of science in their *Leviathan and the Air Pump, Hobbes, Boyle, and the Experimental Life* (Princeton University Press, 1985). Charles Bazerman has shown how Newton deploys mathematical proof in order to eliminate discussion and "reduce disagreement to error," in *Shaping Written Knowledge: The Genre and Activity of the Experimental Article in Science* (Madison: University of Wisconsin Press, 1988), 115–17. Robert Markley asserts that "the fiction of objectivity" allows the Royal Society to subsume disagreement "by furnishing a means to ground scientific fact in shared religious and sociopolitical beliefs." *Fallen Languages: Crises of Representation in Newtonian England, 1640–1740* (Ithaca: Cornell University Press, 1993), 98–99.

2 I. Bernard Cohen, *The Newtonian Revolution* (Cambridge University

Press, 1980). See Rupert Hall, "Newton in France: A New View," *History of Science* 13 (1975): 233–50. Aram Vartanian, *Diderot and Descartes: A Study in Scientific Naturalism in the Enlightenment* (Princeton University Press, 1953). See esp. chapter 3 on scientific method, 203–88. As Ellen McNiven Hine observes, "By the 1730s, it was no longer possible to be either a strict Cartesian or a strict Newtonian." "Dortous de Mairan, the 'Cartonian,'" *Studies on Voltaire and the Eighteenth Century* 266 (1989): 178.

3 Gabrielle-Emilie Le Tonnelier de Breteuil, Marquise du Châtelet, *Institutions physiques*, nouvelle edition (1742). Facsimile edition reprinted in vol. 28 of Christian Wolff, *Gesammelte Werke Materialien und Dokumente*, ed. J. Ecole *et al.* (Heldesheim, Zurich, New York: Georg Olms, 1988) 28:7. The page numbers remain those of the 1742 edition of the *Institutions*.

4 For a detailed analysis of the developments of Du Châtelet's thought as she revised the *Institutions*, see Linda Gardiner Janik, "Searching for the Metaphysics of Science: The Structure and Composition of Madame du Châtelet's *Institutions de physique*, 1737–1740," *Studies in Voltaire and the Eighteenth Century* 201 (1982): 85–113. Carolyn Iltis assesses certain arguments and discusses the status of integrative projects in "Mme du Châtelet's Metaphysics and Mechanics," *Studies in History and Philosophy of Science* 8 (1977): 29–48; W.H. Barber situates Du Châtelet in the context of Leibnizianism in France in "Mme Du Châtelet and Leibnizianism: The Genesis of the *Institutions de physique*," in *The Age of Enlightenment*, ed. Barber *et al.* (Edinburgh: Oliver and Boyd, 1967) and in his broad study, *Leibniz in France from Arnauld to Voltaire: A Study in French Reaction to Leibnizianism, 1670–1760* (Oxford: Clarendon Press, 1955), 135–40 and 182–86. Erica Harth examines Du Châtelet's Cartesianism in the *Institutions* and other writings, in *Cartesian Women*, 189–213. For biographical treatments, see Elisabeth Badinter, *Emilie, Emilie: L'ambition féminine au XVIIIe siècle* (Paris: Flammarion, 1983) and René Vaillot, *Madame du Châtelet* (Paris: Albin Michel, 1978).

5 My discussion, needless to say, is indebted to Erich Auerbach's superb essay, "*Figura*," originally published in 1944 and reprinted in *Scenes from the Drama of European Literature* (Minneapolis: University of Minnesota Press, 1984), 11–76.

6 As when, for example, she refers to the "celebrated Wolf, whom you used to hear me talking about with one of his disciples who was with us for a while and sometimes gave me excerpts from his work (13). The disciple is Du Châtelet's tutor Koenig; one may suppose that this indirect reference to his limited assistance is her response to his accusation that she had plagiarized his work. (See Janik, "Searching for the Metaphysics" 96–97).

7 See also the discussion of the role in her preface to her translation of Mandeville's *Fable of the Bees*, in which she contends with both the

subordination of translators to authors and that of women to men. "Mme du Châtelet's Translation of the 'Fable of the Bees,' " ed. Ira O. Wade, *Studies on Voltaire, with Some Unpublished Papers of Mme du Châtelet* (Princeton University Press, 1947), 131–87.

8 See Hugh M. Davidson, "Voltaire Explains Newton: An Episode in the History of Rhetoric," in *The Dialectic of Discovery*, ed. John Lyons and Nancy Vickers (Lexington, KY: French Forum, 1984), 72–82.

9 Du Châtelet, manuscript of the *Institutions de physique*. BN (Bibliothèque Nationale) f.fr. 12265 (p. 2).

10 See Paul de Man's comments on the "curious choice of examples" in Locke's *Essay*. "The Epistemology of Metaphor," *Critical Inquiry* 5 (1978): 13–30; also Milton Wilson, "Reading Locke and Newton as Literature," *University of Toronto Quarterly* 57 (1988): 471–83, especially his remarks on "negative narration" in conditional or hypothetical statements, pp. 480–82.

11 "Faces ... delimit a field that neutralizes in advance any expressions or connections unamenable to the appropriate significations." Gilles Deleuze and Félix Guattari, *A Thousand Plateaus* (168). See also the discussion 115–16.

12 De Man, "Epistemology," 22–23.

13 For a useful contrast, see Leibniz's fifth paper in the correspondence with Clarke (L 5.47), for his version of "how men come to form to themselves the notion of space" (p. 63).

14 Michel Serres offers an extended reading of the *Monadology*'s reconceptualizing of system as complexity and multiple relations (from the individual to the whole, and from the whole to each individual) as a key to his work. *Le Système de Leibniz et ses modèles mathématiques* (Paris: PUF, 1968), esp. 620–31.

15 A similar technique for maintaining a connection between space and time is offered by the medieval practice of "figural interpretation." In Erich Auerbach's words, "Figural prophecy implies the interpretation of one worldly event through another; the first signifies the second, the second fulfills the first." "*Figura*," 58. The events or persons so related maintain their historical concreteness, but their signification is apprehended in a transhistorical, spiritual act, in which they are "viewed primarily in immediate vertical connection with a divine reality" (72). Thus are (temporal) sequence and (spatial) simultaneity projected onto one another.

16 Leibniz's fourth paper, *The Leibniz-Clarke Correspondence, with Extracts from Newton's Principia and Opticks*, ed. H.G. Alexander (Manchester University Press, 1956), 44–45.

17 See Leibniz's letter XXIII to Arnauld of Oct 6, 1687. *Discourse on Metaphysics, Correspondence with Arnauld, Monadology*, trans. George R. Montgomery (1902; reprint, La Salle, IL: Open Court, 1973), 222–23. For a discussion of the problem of the continuum in Leibniz,

see J.E. McGuire, "'Labyrinthus continui': Leibniz on Substance, Activity, and Matter," in P.K. Machamer and R.G. Turnbull, eds., *Motion and Time, Space and Matter* (Columbus: Ohio State University Press, 1976), 290–326.

18 Laurens Laudan discusses the shift from a similar, implicitly Cartesian, hypotheticalism in Boyle and Glanville to the later belief of Newton and others that improved instrumentation and patient experimentation would unlock all of nature's secrets. "The Clock Metaphor and Probabilism: The Impact of Descartes on English Methodological Thought, 1650–1665," *Annals of Science* 22 (1966): 73–104. It is interesting to note that, although Du Châtelet makes a case similar to Descartes's in arguing that there is no way of knowing which of any number of possible mechanical explanations of a phenomenon is correct (just as we can hypothesize about the internal organization of a clock, but not see inside), her watch analogy makes a different point about the autonomy of explanatory registers.

19 Locke, on the other hand, defines "figure" in terms of the visual perception of boundaries "that really exist in the coherent masses of Matter." *An Essay concerning Human Understanding*, ed. Peter H. Nidditch (Oxford: Clarendon Press, 1975), 168.

20 Walter Benjamin, *Reflections: Essays, Aphorisms, Autobiographical Writings*, ed. Peter Demetz, trans. Edmund Jephcott (New York: Harcourt, Brace, Jovanovich, 1978), 168.

21 In Deleuze's account of Leibniz, such desiring speculation is produced by the system's own dynamics, its emphasis on variety within unity. *Le Pli: Leibniz et le baroque* (Paris: Minuit, 1988), 78.

22 Leibniz claimed that this principle of "the identity of indiscernibles," according to which any two individuals in whom the predicates are entirely the same are indiscernible from one another and are in fact one and the same, was one of the mainstays of his system. As we shall see below, it is also extremely important in Condillac's logic and has strong resonances in Diderot's work. See section 9 of the *Discourse on Metaphysics* as well as Leibniz's Letter 8 to Arnauld (May, 1686) *Discourse on Metaphysics, Correspondence with Arnauld, Monadology*, 14–15, 111.

23 On metaphor as necessity and metonymy as contingency, see Paul de Man, *Allegories of Reading* (New Haven: Yale University Press, 1979), 14–15, 63.

24 For a useful account of the theories of force that Du Châtelet takes over from Leibniz, see Richard S. Westfall, *Force in Newton's Physics: The Science of Dynamics in the Seventeenth Century* (New York and London: Elsevier and Macdonald, 1971), esp. Chapter 6, "Leibnizian Dynamics," 283–322.

25 Westfall, *Force*, 505. See also H.G. Alexander's introduction to the Leibniz-Clarke correspondence, XXIX–XXXII. A different turn on the outcome is offered by David Papineau, who sees it as a revision of

physical thought resulting in "the repudiation of both." "The *Vis viva* Controversy: Do Meanings Matter?" *Studies in History and Philosophy of Science* 8 (1977): 142. See also Thomas Hankins, "Eighteenth-Century Attempts to Resolve the *Vis Viva* Controversy," *Isis* 56 (1965): 281–97. Carolyn Iltis discusses Leibniz's and Du Châtelet's participation in various stages of the debate, and examines the means by which theological, metaphysical, and emotional commitments within the scientific community precluded real debate or objective analysis of the data. "Leibniz and the *Vis viva* Controversy," *Isis* 62 (1971): 21–35; "The Leibnizian-Newtonian Debates: National Philosophy and Social Psychology," *British Journal of the History of Science* 6 (1973): 343–77; and "Madame du Châtelet's Metaphysics and Mechanics," *Studies in History and Philosophy of Science* 8 (1977): 29–48.

26 Jean Jacques Dortous de Mairan, *Dissertation sur l'estimation et la mesure des forces motrices des corps* (1728; rpt. Paris, 1741). Ellen McNiven Hine discusses Mairan's own integrative tendencies in "Dortous de Mairan, the 'Cartonian,'" *Studies on Voltaire and the Eighteenth Century* 266 (1989): 163–79.

27 Without venturing into the physics of the matter himself, René Taton claims that Du Châtelet's quarrel with Mairan and Jurin "exceeded her competence" (and he is also at some pains to minimize her role in Voltaire's *Eléments* and even in her own translation of Newton). "Madame du Châtelet, traductrice de Newton," *Archives internationales d'histoire des sciences* 22 (1969): 185–210. In a more thorough discussion of the scientific issues, however, C. Iltis shows that Du Châtelet "proceeded to reduce the arguments of Jean-Jacques Mairan … to nonsense." "Mme du Châtelet's Metaphysics and Mechanics," 40.

28 On this episode see Badinter, 324–43; Vaillot, 208–11.

29 Iltis, "Metaphysics and Mechanics," 41.

30 R.S. Westfall sees the analysis of imperfectly elastic bodies in Leibniz's *Essay on Dynamics* "the cornerstone of the ultimate principle of the conservation of energy." *Force*, 295.

31 Erica Harth ably characterizes Du Châtelet's frustration and her complex relationships with male mentors, the Academy of Science, and the gendering of "popular science" as feminine, *Cartesian Women*, 199–208.

32 Du Châtelet claims that there is no other difference between the passages "que la différence numérique des mots" (511), a strategically useful assertion, but hardly in keeping with the principle of the identity of indiscernibles!

33 Shapin, "Social Uses of Science," in Rousseau and Porter, *Ferment*, 135–36.

34 Newton's position on hypothesis hardened over time, as Bernard Cohen's study of the revisions of the *Principia* shows. *Introduction to Newton's 'Principia'* (Cambridge: Harvard University Press, 1971) 241–45.

According to Cohen, the final version, "Hypothesis non fingo," is an "absolutely pejorative expression." See also his comparison of Newton and Descartes, *The Newtonian Revolution*, 99–109.

4 CONDILLAC AND THE IDENTITY OF THE OTHER

1 For a general introduction to Condillac, see Isabel Knight, *The Geometric Spirit: The Abbé de Condillac and the French Enlightenment* (New Haven: Yale University Press, 1968). In her chapter on the *Traité des systèmes*, Knight argues that Condillac moves beyond criticism of others to proposing his own program based on the workings of an orderly universe. (As will become apparent, I place more weight on the skeptical strain of the *Traité* than does she.) For Condillac's sources and place in intellectual history, see Ellen McNiven Hine, *A Critical Study of Condillac's Traité des systèmes* (The Hague: Nijhoff, 1979). Sylvain Auroux discusses the *Traité des systèmes* in *La Sémiotique des Encyclopédistes* (Paris: Payot, 1979), 151–55, but looks rather toward his language theory and epistemology in "Empirisme et théorie linguistique chez Condillac," in (along with a number of other fine articles) *Condillac et les problèmes du langage*, ed. Jean Sgard (Genève: Slatkine, 1982), 177–219. I will be citing others of Auroux's articles on Condillac below. See also the suggestive piece by Chantal Hasnaoui, "Condillac, chemins du sensualisme," in *Langues et langages de Leibniz à l'Encyclopédie*, ed. Michèle Duchet and Michèle Jolley (Paris: Union Générale des Editions, 1977), 97–129. Nicolas Rousseau situates Condillac with respect to his contemporaries as well as in twentieth-century philosophy in *Connaissance et langage chez Condillac* (Genève: Droz, 1986); John C. O'Neal discusses Condillac's relevance to sensationism in *The Authority of Experience* (University Park: Pennsylvania State University Press, 1996), 13–59.

2 Michael Foucault, *Naissance de la clinique* (Paris: PUF, 1963), 117. Derrida would go further in claiming that Condillac did not so much "hesitate" between *genèse* and *calcul*, as "travailler à la ruine de cette alternative ... et de tout le système qui en est solidaire" ("L'Archéologie du frivole," intro. to Condillac, *Essai sur l'origine des connaissances humaines*, ed. C. Porset [Paris: Galilée, 1973]), 28.

3 For a general discussion, see David Bates "The Epistemology of Error in Late Enlightenment France," *Eighteenth-Century Studies* 29 (1996): 307–27.

4 On the *langage d'action*, see Condillac, *Essai*, 194–99. Chantal Hasnaoui points out that even in this early "rooted" stage of linguistic development, Condillac cannot effectuate an entire correspondence of sign and referent/motivation: originary languages are "already symbolic" or "rhetorical and metaphorical." "Condillac, chemins du sensualisme," 129 n.77.

5 Condillac, *La Langue des calculs*, ed. Anne-Marie Chouillet (Presses universitaires de Lille, 1981), 1–2.

6 Condillac's aligning of will and error echoes the Fourth Meditation, where Descartes asserts that the will, being infinite, is in the image of God; but that the Creator has chosen to endow humanity with limited understanding. Descartes, *Œuvres*, ed. Adam-Tannery, 12 vols (Paris: Vrin, 1967) 9.1: 46. Descartes's punctuation of the Meditation with the reiterated claim that "ie n'ay certes aucun sujet de me plaindre" suggests a subtle discontentment with what he takes to be the human situation.

7 On Condillac's strategies for circumscribing arbitrariness, see Jürgen Trabant, "La Critique de l'arbitraire du signe chez Condillac et Humboldt," in *Les Idéologues: Sémiotique, théories et politiques linguistiques pendant la Révolution française*, ed. Winfried Busse and Jürgen Trabant (Amsterdam and Philadelphia: John Benjamins, 1986), 73–96. Patrick Tort considers how Condillac grounds semiotic and economic *valeur* and preserves them from the arbitrary in "Condillac, l'économie et les signes," *Condillac et les problèmes du langage*, 421–51.

8 Auroux, *Sémiotique*, 63.

9 S. Auroux, "Condillac ou la vertu des signes," Introduction to Condillac, *Langue des calculs*, XIII–XIV.

10 Ulrich Ricken, "La Liaison des idées et la clarté du français," *Dix-huitième siècle* 1 (1969): 179–93. For the relation of this debate to Diderot's work, see below 153–54.

11 On the impossibility of absolute synonymy in Condillac, see Jean-Claude Choul, "Sémantique synonymique: Une contre-rhétorique Condillac et Diderot," *Papers in the History of Linguistics*, ed. Hans Aarsleff, Louis G. Kelly, and Hans-Josef Niederehe (Amsterdam and Philadelphia: John Benjamins, 1987), 315–26. Du Marsais had also argued against the existence of perfect synonymy, although less on logical and more on practical and empirical grounds, than Condillac. See César-Chesneau du Marsais, *Des tropes*, ed. P. Fontanier, 2 vols. (1818; rpt. Genève: Slatkine, 1984) 1:358–60. For a contemporary view of the estrangement between analogy and univocity, see Deleuze, *Différence et répétition* (Paris: PUF, 1968), 56.

12 Condillac, *Cours d'études: De l'art de penser, Œuvres philosophiques*, ed. Le Roy, 3 vols. (Paris: PUF, 1947) 1: 749.

13 John Locke, *An Essay Concerning Human Understanding*, ed. P.H. Nidditch (Oxford: Clarendon Press, 1975), 609.

14 See C.H. Langford, "Moore's Notion of Analysis," in *Philosophy of G.E. Moore*, ed. P.A. Schilpp (Evanston: Northwestern University Press, 1942), 319–42.

15 G.W. Leibniz, *New Essays on Human Understanding*, trans. Peter Remnant and Jonathan Rennett (Cambridge University Press, 1981), 429. The *New Essays*, published only in 1765, were not available to Condillac.

16 Condillac, *Langue des calculs*, 162–63.

17 On the tense affinities between Condillac and Leibniz, see Derrida, "Archéologie," 65–66n. As Derrida notes, the sites of strongest resemblance are with that part of Leibniz's work which remained unavailable to Condillac. See also Hasnaoui, "Chemins du sensualisme" 120–21, on the relation of *La Langue de calculs* and Leibniz's universal language project.

18 Leibniz, section 8 of the *Discourse on Metaphysics*, in *Leibniz: Discourse on Metaphysics, Correspondence with Arnauld, Monadology*, 13.

19 Leibniz immediately follows with the claim that such events are nonetheless contingent and in no way impinge on the freedom of God or his creatures, an argument which was to remain unknown to the *philosophes*. For an overview of the debate on this issue and continued analysis of the problem, see several of the pieces in *Leibniz: A Collection of Critical Essays*, ed. Harry G. Frankfurt (1972; rpt. University of Notre Dame Press, 1976), especially C.D. Broad, "Leibniz's Predicate-in-Notion Principle and Some of its Alleged Consequences" (1–18), and E.M. Curley, "The Root of Contingency" (69–97).

20 Considering this issue of whether or not universal interconnectedness renders true knowledge impossible, S. Auroux claims that "[p]our les Lumières, la *notion* de 'fait' va fonctionner comme la clôture épistémologique qui assure à la science la sécurité de sa progression et la frontière qui la sépare d'une irrationalité chimérique" (*Sémiotique*, 155). I think that Condillac is at pains to endow empirical "facts" with just such force, but as passages such as the present one suggest, his skepticism frequently obscures that desire.

21 Descartes returns in Chapter 12, "Des Hypothèses" (see esp. pp. 198–203), principally as a foil to Newton. Interestingly, Condillac defends a "limited" use of hypothesis, thus remaining more in the French than the Newtonian tradition. Descartes shadows the text as the precursor who can be neither accepted nor excluded.

22 Aside from philosophizing in an outdated mode, the *Recherche* had been put on the Index in 1709 for its alleged tendencies toward "Spinozism." Malebranche's reputation as an intellectual had, however, remained strong.

23 The considerably less contorted second paragraph of the *Monadology* goes as follows: "There must be simple substances because there are composites; for a composite is nothing else than a collection or aggregate of simple substances." *Leibniz*, trans. Montgomery, 251.

24 Condillac returns to the tensile strength of Leibniz's system a few pages later: "everything is so closely related in Leibniz's system, that one must either accept everything, or reject everything," (164).

25 [Père Boursier], *De l'action de Dieu sur les créatures, traité dans lequel on prouve la prémotion physique* (Paris, 1713). For a discussion of the Jansenist Boursier's role in the debates over free will in the early part of the

century, see Jean Ehrard, *L'Idée de nature en France dans la première moitié du XVIIIe siècle* (1963; rpt. Genève: Slatkine, 1981), 663–65.

26 See his earlier note "the Church does not at all approve of theologians who undertake to explain everything" (126n.).

27 In the only other passage where Condillac gives Spinoza a place in the dialogue, he inserts not himself, but Bayle as the imagined interlocutor – in order to show later (as in the case of Leibniz and Justi) that his own criticism is the stronger (193).

28 As Edwin Curley points out, "Corollaries are often more important than the propositions they follow, and the scholia often offer more intuitive arguments for the propositions just demonstrated, or reply to what Spinoza regards as natural and important objections. The longer scholia, prefaces, and appendices tend to punctuate major divisions within the work and to sum up key contentions." Editor's Introduction to the *Ethics*, *The Collected Works of Spinoza* (Princeton University Press, 1985 –) 1:404. Condillac appears at one point to suspect this complicated relationship among the parts and to find it irritating: "Je me trompe fort, ou la plupart des définitions et des axiomes de Spinosa n'ont été faits qu'après les démonstrations" ["Either I am mistaken, or most of Spinoza's definitions and axioms were only made after the demonstrations"] (178).

29 For an analysis of the way the argument functions in Spinoza, see Jonathan Bennet, *A Study of Spinoza's Ethics* (Indianapolis: Hackett, 1984), 70–75.

30 Arnauld and Nicole, *La Logique ou l'art de penser*, part IV (Paris: Flammarion, 1970), 376.

31 On the place of the geometric method in the history of philosophy and on Spinoza's use of it, see Thomas Carson Marks, "*Ordine Geometrica Demonstrata*: Spinoza's Use of the Axiomatic Method," *Review of Metaphysics* 29 (1975): 263–86.

32 In his discussion of the *Ethics* in terms of what he calls its "hypothetico-deductive order," Bennett sees the self-evidence of the principles as a process, rather than as an originary injunction: only having carefully worked through the entire argument will the reader understand the starting points as true beyond doubt (21). It is this interrelatedness, however, that Condillac condemns as *petitio principi*.

33 Donald Barthelme, "Kierkegaard Unfair to Schlegel," *City Life* (New York: Farrar, Straus, Giroux, 1968), 90–91.

5 DIDEROT – CHANGING THE SYSTEM

1 Herbert Dieckmann, "Système et interprétation dans la pensée de Diderot," *Cinq leçons sur Diderot* (Genève: Droz, 1959), 41–68. More recently, see Pierre Saint-Amand, "Diderot contre la méthode," *Stanford French Review* 8 (1984): 213–28.

2 For example, Pierre Saint-Amand, *Diderot: Le Labyrinthe de la relation* (Paris:

Vrin, 1984). A number of studies have examined Diderot's materialism in relation to Enlightenment critique; in particular Wilda Anderson, *Diderot's Dream* (Baltimore: Johns Hopkins University Press, 1990) and Daniel Brewer, *The Discourse of Enlightenment in Eighteenth-Century France: Diderot and the Art of Philosophizing* (Cambridge University Press, 1993).

3 Ilya Prigogine and Isabelle Stengers, *La Nouvelle alliance: Métamorphose de la science*, 2nd edn. (1979; Paris: Gallimard, 1986), 137.

4 See J. Hayes, "Sequence and Simultaneity in Diderot's *Promenade Vernet* and *Leçons de clavecin*," *Eighteenth-Century Studies* 29 (1996):291–305.

5 The *locus classicus* is Leo Spitzer's essay, "The Style of Diderot," *Linguistics and Literary History: Essays in Linguistics* (Princeton University Press, 1948), 135–91; Georges May, "Diderot, artiste et philosophe du décousu," *Europäische Aufklärung*, ed. H. Friedrich and F. Schalk (Munich: Wilhelm Fink, 1967), 165–88. Expanding on Spitzer's insights, Jean Starobinski pursues the connections between style, experimentalism, and irony in Diderot's writing. "Le Philosophe, le géomètre, l'hybride," *Poétique* 21 (1975): 8–23. Georges Daniel sees parataxis as uniting *enchaînement* and the *style coupé*: *Le Style de Diderot* (Genève: Droz, 1986), 32–38. See also Martin Jay's suggestive comments on parataxis (in Adorno) as "a dialectical model of negations that simultaneously constructed and deconstructed patterns of fluid reality." *Adorno* (Cambridge: Harvard University Press, 1984), 15.

6 Michael Cartwright, "Diderot's Discursive Eye: Peripatetics and the Search for Harmony," in *Diderot: Digression and Dispersion*, ed. Jack Undank and Herbert Josephs (Lexington: French Forum Monographs, 1984), 72–84. For Diderot on undulating and straight lines, see his *Pensées détachées sur la peinture*, in *Œuvres esthétiques*, ed. P. Vernière (Paris: Garnier, 1968), 788.

7 Diderot, *Salon de 1767*, DPV 16:69.

8 See James Creech's discussion of the *modèle idéal* in Diderot's aesthetics and dramatic theory. *Diderot: Thresholds of Representation* (Columbus: Ohio State University Press, 1986), 74–81. On the relation between experimentation or "tâtonnement" and the *modèle idéal*, see Anderson, 204–8.

9 On the *Encyclopédie*'s construction of a critical subject, see Régis *et al.*, "Lire l'*Encyclopédie*," *Littérature* 42 (1981): 20–39; Rosalina de la Carrera, *Success in Circuit Lies: Diderot's Communicational Practice* (Stanford University Press, 1991), 119.

10 See Jack Undank's discussion (appropriately, in a footnote!) on the subject of Diderot and digression, in *Diderot: Inside, Outside, and In-Between* (Madison, WI: Coda Press, 1979), 86–88n.

11 Michel Delon notes in "Savoir totalisant et forme éclatée" (*Dix-huitième siècle* 14 [1982]: 13–26) Diderot's ability to escape the split "between linear composition and synthesizing vision, between unity and diversity" (17); more generally, see Hilary Clark, "Encyclopedic Discourse," *SubStance* 67 (1992): 95.

12 The documentary use of the *Encyclopédie* and especially of its plates is maintained in such portable anthologies as C. G. Gillespie's *A Diderot Pictorial Encyclopedia of Trades and Industry*, 2 vols (New York: Dover, 1959). That such "documents" continue to be regarded by some as impervious to discursive analysis can be seen in a recent popular anthology of articles which deliberately excludes technical articles: see Alain Pons, Introduction, *Encyclopédie ou Dictionnaire raisonné des sciences, des arts et des métiers (articles choisis)*, 2 vols (Paris: Garnier-Flammarion, 1986) 1:18.

13 Jacques Proust, "L'Article *Bas* de Diderot," in *Langue et langages de Leibniz à l'Encyclopédie*, ed. Michèle Duchet and Michèle Jolley (Paris: Union Générale des Editions, 1977), 250. Many of the articles on Diderot and the *Encyclopédie* cited here respond to this call. For readings of the plates, see in particular Roland Barthes, "Image, raison, déraison," in *L'Univers de l'Encyclopédie*, by R. Barthes, Robert Mauzi, and Jean-Pierre Séguin (Paris: Les Libraires associés, 1964), 1–6; Daniel Brewer, *The Discourse of Enlightenment*, 25–35; Stephen Werner, *Blueprint: A Study of Diderot and the Encyclopédie Plates* (Birmingham: Summa Publications, 1993).

14 Christie McDonald sees a productive tension between "the work of the text" in gesturing toward a utopic, monological whole, and "the text of the work," which "disrupts the system." *The Dialogue of Writing*, 88. Different critics emphasize different sides of this effect. Michèle Duchet sees encyclopedic discourse as "a full [*plein*] and continuous text". ("L'Economie du signe dans le *Système des connaissances* et *L'Encyclopédie*," in M. Duchet and M. Jolley, 332); whereas Jean Starobinski downplays the virtual totality of the *système figuré* in favor of an actual *Encyclopédie* of "particularity and multiplicity" ("Remarques sur l'*Encyclopédie*," *Revue de métaphysique et de morale* 75 (1970): 287.

15 Patrick Coleman, "The Idea of Character in the *Encyclopédie*," *Eighteenth-Century Studies* 13 (1979): 21–47.

16 DPV 7:174. All further page references to "Encyclopédie" are from vol. 7 of the DPV.

17 Janie Vanpée discusses the tropological structure of *renvois* with particular reference to the article "Femme," in " 'Tout à la vérité parle en elles, mais un langage équivoque': The *Encyclopédie*'s Ambiguous Definition of Woman," *Studies on Voltaire and the Eighteenth Century* 304 (1992): 749–52.

18 Wilda Anderson offers an analysis of the kinds of readers evoked by the different ordering structures and *renvois* described in "Encyclopédie" (*Diderot's Dream*, 105–10), to which I would add only the possibility for change and increased understanding that the text offers to all.

19 On the problem of attribution, see R.N. Schwab, W.E. Rex, and John Lough, Preface to *Inventory of Diderot's Encyclopédie*, Studies on Voltaire and the Eighteenth Century 80 (1971): 36–44.

20 Michel Serres, *Hermès I: La Communication* (Paris: Minuit, 1969), 20. This

notion of complex systems is also at the heart of Serre's reading of Leibniz, and offers an occasion for again remarking on the "leibnizianism" of the French Enlightenment. On Diderot's acquaintance with the German philosopher's work, see Yvon Belaval, "Note sur Diderot et Leibniz," *Revue des sciences humaines* 112 (1963): 435–51 (rpt. as "Diderot, lecteur de Leibniz," in Belaval, *Etudes leibniziennes* [Paris: Gallimard, 1976], 244–63). For a suggestive account of Leibniz's notion of the encyclopedia, see François Duchesneau, *Leibniz et la méthode de la science* (Paris: PUF, 1993), 18–55.

21 Given the relational structure of the *Encyclopédie*, one senses a kind of "natural fit" in the work being carried out by the ARTFL project (American and French Research on the Treasury of the French Language) to provide a complete online hypertext edition. The electronic text will enable readers to perform not only the connections envisioned by Diderot and d'Alembert – searching either by alphabetic series of articles or by *renvois* – but also those which have been well-nigh impossible in the book format, such as searches by author, by branch of knowledge, or part of speech. In an ideal universe, access to the *Encyclopédie*'s source texts would further prove instructive. As Diderot points out, it would be better to have too many *renvois* than to omit any ("Encyclopédie," 226). ARTFL, University of Chicago, Dept. of Romance Languages and Literatures. Available on the World Wide Web at http://humanities.uchicago.edu/ARTFL/ARTFL.html.

22 See Barbara Stafford's discussion of the powerful interaction of visual and verbal modes in, for example, Pierre Bayle's "deconstructive" page layouts, or the ability of the reader/viewer of Diderot or Piranesi to achieve a critical perspective by pursuing "a multiplicity of intersected paths" and connecting "various pieces of information for which there was no known order." *Body Criticism: Imagining the Unseen in Enlightenment Art and Medicine* (Cambridge: MIT Press, 1991), 166–67, 176, etc.

23 See among others, George Landow, *Hypertext: The Convergence of Contemporary Critical Theory and Technology* (Baltimore: Johns Hopkins University Press, 1992), esp. 162–201. Gregory Ulmer offers an instructive comparison with Pierre Ramus's logical innovations in *Heuretics: The Logic of Invention* (Baltimore: Johns Hopkins University Press, 1994), 16–38.

24 See Thomas Kavanagh, *Enlightenment and the Shadows of Chance*, 229–47; Jean-Claude Guédon, "Lecture encyclopédique de *Jacques le fataliste*: Pour une épistémologie du *trouble*," *Stanford French Review* 8 (1984): 335–47.

25 Diderot, *Plan d'une université pour le gouvernement de Russie*, in A-T 3:430. All subsequent references to the *Plan* refer to vol. 3 of the A-T edition. On the curriculum's inherent tensions, see Kathryn Ascheim, "*Belles-Lettres* and the University: Diderot's *Plan d'une université ou d'une éducation publique*

dans toutes les sciences," *Yale French Studies* 77 (1990): 61–75; E.S. Burt, "Ordering Education: Diderot's *Plan d'une université pour le gouvernement de Russie.*" Session on "How-To Manuals and Familiar Letters: Prescriptive Texts," ASECS Conference, Cincinnati, 25 April, 1987.

26 In DPV 4:1–107 and 109–233, respectively. References to both texts should be understood as referring to vol. 4 of the DPV.

27 *The Aeneid of Virgil,* trans. Rolfe Humphries (New York: MacMillan, 1987). Book IV, lines 733–38.

28 Bracketed portion not included in Diderot's quotation. Lucretius, *On the Nature of Things,* trans. Frank O. Copley (New York: Norton, 1977). Book I, lines 809–11.

29 Thanks to the conscientiousness of the DPV editors, who include both images, the modern reader does not have to follow this *renvoi* to the point of seeking out the Havercamp *De rerum natura* (see *Sourds* 132 and 186).

30 Diderot cites the aria, "Non ha ragione, ingrato, un core abbandonato," from the Sarro-Metastasio *Didone* of 1724 in the *Salon de 1767* (DPV 16:82).

31 See Marian Hobson's reading of the text's tropological dimension, "*La Lettre sur les sourds et les muets* de Diderot: Labyrinthe et langage," *Semiotica* 16 (1976): 291.

32 The DPV editor gives the following gloss of Diderot's version: "Les ayant pris après avoir tourné leurs empreintes en sens inverse pour qu'ils ne laissassent point de traces en marchant droit devant eux" (*Sourds,* 130). The lines are to be found in Book VIII, lines 216–19 in the Humphries translation of the *Aeneid.*

33 James Doolittle calls attention to the "misquote" and offers this gloss: "[Diderot] apparently intends to show ... that the inversion is as insignificant in Latin as it would be in French." "Hieroglyph and Emblem in Diderot's *Lettre sur les sourds et les muets,*" *Diderot Studies* 2 (1952): 165, n. 17. Obviously, I disagree.

34 Jacques Derrida offers suggestive remarks on Diderot as "a thinker of mimesis who was haunted by blindness," in *Memoirs of the Blind,* trans. P-A Brault and M. Naas (University of Chicago Press, 1993), 102. On the *Lettre sur les aveugles,* see esp. Daniel Brewer, *The Discourse of Enlightenment,* 98–102; Suzanne Pucci, "Vision and the 'I' of the Beholder," *Esprit créateur* 24 (1984): 108–22; William R. Paulson, *Enlightenment, Romanticism, and the Blind in France* (Princeton University Press, 1987). Paulson discusses the Molyneux problem, 21–38.

35 Martin Jay, *Downcast Eyes: The Denigration of Vision in Twentieth-Century French Thought* (Berkeley: University of California Press, 1993), 100. Jay calls the *Lettre* a "challenge to the primacy of vision" in an age of "spectacular cultural politics" and ocularocentric epistemologies. Jay, however, tends to substitute a new primacy of touch for the primacy of sight; I would argue that, while touch is clearly emphasized in the *Lettre*

sur les aveugles and resonates well with Diderot's materialism, Diderot nevertheless resists the temptation to overturn one hierarchy only to replace it with another, but instead demonstrates *one possible* alternative perceptual configuration.

36 For background and analysis of the debate, see Ulrich Ricken, *Grammaire et philosophie au siècle des Lumières* (Publications de l'université de Lille, 1978); Gérard Genette, *Mimologiques: Voyage en Cratylie* (Paris: Seuil, 1976), esp. "Blanc bonnet versus bonnet blanc" (183–226); and Marian Hobson's "Labyrinth et langage" article, cited earlier.

37 James Creech relates this view of language as a "deferral of ideal expression" to Diderot's preoccupations with posterity, self-projection, and a temporality that can only be overcome through a general strategy of proleptic *renvois*. *Thresholds of Representation*, 144–48. See also Suzanne Pucci on "inversion" in Diderot's understanding as a "reversal of chronology" that dislocates a priori reasoning and the privilege of subject over object. *Diderot and a Poetics of Science* (New York: Peter Lang, 1986), 108–9.

38 See Hobson, "Labyrinth," 306. In his dramatic theory, Diderot makes a notably different use of the term "tissu," as referring to factitious juxtapositions that distort reality, as opposed to the seamless *enchaînement* of his *système dramatique*. The conceptual linkage of *enchaînement* and *système*, in both the dramatic texts and the present *Lettre*, is highly significant. See my *Identity and Ideology: Diderot, Sade, and the Serious Genre* (Amsterdam: John Benjamins, 1991), 25–79.

39 James Doolittle has argued that we should understand "hieroglyph" as a particularly resonant fragment, and "emblème" as a complete poem ("Hieroglyph and Emblem," 155). Following this idea, it is tempting to link the subtle power of the hieroglyph with the compelling attraction of the fragmentary, analyzed by Jay Caplan as "the aesthetics of sacrifice" in *Framed Narratives: Diderot's Genealogy of the Beholder* (Minneapolis: University of Minnesota Press, 1985). Or, as Diderot writes in the *Salon de 1767*, "Je suis inspiré par le souffle divin de l'artiste, *Agnosco veteris vestigia flammae*; c'est un mot qui révèle en moi une grande pensée. Dans les transports violents de la passion, l'homme supprime les liaisons, commence une phrase sans la finir, laisse échapper un mot, pousse un cri et se tait; cependant j'ai tout entendu; c'est l'esquisse d'un discours. La passion ne fait que des esquisses." *Salons*, ed. Jean Seznec, 2nd edn., 4 vols. (Oxford: The Clarendon Press, 1983) 3:248. (This passage is not included in the DPV, which is based on a different manuscript source.) The "passion" evoked by the lines from Virgil is, of course, Dido's.

40 Warburton, *Essai sur les hiéroglyphes des Egyptiens*, trans. L. des Malpeines, ed. Patrick Tort, with introductions by Jacques Derrida ("Scribble: Pouvoir/Ecrire") and Patrick Tort (Paris: Aubier Flammarion, 1977). In Derrida's reading, Warburton remains torn between views of hiero-

glyphics as "natural" writing, fulfilling ordinary communicative functions, and as a perversely "veiled" or "encrypted" writing, *écrypture*
meant to preserve the authority of the priestly elite, a conflict that
cannot be wholly resolved, as Warburton attempts to do, by chronolo-
gizing. See also Gérard Genette on Court de Gébelin's understanding
of hieroglyphics as perfectly motivated, mimetic writing ("L'Hiéroglyphe généralisé," *Mimologiques*, 119–48).

41 As Derrida observes of Warburton: "l'écriture hiéroglyphique n'entoure
pas le savoir comme la forme détachable d'un contenant ou d'un
signifiant. Elle structure le contenu de la science." "Scribble," 24. See
also Richard Kroll on Warburton's and others' projects where "visu-
alism seeks to reinforce the primacy of written or printed over aural
media." *Material Word*, 181–86.

42 A similar sensibility echoes in the practice of contemporary Moroccan
writer Abdelkebir Khatibi, who juxtaposes Arabic calligraphy with
French in his novel *Amour bilingue*. As Thomas O. Beebee observes,
"Calligraphy bypasses mimesis by locating the meaning of the word
within the grapheme rather than in anything exterior to language."
"The Fiction of Translation: Abdelkabir Khatibi's *Love in Two Languages*," *Sub-Stance* 73 (1994): 69. The material action of calligraphy in
Islamic culture is further explored by Brinkley Messick, who explains
that although in Islamic society writing initially marks a fall away from
the immediacy of the divine injunction given the Prophet, "Recite...,"
the status of the document throughout the shift from calligraphy to
print embodies and structures social relations: "The poetics of written
space then can be extended to general domains of spatial organization:
towns, architecture, and the space of the state." *The Calligraphic State:
Textual Domination in a Muslim Society* (Berkeley: University of California
Press, 1993), 231.

43 The *Encyclopédie* itself can be seen as another such avatar, as can certain
of Diderot's ideas on music. See Downing A. Thomas, "Musicology
and Hieroglyphics: Questions of Representation in Diderot," *The
Eighteenth Century: Theory and Interpretation* 35 (1994): 64–77. On the
"hieroglyphic" qualities of the *renvois*, see p. 75.

44 See Wilda Anderson's discussion of the "miniarticle 'Langue.'" *Diderot's
Dream*, 95–104.

45 " 'Le premier serment que se firent deux êtres de chair, ce fut au pied
d'un rocher qui tombait en poussière; ils attestèrent de leur constance
un ciel qui n'est pas un instant le même, tout passait en eux et autour
d'eux, et ils croyaient leurs coeurs affranchis de vicissitudes. O enfants
toujours enfants!...' " *Jacques le fataliste* (DPV 23:128).

46 The etymological momentum can be felt in the writing of a number of
contemporary theorists of translation, who emphasize the dynamic
qualities of its hermeneutic leap (Steiner), its "anticipatory, annuncia-
tory" mode (Derrida), and its collaborative, mediating "doubleness"

(Barnstone), as opposed to a monological, transparent notion of linguistic meaning. George Steiner, *After Babel: Aspects of Language and Translation*, 2nd edn. (1975; London: Oxford University Press, 1992); Willis Barnstone, *The Poetics of Translation* (New Haven: Yale University Press, 1993), 15–16; Jacques Derrida, "Des tours de Babel," in *Difference in Translation*, ed. Joseph F. Graham (Ithaca: Cornell University Press, 1985), 230. (Graham's English translation also appears, 165–205. (Elsewhere, Derrida speaks of two alternating modes of translation: "one governed by the classical model of transportable univocality or of a formalizable polysemia, and the other, which goes into dissemination." "Living On/Border Lines," in Bloom *et al.*, *Deconstruction and Criticism* (New York: Seabury Press, 1979), 92n.

47 See Undank's discussion of Diderot as translator (*Inside*, 12–20). Peter France offers a useful historical perspective on translators' freedom and cultural appropriation, in "Translating the British," *Politeness and its Discontents: Problems in French Classical Culture* (Cambridge University Press, 1992), 151–72.

48 Cf. Jean-Claude Choul, "Sémantique synonymique: Une contre-rhétorique Condillac et Diderot," in *Papers in the History of Linguistics*, ed. Hans Aarsleff, L. Kelly, H-J. Niederehe (Amsterdam and Philadelphia: John Benjamins, 1987) 315–26; and Christine Clark-Evans, "Incommensurability and Language Theory in Diderot's 'Encyclopédie,'" *Journal of the Australian Language and Literature Association* 70 (1988): 260–75.

49 Umberto Eco, "Semantics of Metaphor," *The Role of the Reader: Explorations in the Semiotics of Texts* (Bloomington: Indiana University Press, 1984).

50 Walter Benjamin, "The Task of the Translator," *Illuminations*, trans. Harry Zohn (London: Jonathan Cape, 1970), 75.

51 Derrida, *Mémoirs of the Blind*, 102.

52 Denis Diderot, *Lettres à Sophie Volland*, ed. André Babelon, 3 vols (1930; rpt. Paris: Editions d'aujourd'hui, 1978) 1:46.

53 Key references include Georges Bataille, *L'Erotisme* (Paris: Union Générale d'éditions, 1964) 70–77; Mary Douglas, *Purity and Danger: An Analysis of Concepts of Pollution and Taboo* (London: Routledge and Kegan Paul, 1966), 96–104; Peter Stallybrass and Allon White, *The Poetics and Politics of Transgression* (Ithaca: Cornell University Press, 1986).

54 See Neil Hertz, on plagiarism as the fear of "interior difference," ("Two Extravagant Teachings," in *The End of the Line: Essays on Psychoanalysis and the Sublime* [New York: Columbia University Press, 1985], 144–59); Marilyn Randall, on plagiarism as a "revolutionary move" in post-colonial critique ("'Appropriate(d) Discourse: Plagiarism and Decolonization," *New Literary History* 22 [1991]: 525–41).

55 Natalie Zemon Davis points out that du Tilh was actually only found guilty of "imposture and false supposition of name and person and of

adultery"; the additional crimes were added in the 1561 account by Jean de Coras. *The Return of Martin Guerre* (Cambridge: Harvard University Press, 1983), 86, 109.

56 François Gayot de Pitaval, *Causes célèbres et intéressantes, avec les jugements qui les ont décidées*, nouvelle edn., 20 vols. (Paris: Chez Théodore Legras, 1738–43) 1: 49.

57 I have explored this issue at greater length in J. Hayes, "Plagiarism and Legitimation in Eighteenth-Century France," *The Eighteenth Century: Theory and Interpretation* 34 (1993): 115–31.

58 Diderot, *Essai sur les règnes de Claude et de Néron*. DPV 25: 228. For Naigeon's footnote, see the appendix pp. 436–7. All references to the *Essai* are to vol. 25 of the DPV.

59 See Herbert Josephs, *"Essai sur les règnes de Claude et de Néron*: A Final Borrowing," in *Diderot: Digression and Dispersion*, ed. Jack Undank and Herbert Josephs (Lexington: French Forum Publishers, 1984), 138–49.

60 Denis Diderot, *Sur la liberté de la presse*, ed. Jacques Proust (Paris: Editions sociales, 1964). All subsequent references are to this edition.

61 Volume 12 of the DPV, from which come all subsequent references, rectifies the situation. Carol Sherman, one of the few critics to underscore the relationship among the three works and to treat them together, nevertheless reads them out of order and is more concerned with analyzing their rhetorical and formal parallels, than with reading them as a single work. See her *Diderot and the Art of Dialogue* (Genève: Droz, 1976).

62 Jeffrey Mehlman reads the clouds as part of an ongoing textual instantiation of the Lucretian fall of atoms in Diderot's work. The Lucretian subtext lends a subversive reverberation to the triptych's weather picture, offering chance and dissipation in the place of predictability and order. *Cataract: A Study in Diderot* (Middletown, CT: Wesleyan University Press, 1979), 27–32.

63 The destabilizing of authority, productivity, and even representation has of course already been inaugurated in the dissonance between the dialogue's negative title and its opening words. See Suzanne R. Pucci, "*'Ceci n'est pas ...'* Negative Framing in Diderot and Magritte," *Mosaic* 20, no. 3 (1987): 1–14. For a narratological reading of the frame as commentary, see William Edmiston, "The Role of the Listener: Narrative Technique in Diderot's 'Ceci n'est pas un conte,'" *Diderot Studies* 20 (1981): 61–75.

64 In Virginia Swain's account of narrative contracts in the dialogue, the traditional narrative pact is replaced with a grimmer convention, that of blackmail or agreed dissimulation, which *"unites* 'self' and 'other' in alienation and *duplicity.*" Conventional Wisdom and Conventional Acts: The Narrative Contract in Diderot's 'Ceci n'est pas un conte,'" *Eighteenth-Century Studies* 17 (1983): 14–27.

65 Tony Tanner, *Adultery and the Novel: Contract and Transgression* (Baltimore:

Johns Hopkins University Press, 1979). Eighteenth-century legal scholar Jean-François Fournel deplores the "inégalité" in the ways that the law views infidelity in men and women ("étrange distinction qui annonce assez que ce sont les *hommes* qui ont fait les Loix!") but rationalizes it in reflecting that the law sets so heavy a burden of proof on aggrieved husbands, that women are de facto as exempt from prosecution as men are de jure. *Traité de l'adultère, considéré dans l'ordre judiciaire* (Paris: Chez J-F Bastien, 1778), XVII.

66 Carlière's language is echoed in J-F Fournel's discussion of a husband's "possession" of his wife: "Posséder une femme, ce n'est pas seulement être en droit de disposer de sa personne (disposition que l'Adultere des femmes enleve souvent au mari), c'est occuper son coeur, être l'objet de ses attentions, de ses craintes, de ses alarmes; c'est diriger ses idées, gouverner son esprit, maîtriser ses volontés: voilà la véritable jouissance d'un mari, & c'est précisément celle qu'un Adultere lui enleve." *Traité de l'adultère*, 276–67.

67 Wilda Anderson, *Diderot's Dream*, 127–77. See Georges Van Den Abbeele, "Utopian Sexuality and its Discontents: Exoticism and Colonialism in the *Supplément au Voyage de Bougaineville*," *Esprit créateur* 24.1 (1984): 43–52.

68 An additional irony of which Diderot may not have been aware: the Polly Baker story, while neither Diderot nor Raynal's invention – its source was a London newspaper account – was nevertheless a fiction, a mystification by Benjamin Franklin (DPV 12:614 n.50). On the tale's odd paternity and its reappropriation in contemporary bio-politics, see Christie McDonald, "Opérateurs du changement: De Miss Polly Baker à Murphy Brown," *Œuvres et critiques* 19.1 (1994): 68–78.

69 Although her emphasis on the efficacy of "communicative action" differs from the approach taken here, Diane Fourny comes to many similar conclusions in her reading of the triptych. "Ethics and Otherness: An Exploration of Diderot's Conte moral," *Studies in Eighteenth-Century Culture* 27 (1998): 283–306.

70 William R. Paulson, *The Noise of Culture: Literary Texts in a World of Information* (Ithaca: Cornell University Press, 1988), 146.

71 Niklas Luhmann, *Love as Passion: The Codification of Intimacy*, trans. J. Gaines and D.L. Jones (Cambridge: Harvard University Press, 1986).

72 Although I encountered her work after the present analysis was complete, I wish to signal Marilynn Desmond's *Reading Dido: Gender, Textuality, and the Medieval Aeneid* (Minneapolis: University of Minnesota Press, 1994), for another range of responses to the Dido variant. Desmond presents woman-centered evocations of Dido in a rich medieval counter-tradition leading up to the "feminist self-fashioning" of Christine de Pizan.

73 Mohammed Dib, *Qui se souvient de la mer* (Paris: Seuil, 1962), 185. English translation: "'Exploding one after the other, the new constructions all

went up in smoke, to the very last one, following which the walls fell apart and collapsed: the city was dead, its remaining inhabitants standing in the middle of the ruins like desiccated trees, in the pose in which the cataclysm had surprised them, until the arrival of the sea, whose tumult had long been heard, and which quickly covered them beneath the endless rocking of its waves.'

At times there still comes to me a sound of something shattering, of muffled singing, and I let my thoughts wander, I remember the sea." *Who Remembers the Sea*, trans. Louis Tremaine (Washington, DC: Three Continents Press, 1985).

CONCLUSION – LABYRINTHS OF ENLIGHTENMENT

1 On the evolution of Le Nôtre's gardens, see Allen S. Weiss, *Mirrors of Infinity: The French Formal Garden and Seventeenth-Century Metaphysics* (New York: Princeton Architectural Press, 1995); F. Hamilton Hazlehurst, *Gardens of Illusion: The Genius of André Le Nostre* (Nashville: Vanderbilt University Press, 1980). For an account of the labyrinth, see Michel Conan, "Les Jardins infinis," postface to Charles Perrault, *Le Labyrinthe de Versailles*, facsimile edn. with engravings by Sébastien Le Clerc (1677; rpt. Paris: Editions du Moniteur, 1982), n.p.

2 Louis XIV, *Manière de montrer les jardins de Versailles*, preface by Raoul Girardet (Paris: Plon, 1951), 20. As Girardet observes in the preface, "Le texte de Louis XIV ne laisse aucune place à l'abandon, à la flânerie, au vagabondage. La promenade est un acte de la vie du souverain et elle doit être réglée selon les mêmes principes qui régissent tous les autres actes de la vie royale" (4).

3 Madeleine de Scudéry, *La Promenade de Versailles* (1669; rpt. Paris: Devambez, 1920), 52.

4 See Elizabeth J. MacArthur, "Nature Made Word: Guidebooks to the Gardens at Versailles," *Cahiers du dix-septième siècle* 5, no. 1 (1991): 183–94.

5 Louis Marin, "Classical, Baroque: Versailles, or the Architecture of the Prince," *Yale French Studies* 80 (1991): 180. See also Jean-Marie Apostolidès on "mythistoire," *Le Roi-machine: Spectacle et politique au temps de Louis XIV* (Paris: Minuit, 1981), esp. the reading of the gardens, pp. 89–92.

6 I am indebted here to Penelope Reed Doob's fine study, *The Idea of the Labyrinth from Classical Antiquity through the Middle Ages* (Ithaca: Cornell University Press, 1990).

7 William Bouwsma, *John Calvin: A Sixteenth-Century Portrait* (New York: Oxford University Press, 1988), 32–48. It is interesting to notice that "labyrinth" and "abyss" have become synonyms for Voltaire, as he indicates in his letter on Newton's calculus, speaking of "the labyrinth and the abyss of the infinite" (*Lettres philosophiques*, XVII).

8 G. Nador, "Métaphores de chemins et labyrinthes chez Descartes," *Revue philosophique* 152 (1962): 48.

9 Roger Herzel, "The Scenery for the Original Production of *Don Juan*," in *The Age of Theatre in France: Dramatic Literature and Performance from Corneille to Beaumarchais*, ed. David Trott and Nicole Boursier (Edmonton: Academic Printing and Publishing, 1988), 247–55.

10 See Jean Ehrard, "L'Arbre et le labyrinthe," in *L'Encyclopédie, Diderot, l'esthétique: Mélanges en hommage à Jacques Chouillet*, eds. S. Auroux *et al.* (Paris: PUF, 1991), 239.

11 Jean-Marie Benoist makes a similar argument in his analysis of the "return of Leibniz" in poststructuralist thought. *La Révolution structurale* (Paris: Grasset, 1975). As we have seen, Leibniz also "returns" in various forms, throughout the eighteenth century.

12 N. Katherine Hayles, *Chaos Bound: Orderly Disorder in Contemporary Literature and Science* (Ithaca: Cornell University Press, 1990), esp. 209–35. For an account specifically relating Diderot to theories of complexity, see Huguette Cohen, "Diderot's Cosmic Games: Revisiting a Dilemma," *Diderot Studies* 26 (1995): 71–87.

13 *L'Année dernière à Marienbad*, directed by Alain Resnais, screenplay Alain Robbe-Grillet, Astor Pictures, 1961, 90 min. English translation: "The park of this hotel was a kind of garden à la française without any trees or flowers, without any foliage ... Gravel, stone, marble and straight lines marked out rigid spaces, surfaces without mystery. It seemed, at first glance, impossible to get lost here ... at first glance ... down straight paths, between the statues with frozen gestures and the granite slabs, where you were now already getting lost, forever, in the calm night, alone with me." *Last Year at Marienbad* [screenplay], trans. Richard Howard (New York: Grove Press, 1962), 165.

Bibliography

Adorno, Theodor. *Negative Dialectics*. trans. E.B. Ashton. New York: Seabury Press, 1973.

d'Alembert, Jean le Rond. *Recherches sur differents points importants du système du monde*. 3 vols. Paris: David l'aîné, 1754.

[Alletz, Pons-Augustin.] *Manuel de l'homme du monde, ou Connoissance générale des principaux états de la Société, & de toutes les matières qui sont le sujet des conversations ordinaires*. Paris: Chez Guillyn, 1761.

Altman, Janet. *Epistolarity: Approaches to a Form*. Columbus: Ohio State University Press, 1982.

"The Letter Book as a Literary Institution 1539–1789: Toward a Cultural History of Published Correspondences in France." Porter 17–62.

Anderson, Benedict. *Imagined Communities: Reflections on the Origin and Spread of Nationalism*. Revised edn. 1983; London: Verso, 1991.

Anderson, Wilda. *Diderot's Dream*. Baltimore: Johns Hopkins University Press, 1990.

Apostolidès, Jean-Marie. *Le Roi-machine: Spectacle et politique au temps de Louis XIV*. Paris: Minuit, 1981.

Arnauld, Antoine, and Lancelot Nicole. *La Logique ou l'art de penser*. Paris: Flammarion, 1970.

Ascheim, Kathryn. "*Belles-Lettres* and the University: Diderot's *Plan d'une université ou d'une éducation publique dans toutes les sciences*." *Yale French Studies* 77 (1990): 61–75.

Auerbach, Erich. "*Figura*." *Scenes from the Drama of European Literature*. Minneapolis: University of Minnesota Press, 1984, 11–76.

Auroux, Sylvain. "Condillac ou la vertu des signes." Introduction to *La Langue des calculs*, by Condillac. XIII–XIV.

"Empirisme et théorie linguistique chez Condillac." Sgard 177–219.

La Sémiotique des encyclopédistes. Paris: Payot, 1979.

Badinter, Elisabeth. *Emilie, Emilie: L'ambition féminine au XVIIIe siècle*. Paris: Flammarion, 1983.

[Bailly, Jean-Sylvain.] *Eloge de Leibnitz, qui a remporté le prix à l'académie royale des Sciences & Belles-Lettres de Prusse en 1768*. n.p.: n.d. [Pages numbered 129–218 in the copy at the Bibliothèque nationale.]

Histoire de l'astronomie moderne depuis la fondation de l'école d'Alexandrie, jusqu'à l'époque de M.D.C.C.X.X.X. 3 vols. Paris: Chez les Frères de Bure, 1779–82.

Baldi, Camillo. *La Lettre déchiffrée.* trans. Anne-Marie Debet and Alessandro Fontana. Paris: Les Belles Lettres, 1993. Translation of *Trattato come da una lettera missiva si conoscano la natura e le qualità dello scrittore.* 1622.

Barber, William H. *Leibniz in France from Arnauld to Voltaire: A Study in French Reaction to Leibnizianism, 1670–1760.* Oxford: Clarendon Press, 1955.

"Mme Du Châtelet and Leibnizianism: The Genesis of the *Institutions de physique.*" *The Age of Enlightenment: Studies Presented to Theodore Besterman.* ed. Barber *et al.* Edinburgh and London: Oliver and Boyd, 1967, 200–22.

Barnstone, Willis. *The Poetics of Translation.* New Haven: Yale University Press, 1993.

Barthes, Roland. *Fragments d'un discours amoureux.* Paris: Seuil, 1977.

"Image, raison, déraison." *L'Univers de l'Encyclopédie,* by Barthes, Robert Mauzi, and Jean-Pierre Séguin. Paris: Les Libraires associés, 1964, 1–6.

Bataille, Georges. *L'Erotisme.* Paris: Union Générale d'éditions, 1964.

Bates, David. "The Epistemology of Error in Late Enlightenment France." *Eighteenth-Century Studies* 29 (1996): 307–27.

Bazerman, Charles. *Shaping Written Knowledge: The Genre and Activity of the Experimental Article in Science.* Madison: University of Wisconsin Press, 1988.

Beebee, Thomas O. "The Fiction of Translation: Abdelkabir Khatibi's *Love in Two Languages.*" *SubStance* 73 (1994): 63–78.

Belaval, Yvon. "Note sur Diderot et Leibniz." *Revue des sciences humaines* 112 (1963): 435–51. Rpt. as "Diderot, lecteur de Leibniz," in Belaval, *Etudes leibniziennes.* Paris: Gallimard, 1976, 244–63.

Benhabib, Seyla. *Critique, Norm and Utopia: A Study of the Foundations of Critical Theory.* New York: Columbia University Press, 1986.

Benjamin, Walter. *Illuminations.* trans. Harry Zohn. ed. Hannah Arendt. London: Jonathan Cape, 1970.

Reflections: Essays, Aphorisms, Autobiographical Writings. ed. Peter Demetz. trans. Edmund Jephcott. New York: Harcourt, Brace, Jovanovich, 1978.

Bennet, Jonathan. *A Study of Spinoza's Ethics.* Indianapolis: Hackett, 1984.

Benoist, Jean-Marie. *La Révolution structurale.* Paris: Grasset, 1975.

Benrekassa, Georges. *Le Langage des Lumières: Concepts et savoir de la langue.* Paris: PUF, 1995.

Berman, Morris. *The Reenchantment of the World.* Ithaca: Cornell University Press, 1981.

Bernstein, Richard J. "Foucault: Critique as a Philosophical Ethos." *Philosophical Interventions in the Unfinished Project of Enlightenment.* ed. Axel Honneth *et al.* Cambridge: MIT Press, 1992, 280–310.

"The Rage Against Reason." *Construction and Constraint: The Shaping of Scientific Reason.* ed. Ernan McMullin. University of Notre Dame Press, 1988, 189–221.

Bonfiglio, Thomas P. "The Patrilineal Discourse of Enlightenment: Reading Foucault Reading Kant." *Bulletin de la société américaine de philosophie française* 6 (1994): 104–15.

Bordo, Susan. *The Flight to Objectivity: Essays on Cartesianism and Culture.* Albany: SUNY Press, 1987.

Bossis, Mireille. "Methodological Journeys Through Correspondences." Porter 63–75.

[Bouhours, Père Dominique.] *Remarques nouvelles sur la langue françoise.* Paris: Chez Sébastien Marbre-Cramoisy, 1675.

Bouwsma, William. *John Calvin: A Sixteenth-Century Portrait.* New York: Oxford University Press, 1988.

Brewer, Daniel. *The Discourse of Enlightenment in Eighteenth-Century France: Diderot and the Art of Philosophizing.* Cambridge University Press, 1993.

Broberg, Gunnar. "The Broken Circle." Frängsmyr 45–71.

Bryson, Norman. *Word and Image: French Painting of the Ancien Regime.* Cambridge University Press, 1981.

Buffat, Marc. "Conversation par écrit." *Recherches sur Diderot et l'Encyclopédie* 9 (1990): 55–69.

"Les Lettres à Sophie Volland: Relation amoureuse et relation épistolaire." Diaz 33–45.

Buffon, Georges-Louis Leclerc, comte de. "Histoire naturelle: Premier discours." *Œuvres philosophiques.* ed. Jean Piveteau. Paris: PUF, 1954.

Burt, E.S. "Ordering Education: Diderot's *Plan d'une université pour le gouvernement de Russie.*" Unpublished essay.

Callot, Emile. "Système et méthode dans l'histoire de la botanique." *Revue d'histoire des sciences* 18 (1965): 45–53.

Caplan, Jay. *Framed Narratives: Diderot's Genealogy of the Beholder.* Minneapolis: University of Minnesota Press, 1985.

Cartwright, Michael. "Diderot's Discursive Eye: Peripatetics and the Search for Harmony." Undank and Josephs 72–84.

Cassirer, Ernst. *The Philosophy of the Enlightenment.* trans. F.C.A. Koelln and J.P. Pettegrove. Princeton University Press, 1951.

Castle, Terry. "The Female Thermometer." *Representations* 17 (1987): 1–27.

Chouillet, Jacques. "La Promenade Vernet." *Recherches sur Diderot et l'Encyclopédie* 2 (1987): 123–63.

Choul, Jean-Claude. "Sémantique synonymique: Une contre-rhétorique Condillac et Diderot." *Papers in the History of Linguistics.* ed. Hans Aarsleff, Louis G. Kelly, and Hans-Josef Niederehe. Amsterdam and Philadelphia: John Benjamins, 1987, 315–26.

Christensen, Jerome. *Practicing Enlightenment: Hume and the Formation of a Literary Career.* Madison: University of Wisconsin Press, 1987.

Clark, Hilary. "Encyclopedic Discourse." *SubStance* 67 (1992): 95–110.

Clark-Evans, Christine. "Incommensurability and Language Theory in Diderot's 'Encyclopédie.'" *Journal of the Australian Language and Literature Association* 70 (1988): 260–75.

Cohen, Huguette. "Diderot's Cosmic Games: Revisiting a Dilemma." *Diderot Studies* 26 (1995): 71–87.

Cohen, I. Bernard. *Introduction to Newton's "Principia."* Cambridge: Harvard University Press, 1971.

The Newtonian Revolution. Cambridge University Press, 1980.

Coleman, Patrick. "Character in an Eighteenth-Century Context." *The Eighteenth Century: Theory and Interpretation* 24 (1983): 51–63.

"The Idea of Character in the *Encyclopédie.*" *Eighteenth-Century Studies* 13 (1979): 21–47.

Condillac, Etienne Bonnot, Abbé de. *La Langue des calculs.* ed. Anne-Marie Chouillet. Presses Universitaires de Lille, 1981.

Œuvres philosophiques. ed. Le Roy. 3 vols. Paris: PUF, 1947.

Creech, James. *Diderot: Thresholds of Representation.* Columbus: Ohio State University Press, 1986.

Crocker, Lester. "The Enlightenment: What and Who?" *Studies in Eighteenth-Century Culture* 17 (1987): 335–47.

[Cureau de la Chambre, Marin.] *Le Systeme de l'ame.* Paris: Chez Jacques d'Allin, 1664.

Daniel, Georges. *Le Style de Diderot.* Genève: Droz, 1986.

Daston, Lorraine. *Classical Probability in the Enlightenment.* Princeton University Press, 1988.

Davidson, Hugh M. "The Problem of Scientific Order versus Alphabetical Order in the *Encyclopédie.*" *Studies in Eighteenth-Century Culture* 2 (1972): 33–49.

"Voltaire Explains Newton: An Episode in the History of Rhetoric." *The Dialectic of Discovery.* ed. John Lyons and Nancy Vickers. Lexington, KY: French Forum, 1984. 72–82.

Davis, Natalie Zemon. *The Return of Martin Guerre.* Cambridge: Harvard University Press, 1983.

DeJean, Joan. *Tender Geographies: Women and the Origins of the Novel in France.* New York: Columbia University Press, 1991.

De la Carrera, Rosalina. *Success in Circuit Lies: Diderot's Communicational Practice.* Stanford University Press, 1991.

Deleuze, Gilles. *Différence et répétition.* Paris: PUF, 1968.

Le Pli: Leibniz et le baroque. Paris: Minuit, 1988.

Deleuze, Gilles and Félix Guattari. *Capitalisme et schizophrénie I: L'Anti-Œdipe.* Paris: Minuit, 1972. *Anti-Œdipus: Capitalism and Schizophrenia,* trans. Robert Hurley, Mark Stern, and Helen Lane. Minneapolis: University of Minnesota Press, 1983.

Capitalisme et schizophrénie II: Mille plateaux. Paris: Minuit, 1980. *A Thousand Plateaus,* trans. Brian Massumi. Minneapolis: University of Minnesota Press, 1987.

Delon, Michel. "Savoir totalisant et forme éclatée." *Dix-huitième siècle* 14 (1982): 13–26.

De Man, Paul. *Allegories of Reading: Figural Language in Rousseau, Nietzsche, Rilke, and Proust.* New Haven: Yale University Press, 1979.

"The Epistemology of Metaphor." *Critical Inquiry* 5 (1978): 13–30.

Deprun, Jean. *La Philosophie de l'inquiétude en France au XVIIIe siècle.* Paris: Vrin, 1979.

Derathé, Robert. *Jean-Jacques Rousseau et la science politique de son temps.* 2nd edn. Paris: Vrin, 1974.

Derrida, Jacques. "L'Archéologie du frivole." Intro. to *Essai sur l'origine des connaissances humaines*, by Condillac. ed. Charles Porset. Paris: Galilée, 1973.

"Des tours de Babel." *Difference in Translation.* ed. Joseph F. Graham, Ithaca: Cornell University Press, 1985. 209–48. Rpt. in Derrida, *Psyché: Inventions de l'autre.* Paris: Galilée, 1987.

"Envois." In *The Post Card from Socrates to Freud and Beyond*, trans. Alan Bass (University of Chicago Press, 1987).

"La Langue et le discours de la méthode." *Cahiers du groupe de recherches sur la philosophie et le langage* 3 (1983): 35–51.

"Living On/Border Lines." trans. James Hulbert. *Deconstruction and Criticism.* By Harold Bloom *et al.* New York: Seabury Press, 1979, 75–176.

Memoirs of the Blind. trans. P-A Brault and M. Naas. University of Chicago Press, 1993.

"Scribble." Intro. to Warburton 7–43. Translated by Cary Plotkin as "Scribble (writing-power), *Yale French Studies* 58 (1979): 117–47.

Descartes, René. *Descartes, la princesse Elisabeth et la reine Christine, d'après des lettres inédites.* ed. Louis-Antoine Foucher de Careil. Paris and Amsterdam: Germer-Baillière and Mulier, 1879.

Lettres sur la morale: Correspondance avec la princesse Elisabeth, Chanut et la reine Christine. ed. Jacques Chevalier. Paris: Boivin, 1953.

Œuvres. ed. C. Adam and P. Tannery. 12 vols. Paris: Vrin, 1967.

Desjardins, Marie-Catherine. *Lettres et billets galants.* ed. Micheline Cuénin. Paris: Publications de la société d'étude du XVIIe siècle, 1975.

Desmond, Marilynn. *Reading Dido: Gender, Textuality, and the Medieval Aeneid.* Minneapolis: University of Minnesota Press, 1994.

Détienne, Marcel, and Jean-Pierre Vernant. *Cunning Intelligence in Greek Culture and Society.* trans. Janet Lloyd. Atlantic Highlands, NJ: Humanities Press, 1978.

D'Holbach, Paul Henri Thiry, baron. *Systême de la nature, ou des loix du monde physique & du monde moral.* 2 vols. London, 1770; Genève: Slatkine, 1973.

Diaz, Jean-Louis, ed. *La Lettre d'amour.* Special issue of *Textuel* 24 (1992).

Diderot, Denis. *Lettres à Sophie Volland.* ed. André Babelon. 3 vols. 1930. Rpt. Paris: Editions d'aujourd'hui, 1978.

Œuvres complètes. ed. Herbert Dieckmann, Jacques Proust, Jean Varloot *et al.* 33 vols. Paris: Hermann, 1975–.

"Pensées détachées sur la peinture." *Œuvres esthéthiques.* ed. Paul Vernière. Paris: Garnier, 1968. 749–840.

Plan d'une université pour le gouvernement de Russie. Œuvres de Diderot. eds. J. Assezat and M. Tourneux. 20 vols. 1875–77. Rpt. Nedeln, Liechtenstein: Kraus, 1966. 3:409–534.

Salons. ed. Jean Seznec. 2nd edn. 4 vols. Oxford: Clarendon Press, 1983.

Sur la liberté de la presse. ed. Jacques Proust. Paris: Editions sociales, 1964.

Diderot, Denis, and Jean le Rond d'Alembert. *Encyclopédie ou dictionnaire raisonné des sciences, des arts & des métiers.* 1751–1761; New York: Readex Microprint Corporation, 1969.

Didier, Béatrice. "L'Ecoute musicale chez Diderot." *Diderot Studies* 23 (1988): 55–73.

Dieckmann, Herbert. *Cinq leçons sur Diderot.* Genève: Droz, 1959.

Doob, Penelope Reed. *The Idea of the Labyrinth from Classical Antiquity through the Middle Ages.* Ithaca: Cornell University Press, 1990.

Doolittle, James. "Hieroglyph and Emblem in Diderot's *Lettre sur les sourds et les muets.*" *Diderot Studies* 2 (1952): 148–67.

Dortous de Mairan, Jean Jacques. *Dissertation sur l'estimation et la mesure des forces motrices des corps.* 1728. Reprinted in the 2nd edn. of Du Châtelet's *Institutions* (1741; see ref. under Du Châtelet).

Douglas, Mary. *Purity and Danger: An Analysis of Concepts of Pollution and Taboo.* London: Routledge and Kegan Paul, 1966.

Du Châtelet, Gabrielle-Emilie Le Tonnelier de Breteuil, Marquise. *Institutions physiques,* nouvelle edition. 1742. Rpt. in Vol. 28 of Christian Wolff, *Gesammelte Werke Materialien und Dokumente.* eds. J. Ecole *et al.* Heldesheim, Zurich, New York: Georg Olms, 1988.

Institutions de physique. Manuscript. BN f.fr. 12265. Bibliothèque Nationale, Paris.

Les Lettres de la marquise du Châtelet. ed. Theodore Besterman. 2 vols. Genève: Institut et Musée Voltaire, 1958.

Trans. "Mme du Châtelet's Translation of the 'Fable of the Bees.' " ed. Ira O. Wade. *Studies on Voltaire, with Some Unpublished Papers of Mme du Châtelet.* Princeton University Press, 1947, 131–87.

Trans. *Les Principes de Newton.* Manuscript. BN f.fr. 12267. Bibliothèque Nationale, Paris.

Duchesneau, François. *Leibniz et la méthode de la science.* Paris: PUF, 1993.

Duchet, Michèle. "L'Economie du signe dans le *Système des connaissances* et l'*Encyclopédie.*" Duchet and Jolley 323–49.

Duchet, Michèle, and Michèle Jolley, eds. *Langues et langages de Leibniz à l'Encyclopédie.* Paris: Union Générale des Editions, 1977.

Du Marsais, César-Chesneau. *Des tropes.* ed. P. Fontanier. 2 vols. 1818. Rpt. Genève: Slatkine, 1984.

Durand-Serail, Béatrice. Intro. to *Leçons de clavecin*. Diderot, *Ecrits sur la musique*. Paris: Lattès, 1987.

Eagleton, Terry. *The Rape of Clarissa*. Minneapolis: University of Minnesota Press, 1982.

Eco, Umberto. "Semantics of Metaphor." *The Role of the Reader: Explorations in the Semiotics of Texts*. Bloomington: Indiana University Press, 1984, 67–89.

Edmiston, William. "The Role of the Listener: Narrative Technique in Diderot's 'Ceci n'est pas un conte.'" *Diderot Studies* 20 (1981): 61–75.

Ehrard, Jean. "L'Arbre et le labyrinthe." *L'Encyclopédie, Diderot, l'esthétique: Mélanges en hommage à Jacques Chouillet*. ed. S. Auroux, D. Bourel, and C. Porset. Paris: PUF, 1991. 233–39.

L'Idée de nature en France dans la première moitié du XVIIIe siècle. 1963. Rpt. Genève: Slatkine, 1981.

Encyclopédie Project. ARTFL, University of Chicago, Dept. of Romance Languages and Literatures. Available on World Wide Web at http://humanities.uchicago.edu/ARTFL/ARTFL.html.

Flax, Jane. "Is Enlightenment Emancipatory?" *Disputed Subjects: Essays on Psychoanalysis, Politics, and Philosophy*. New York: Routledge, 1993, 75–91.

Fontenelle, Bernard Le Bovier de. "Sur l'utilité des Mathématiques et de la Physique." *Histoire du renouvellement de l'Académie royale des sciences en MDCXCIX et les éloges historiques de tous les Académiciens morts depuis ce Renouvellement*. Amsterdam: Chez Pierre de Coup, 1709.

Foucault, Michel. *Les Mots et les choses: Une Archéologie des sciences humaines*. Paris: Gallimard, 1966. Translated as *The Order of Things: An Archeology of the Human Sciences*. New York: Random House, 1970.

Naissance de la clinique. Paris: PUF, 1963.

Surveiller et punir: Naissance de la prison. Paris: Gallimard, 1975.

"Qu'est-ce que les Lumières?" *Dits et écrits 1954–1988*. ed. Daniel Defert and François Ewald, 4 vols. Paris: Gallimard, 1994. 4:562–78. Translated as "What is Enlightenment?" trans. Catherine Porter. *The Foucault Reader*, ed. Paul Rabinow. New York: Pantheon, 1984. 32–50.

Foucault, Michel, and Richard Sennet. "Sexuality and Solitude." *Humanities in Review* 1 (1982): 3–21.

Fournel, Jean-François. *Traité de l'adultère, considéré dans l'ordre judiciaire*. Paris: Chez J-F Bastien, 1778.

Fourny, Diane. "Ethics and Otherness: An Exploration of Diderot's Conte moral." *Studies in Eighteenth-Century Culture* 27 (1998): 283–306.

France, Peter. "Translating the British." *Politeness and its Discontents: Problems in French Classical Culture*. Cambridge University Press, 1992, 151–72.

Frängsmyr, Tore, J.L. Heilbron, and Robin E. Rider, eds. *The Quantifying Spirit in the Eighteenth Century*. Berkeley: University of California Press, 1987.

Frankfurt, Harry G., ed. *Leibniz: A Collection of Critical Essays*. 1972. Rpt. University of Notre Dame Press, 1976.

Fraser, Nancy. "Foucault on Modern Power: Empirical Insights and Normative Confusions." *Praxis International* 1 (1981, October): 272–88.

Fried, Michael. *Absorption and Theatricality: Painting and the Beholder in the Age of Diderot.* Berkeley: University of California Press, 1980.

[Gamaches, Etienne-Simon]. *Système du coeur, ou conjectures sur la manière dont naissent les différentes affections de l'ame, principalement par rapport aux objects sensibles.* Paris: Chez Denys Dupuis, 1704. [Author given as "M. de Clarigny" on title page.]

Gayot de Pitaval, François. *Causes célèbres et intéressantes, avec les jugements qui les ont décidées.* Nouvelle edn., 20 vols. Paris: Chez Théodore Legras, 1738–43.

Genette, Gérard. *Mimologiques: Voyage en Cratylie.* Paris: Seuil, 1976.

Gillespie, C. G., ed. *A Diderot Pictorial Encyclopedia of Trades and Industry.* 2 vols. New York: Dover, 1959.

Goldsmith, Elizabeth. *Exclusive Conversations: The Art of Interaction in Seventeenth-Century France.* Philadelphia: University of Pennsylvania Press, 1988.

——— "Publishing Passion: Madame de Villedieu's *Lettres et billets galants.*" *Papers on Seventeenth-Century French Literature* 37 (1987): 439–50.

——— ed. *Writing the Female Voice.* Boston: Northeastern University Press, 1989.

Goodman, David. "Buffon's *Histoire naturel* as a Work of the Enlightenment." North and Roche 57–65.

Goodman, Dena. "Enlightenment Salons: The Convergence of Female and Philosophic Ambitions." *Eighteenth-Century Studies* 22 (1989): 329–50.

——— *The Republic of Letters: A Cultural History of the French Enlightenment.* Ithaca: Cornell University Press, 1994.

Graffigny, Françoise d'Issemberg d'Happencourt de. *Correspondance de Madame de Graffigny.* ed. J.A. Dainard *et al.* 4 vols. to date. Oxford: Voltaire Foundation, 1985 – .

Grassi, Marie-Claire. "Friends and Lovers (or the Codification of Intimacy)." Porter 77–92.

——— "Lettres d'amour en archives." Diaz 47–55.

Guédon, Jean-Claude. "Lecture encyclopédique de *Jacques le fataliste*: Pour une épistémologie du trouble." *Stanford French Review* 8 (1984): 335–47.

Habermas, Jürgen. *The Philosophical Discourse of Modernity: Twelve Lectures.* trans. Frederick Lawrence. Cambridge: MIT Press, 1987.

——— "Taking Aim at the Heart of the Present," *Foucault: A Critical Reader.* ed. David Couzens Hoy. Oxford: Blackwell, 1986, 103–8.

Hall, Rupert. "Newton in France: A New View." *History of Science* 13 (1975): 233–50.

Hankins, Thomas L. "Eighteenth-Century Attempts to Resolve the *Vis Viva* Controversy." *Isis* 56 (1965): 281–97.

——— *Science and the Enlightenment.* Cambridge University Press, 1985.

Harpham, Geoffrey Galt. "So ... What *Is* Enlightenment? An Inquisition into Modernity." *Critical Inquiry* 20 (1994): 524–56.

Harth, Erica. *Cartesian Women: Versions and Subversions of Rational Discourse in the Old Regime*. Ithaca: Cornell University Press, 1992.

Hasnaoui, Chantal. "Condillac, chemins du sensualisme." Duchet and Jolley 97–129.

Hayes, Julie C. *Identity and Ideology: Diderot, Sade, and the Serious Genre*. Amsterdam: John Benjamins, 1991.

——. "Plagiarism and Legitimation in Eighteenth-Century France." *The Eighteenth Century: Theory and Interpretation* 34 (1993): 115–31.

——. "Sequence and Simultaneity in Diderot's *Promenade Vernet* and *Leçons de clavecin*." *Eighteenth-Century Studies* 29 (1996): 291–305.

——. "Sophistry and Displacement: The Poetics of Sade's Ciphers." *Studies on Voltaire and the Eighteenth Century* 242 (1986): 335–43.

Hayles, N. Katherine. *Chaos Bound: Orderly Disorder in Contemporary Literature and Science*. Ithaca: Cornell University Press, 1990.

Hazlehurst, F. Hamilton. *Gardens of Illusion: The Genius of André Le Nostre*. Nashville: Vanderbilt University Press, 1980.

Hertz, Neil. "Two Extravagant Teachings." *The End of the Line: Essays on Psychoanalysis and the Sublime*. New York: Columbia University Press, 1985, 144–59.

Herzel, Roger. "The Scenery for the Original Production of *Dom Juan*." *The Age of Theatre in France: Dramatic Literature and Performance from Corneille to Beaumarchais*. ed. David Trott and Nicole Boursier. Edmonton: Academic Printing and Publishing, 1988, 247–55.

Hiley, David R. *Philosophy in Question: Essays on a Pyrrhonian Theme*. University of Chicago Press, 1988.

Hine, Ellen McNiven. "Dortous de Mairan, the 'Cartonian.'" *Studies on Voltaire and the Eighteenth Century* 266 (1989): 163–79.

——. *A Critical Study of Condillac's Traité des systèmes*. The Hague: Nijhoff, 1979.

Hobbes, Thomas. *Leviathan*. ed. C.B. MacPherson. 1968; London: Penguin, 1985.

Hobson, Marian. "La *Lettre sur les sourds et les muets* de Diderot: Labyrinthe et langage." *Semiotica* 16 (1976): 291–327.

Horkheimer, Max, and Theodor Adorno. *Dialectic of Enlightenment*. trans. John Cummings. 1972; reprint, New York: Continuum, 1987.

Horowitz, Louise. "The Correspondence of Madame de Sévigné: Letters or Belles-Lettres?" *French Forum* 6 (1981): 13–27.

[Huber, Marie.] *Le Sisteme des anciens et des modernes, concilié par l'Exposition des Sentimens de quelques Theologiens, sur l'état des âmes séparées des corps. En quatorze lettres*. 2nd edn. 1731. Amsterdam: Wetsteins & Smith, 1733.

Iltis [Merchant], Carolyn. "Leibniz and the *Vis viva* Controversy." *Isis* 62 (1971): 21–35.

——. "The Leibnizian-Newtonian Debates: National Philosophy and Social Psychology." *British Journal of the History of Science* 6 (1973): 343–77.

——. "Madame du Châtelet's Metaphysics and Mechanics." *Studies in History and Philosophy of Science* 8 (1977): 29–48.

Jacobs, Margaret C. *The Radical Enlightenment: Pantheists, Freemasons, and Republicans*. London: George Allen and Unwin, 1981.

Janik, Linda Gardiner. "Searching for the Metaphysics of Science: The Structure and Composition of Madame Du Châtelet's *Institutions de physique*, 1737–1740." *Studies on Voltaire and the Eighteenth Century* 201 (1982): 85–113.

Jay, Martin. *Adorno*. Cambridge: Harvard University Press, 1984.

—— *Downcast Eyes: The Denigration of Vision in Twentieth-Century French Thought*. Berkeley: University of California Press, 1993.

Jensen, Katharine Ann. *Writing Love: Letters, Women, and the Novel in France 1605–1776*. Carbondale: Southern Illinois University Press, 1995.

Josephs, Herbert. "*Essai sur les règnes de Claude et de Néron*: A Final Borrowing." Undank and Josephs 138–49.

Kamuf, Peggy. *Fictions of Feminine Desire: Disclosures of Heloise*. Lincoln: University of Nebraska Press, 1982.

Kauffman, Linda S. *Discourses of Desire: Gender, Genre, and Epistolary Fictions*. Ithaca: Cornell University Press, 1986.

Kaufmann, Vincent. *L'Equivoque epistolaire*. Paris: Minuit, 1990.

Kavanagh, Thomas M. *Enlightenment and the Shadows of Chance: The Novel and the Culture of Gambling in Eighteenth-Century France*. Baltimore: Johns Hopkins University Press, 1993.

—— *Writing the Truth: Authority and Desire in Rousseau*. Berkeley: University of California Press, 1987.

Keller, Evelyn Fox. *Reflections on Gender and Science*. New Haven: Yale University Press, 1985.

Kermode, Frank, and Anita Kermode. *The Oxford Book of Letters*. Oxford University Press, 1995.

Knight, David. *Ordering the World: A History of Classifying Man*. London: Burnett Books, 1981.

Knight, Isabel. *The Geometric Spirit: The Abbé de Condillac and the French Enlightenment*. New Haven: Yale University Press, 1968.

Kroll, Richard W.F. *The Material Word: Literate Culture in the Restoration and Early Eighteenth Century*. Baltimore: Johns Hopkins University Press, 1991.

Laclau, Ernesto, and Chantal Mouffe. *Hegemony and Socialist Strategy: Toward a Radical Democratic Politics*. trans. Winston Moore and Paul Cammack. London: Verso, 1985.

Lacour, Claudia Brodsky. *Lines of Thought: Discourse, Architectonics, and the Origin of Modern Philosophy*. Durham: Duke University Press, 1996.

Landow, George. *Hypertext: The Convergence of Contemporary Critical Theory and Technology*. Baltimore: Johns Hopkins University Press, 1992.

Langford, C.H. "Moore's Notion of Analysis." *Philosophy of G.E. Moore*. ed. P.A. Schilpp. Evanston: Northwestern University Press, 1942, 319–42.

Langford, Larry. "Postmodernism and Enlightenment, Or, Why Not a Fascist Aesthetics." *Sub-Stance* 67 (1992): 24–43.

Larson, James L. *Reason, and Experience: The Representation of Natural Order in the Work of Carl von Linné.* Berkeley: University of California Press, 1971.

Laudan, Laurens. "The Clock Metaphor and Probabilism: The Impact of Descartes on English Methodological Thought, 1650–1665." *Annals of Science* 22 (1966): 73–104.

Leibniz, Gottfried Wilhelm. *Discourse on Metaphysics, Correspondence with Arnauld, Monadology.* trans. George R. Montgomery. 1902. Rpt. La Salle, IL: Open Court, 1973.

New Essays on Human Understanding. trans. Peter Remnant and Jonathan Rennett. Cambridge University Press, 1981.

Leibniz, Gottfried Wilhelm, and Samuel Clarke. *The Leibniz-Clarke Correspondence, with Extracts from Newton's Principia and Opticks.* ed. H.G. Alexander. Manchester University Press, 1956.

Lemert, Charles C. and Garth Gillam. *Michel Foucault: Social Theory and Transgression.* New York: Columbia University Press, 1982.

Lesche, John E. "Systematics and the Geometrical Spirit" Frängsmyr 73–111.

Lespinasse, Julie de. *Lettres.* 1893. Rpt. Paris: Editions d'aujourd'hui, 1978.

Lettres à Condorcet. ed. Jean-Noël Pascal. Paris: Desjonquières, 1990.

Locke, John. *An Essay concerning Human Understanding.* ed. Peter H. Nidditch. Oxford: Clarendon Press, 1975.

Lough, John. *Essays on the Encyclopédie of Diderot and d'Alembert.* London: Oxford University Press, 1968.

Louis XIV. *Manière de montrer les jardins de Versailles.* Intro. Raoul Girardet. Paris: Plon, 1951.

Lovejoy, Arthur O. *The Great Chain of Being: A Study of the History of an Idea.* Cambridge: Harvard University Press, 1936.

Loveland, Jeff. "Buffon's *Histoire et théorie de la terre* in the Quarrel over Systems." *Studies on Voltaire and the Eighteenth Century,* forthcoming.

Lucie, ou le systême d'amour, comédie en un acte et en vers, par M. R****, representée, pour la première fois à Lyon, le 15 décembre, 1789. Lyon: n.p., 1791.

Lucretius. *On the Nature of Things.* trans. Frank O. Copley. New York: Norton, 1977.

Luhmann, Niklas. *Love as Passion: The Codification of Intimacy.* trans. J. Gaines and D.L. Jones. Cambridge: Harvard University Press, 1986.

Lyotard, Jean-François. *The Differend: Phrases in Dispute.* trans. Georges Van Den Abbeele 1983. Minneapolis: University of Minnesota Press, 1988.

The Postmodern Condition: A Report on Knowledge. trans. G. Bennington and B. Massumi. 1979. Minneapolis: University of Minnesota Press, 1984.

MacArthur, Elizabeth J. *Extravagant Narratives: Closure and Dynamic Form in the Epistolary Form.* Princeton University Press, 1990.

"Nature Made Word: Guidebooks to the Gardens at Versailles." *Cahiers du dix-septième siècle* 5, no. 1 (1991): 183–94.

Marin, Louis. "Classical, Baroque: Versailles, or the Architecture of the Prince." *Yale French Studies* 80 (1991): 167–82.

Markley, Robert M. *Fallen Languages: Crises of Representation in Newtonian England, 1640– 1740.* Ithaca: Cornell University Press, 1993.

Marks, Thomas Carson. "*Ordine Geometrica Demonstrata*: Spinoza's Use of the Axiomatic Method." *Review of Metaphysics* 29 (1975): 263–86.

Marx, Jacques. "L'Art d'observer au XVIIIe siècle: Jean Senebier et Charles Bonnet." *Janus* 61 (1974): 201–20.

May, Georges. "Diderot, artiste et philosophe du décousu." *Europäische Aufklärung.* ed. H. Friedrich and F. Schalk. Munich: Wilhelm Fink, 1967, 165–88.

McDonald, Christie V. *The Dialogue of Writing: Essays in Eighteenth-Century French Literature.* Waterloo, Ontario: Wilfrid Laurier Press, 1984.

"Opérateurs du changement: De Miss Polly Baker à Murphy Brown." *Œuvres et critiques* 19, no. 1 (1994): 68–78.

McGuire, J.E. "'Labyrinthus continui': Leibniz on Substance, Activity, and Matter." *Motion and Time, Space and Matter.* ed. P.K. Machamer and R.G. Turnbull. Columbus: Ohio State University Press, 1976, 290–326.

Mehlman, Jeffrey. *Cataract: A Study in Diderot.* Middletown, CT: Wesleyan University Press, 1979.

Melançon, Benoit. *Diderot épistolier: Contribution à une poétique de la lettre familière au XVIIIe siècle.* [Saint-Laurent, Québec]: Fides, 1996.

Merchant, Carolyn. See Iltis, Carolyn.

Messick, Brinkley. *The Calligraphic State: Textual Domination in a Muslim Society.* Berkeley: University of California Press, 1993.

Mintz, Samuel I. *The Hunting of Leviathan: Seventeenth-Century Reactions to the Materialism and Moral Philosophy of Thomas Hobbes.* Cambridge University Press, 1969.

Moser, Walter. "D'Alembert: L'Ordre philosophique de ce discours." *MLN* 91 (1976): 722–33.

"Le Discours dans le *Discours préliminaire*." *Romanic Review* 67 (1976): 102–16.

Nador, G. "Métaphores de chemins et labyrinthes chez Descartes." *Revue philosophique* 152 (1962): 37–51.

Nietzsche, Friedrich. *On the Genealogy of Morals.* trans. Walter Kaufmann and R.J. Hollingdale. 1967. New York: Vintage-Random House, 1989.

Norris, Christopher. *The Truth About Postmodernism.* Oxford: Blackwell, 1993.

North, J.D. and J.J. Roche, eds. *The Light of Nature.* Dordrecht: Nijhoff, 1985.

O'Neal, John C. *The Authority of Experience: Sensationist Theory in the French Enlightenment.* University Park: Pennsylvania State University Press, 1996.

Ong, Walter J. *Ramus, Method, and the Decay of Dialogue.* 2nd edn. 1958. Cambridge: Harvard University Press, 1983.

"System, Space, and Intellect in Renaissance Symbolism." *Bibliothèque d'humanisme et de renaissance* 18 (1956): 222–39.

Papineau, David. "The *Vis viva* Controversy: Do Meanings Matter?" *Studies in History and Philosophy of Science* 8 (1977): 111–42.

Parrochia, Daniel. *La Raison systématique: Essai d'une morphologie des systèmes philosophiques*. Paris: Vrin, 1993.

Paulson, William R. *Enlightenment, Romanticism, and the Blind in France*. Princeton University Press, 1987.

——. *The Noise of Culture: Literary Texts in a World of Information*. Ithaca: Cornell University Press, 1988.

Perrault, Charles. *Le Labyrinthe de Versailles*. 1677. Paris: Editions du Moniteur, 1982.

Pons, Alain, (ed.) *Encyclopédie ou Dictionnaire raisonné des sciences, des arts et des métiers (articles choisis)*. 2 vols. Paris: Garnier-Flammarion, 1986.

Porset, Charles. "Figures de l'encyclopédie." *Le Siècle de Voltaire: Hommage à René Pomeau*. ed. Christiane Mervaud and Sylvain Menant. 2 vols. Oxford: Voltaire Foundation, 1982. 2:719–33.

Porter, Charles, (ed). *Men/Women of Letters*. Special number of *Yale French Studies* 71 (1986).

Pratt, Vernon. "System-Building in the Eighteenth Century." North and Roche 421–31.

Prigogine, Ilya, and Isabelle Stengers. *La Nouvelle alliance: Métamorphose de la science*. Paris: Gallimard, 1979.

Proust, Jacques. "L'Article **Bas* de Diderot." Duchet and Jolley 245–78.

Pucci, Suzanne R. "'*Ceci n'est pas …* ' Negative Framing in Diderot and Magritte." *Mosaic* 20, no. 3 (1987): 1–14.

——. *Diderot and a Poetics of Science*. New York: Peter Lang, 1986.

——. "Vision and the 'I' of the Beholder." *Esprit créateur* 24 (1984): 108–22.

Racevskis, Karlis. *Postmodernism and the Search for Enlightenment*. Charlottesville: University of Virginia Press, 1993.

Radice, Betty, (ed.) *The Letters of Heloise and Abelard*. Middlesex: Penguin, 1973.

Randall, Marilyn. "Appropriate(d) Discourse: Plagiarism and Decolonization." *New Literary History* 22 (1991): 525–41.

Redford, Bruce. *The Converse of the Pen: Acts of Intimacy in the Eighteenth-Century Familiar Letter*. University of Chicago Press, 1986.

Régis, Isabelle, *et al.* "Lire l'*Encyclopédie*." *Littérature* 42 (1981): 20–39.

Reiss, Timothy. "Descartes, the Palatinate, and the Thirty Years War: Political Theory and Political Practice." *Yale French Studies* 80 (1991): 108–45.

——. *The Discourse of Modernism*. Ithaca: Cornell University Press, 1982.

Ricken, Ulrich. *Linguistics, Anthropology and Philosophy in the French Enlightenment: Language Theory and Ideology*. trans. Robert Norton. London: Routledge, 1994.

Roger, Jacques. *Buffon: Un philosophe au Jardin du Roi*. Paris: Fayard, 1989.

——. "The Living World." Rousseau and Porter 255–83.

Rorty, Richard. *Contingency, Irony, and Solidarity*. Cambridge University Press, 1989.

Rousseau, G.S., and Roy Porter, eds. *The Ferment of Knowledge: Studies in the Historiography of Eighteenth-Century Science*. Cambridge University Press, 1980.

Rousseau, Jean-Jacques. *Œuvres complètes*. ed. Bernard Gagnebin and Marcel Raymond. 5 vols. Paris: Gallimard, 1964–1995.

Rousseau, Nicolas. *Connaissance et langage chez Condillac*. Genève: Droz, 1986.

Ryan, Michael. *Marxism and Deconstruction: A Critical Articulation*. Baltimore: Johns Hopkins University Press, 1982.

Saint-Amand, Pierre. "Diderot contre la méthode." *Stanford French Review* 8 (1984): 213–28.

Diderot: Le Labyrinthe de la relation. Paris: Vrin, 1984.

Les Lois de l'hostilité: La Politique à l'âge des Lumières. Paris: Seuil, 1992.

Sainte-Beuve, Charles-Augustin. *Causeries de lundi*. 9th edn. Paris: Garnier, n.d.

Schmidt, James, ed. *What is Enlightenment? Eighteenth-Century Answers and Twentieth-Century Questions*. Berkeley: University of California Press, 1996.

Schwab, R.N., Walter E. Rex, and John Lough. *Inventory of Diderot's Encyclopédie, Studies on Voltaire and the Eighteenth Century* 80, 83, 85, 91–3, 223 (1971–1984).

Scudéry, Madeleine de. *La Promenade de Versailles*. 1669. Rpt. Paris: Devambez, 1920.

Segal, Naomi. *The Unintended Reader: Feminism and Manon Lescaut*. Cambridge University Press, 1986.

Senebier, Jean. *Essai sur l'art d'observer et de faire des expériences*. 2nd edn. 3 vols. 1775; Genève: J.J. Paschoud, 1802.

Serres, Michel. *Hermès I: La Communication*. Paris: Minuit, 1969.

Le Système de Leibniz et ses modèles mathématiques. Paris: PUF, 1968.

Sgard, Jean, ed. *Condillac et les problèmes du langage*. Genève: Slatkine, 1982.

Shapin, Steven. "Of Gods and Kings: Natural Philosophy and Politics in the Leibniz-Clarke Disputes." *Isis* 72 (1981): 187–215.

"Social Uses of Science." Rousseau and Porter 93–109.

Shapin, Steven, and Simon Shaffer. *Leviathan and the Air-Pump: Hobbes, Boyle, and the Experimental Life*. Princeton University Press, 1985.

Sherman, Carol. *Diderot and the Art of Dialogue*. Genève: Droz, 1976.

Showalter, English. "Authorial Consciousness and the Familiar Letter: The Case of Madame de Graffigny." Porter 113–30.

"Graffigny at Cirey: A Fraud Exposed." *French Forum* 21 (1996): 29–44.

Slaughter, M.M. *Universal Languages and Scientific Taxonomy in the Seventeenth Century*. Cambridge University Press, 1982.

Sloan, Philip R. "The Buffon-Linnaeus Controversy." *Isis* 67 (1976): 356–75.

Sloterdijk, Peter. *The Critique of Cynical Reason*. trans. Michael Eldred. Minneapolis: University of Minnesota Press, 1987.

Spacks, Patricia Meyer. *Gossip*. New York: Knopf, 1985.

Spinoza, Benedictus de. *The Collected Works of Spinoza.* ed. and trans. Edwin M. Curley. 2 vols. Princeton University Press, 1985–.

Spitzer, Leo. "The Style of Diderot." *Linguistics and Literary History: Essays in Linguistics.* Princeton University Press, 1948, 135–91.

Spragens, Thomas A. *The Politics of Motion: The World of Thomas Hobbes.* Lexington: University Press of Kentucky, 1973.

Stafford, Barbara. *Body Criticism: Imagining the Unseen in Enlightenment Art and Medicine.* Cambridge: MIT Press, 1991.

Stallybrass, Peter, and Allon White. *The Poetics and Politics of Transgression.* Ithaca: Cornell University Press, 1986.

Starobinski, Jean. "Le Philosophe, le géomètre, l'hybride." *Poétique* 21 (1975): 8–23.

"Remarques sur l'*Encyclopédie.*" *Revue de métaphysique et de morale* 75 (1970):284– 91.

Steiner, George. *After Babel: Aspects of Language and Translation.* 2nd edn. 1975. London: Oxford University Press, 1992.

Swain, Virginia. "Conventional Wisdom and Conventional Acts: The Narrative Contract in Diderot's 'Ceci n'est pas un conte.' " *Eighteenth-Century Studies* 17 (1983): 14–27.

Le Système des colonies. n.p.:n.d. B.N., coll.des imprimés, 9K79.

Le Système du melange dans l'oeuvre des convulsions, Confondu par ses ressemblances avec le Système des Augustinistes, & par les erreurs, & les défauts qu'il renferme. n.p., 1735.

Tanner, Tony. *Adultery and the Novel: Contract and Transgression.* Baltimore: Johns Hopkins University Press, 1979.

Taton, René. "Madame du Châtelet, traductrice de Newton." *Archives internationales d'histoire des sciences* 22 (1969): 185–210.

Taylor, Charles. *The Sources of the Self: The Making of Modern Identity.* Cambridge: Harvard University Press, 1989.

Terdiman, Richard. *Discourse/Counter-Discourse: The Theory and Practice of Symbolic Resistance in Nineteenth-Century France.* Ithaca: Cornell University Press, 1985.

Thomas, Downing A. "Musicology and Hieroglyphics: Questions of Representation in Diderot." *The Eighteenth Century: Theory and Interpretation* 35 (1994): 64–77.

Tort, Michel. "L'Effet Sade." *Tel quel* 28 (1967): 66–83.

Tort, Patrick. "Condillac, l'économie et les signes," Sgard 421–51.

Trabant, Jürgen. "La Critique de l'arbitraire du signe chez Condillac et Humboldt." *Les Idéologues: Sémiotique, théories et politiques linguistiques pendant la Révolution française.* ed. Winfried Busse and Jürgen Trabant. Amsterdam and Philadelphia: John Benjamins, 1986, 73–96.

Tyard, Pontus de. *Solitaire second ou discours sur la musique.* ed. Cathy Yandell. Genève: Droz, 1980.

Ulmer, Gregory. *Heuretics: The Logic of Invention.* Baltimore: Johns Hopkins University Press, 1994.

Undank, Jack. "An Ethics of Discourse." Undank and Josephs 231–49.
Diderot: Inside, Outside, and In-Between. Madison, WI: Coda Press, 1979.
Undank, Jack, and Herb Josephs, eds. *Diderot: Digression and Dispersion.* Lexington: French Forum Monographs, 1984.
Vaillot, René. *Madame du Châtelet.* Paris: Albin Michel, 1978.
Van Den Abbeele, Georges. "Utopian Sexuality and its Discontents: Exoticism and Colonialism in the *Supplément au Voyage de Bougaineville.*" *Esprit créateur* 24, no. 1 (1984): 43–52.
Vandendorpe, Christian, ed. *Le Plagiat,* Actes du colloque tenu à l'Université d'Ottawa du 26 au 28 septembre 1991. Ottawa: Presses de l'Université d'Ottawa, 1992.
Vanpée, Janie. " 'Tout à la vérité parle en elles, mais un langage équivoque': The *Encyclopédie*'s Ambiguous Definition of Woman." *Studies on Voltaire and the Eighteenth Century* 304 (1992): 749–52.
Vartanian, Aram. *Diderot and Descartes: A Study in Scientific Naturalism in the Enlightenment.* Princeton University Press, 1953.
Vaugelas, Claude Favre de. *Remarques sur la langue françoise.* 1747. Rpt. Paris: Droz, 1934.
Virgil. *Aeneid.* trans. Rolfe Humphries. New York: MacMillan, 1987.
Voltaire, François-Marie Arouet de. *Correspondance.* ed. Theodore Besterman. Coll. Pléiade. Paris: Gallimard, 1963–
Les Systèmes. Œuvres. 1833. ed. M. Beuchot. 14:251. 72 vols. Paris: Lefèvre, 1829–1840. The Bibliothèque Nationale possesses an anonymous pamphlet copy, B.N. res. Beuchot, 83S.
Warburton, William. *Essai sur les hiéroglyphes des Égyptiens.* trans. L. des Malpeines. 1744. ed. Patrick Tort. Paris: Aubier Flammarion, 1977.
Watkins, J.W.N. *Hobbes's System of Ideas: A Study in the Political Significance of Philosophical Theories.* New York: Barnes and Noble, 1968.
Weiss, Allen S. *Mirrors of Infinity: The French Classical Garden and Seventeenth-Century Metaphysics.* New York: Princeton Architectural Press, 1995.
Werner, Stephen. *Blueprint: A Study of Diderot and the Encyclopédie Plates.* Birmingham: Summa Publications, 1993.
Westfall, Richard S. *Force in Newton's Physics: The Science of Dynamics in the Seventeenth Century.* New York and London: Elsevier and Macdonald, 1971.
Wilden, Anthony. *System and Structure: Essays in Communication and Exchange.* 2nd edn. New York: Tavistock, 1980.
Williams, Raymond. "Base and Superstructure in Marxist Cultural Theory." *Problems in Materialism and Culture: Selected Essays.* London: Verso, 1980, 31–49.
Wilson, Milton. "Reading Locke and Newton as Literature." *University of Toronto Quarterly* 57 (1988): 471–83.

Index

Printed in the United Kingdom
by Lightning Source UK Ltd.
121953UK00001B/263/A

9 780521 030960